SHIP OF STATE

The Nautical Metaphors of Thomas Jefferson

With Numerous Examples by Other Writers From Classical Antiquity to the Present

Charles A. Miller

University Press of America,® Inc.
Lanham · New York · Oxford

ISBN 0-7618-2516-9 (paperback : alk. ppr.)

CONTENTS

SECTION 1

INTRODUCTION

NO DEMONSTRATION is needed to show that Thomas Jefferson wrote in an elevated style. He would have called it "rational and chaste";[1] we may call it classical. It is a style that cannot be mistaken for Franklin's (sprightly), Washington's (practical), Adams's (passionate), Paine's (declamatory), Madison's (precise), or Hamilton's (energetic).

This essay is a study of a small but abundant feature of Jefferson's classical style, his metaphors of the sea. Originating in a collection of about a hundred of Jefferson's nautical metaphors, the essay examines these metaphors from several perspectives. It finds their source in his education in the classics. It explores their uses over the course of his life. It contrasts his nautical metaphors with two other collections: his own metaphors on non-nautical subjects and the nautical metaphors of other writers. Finally, it places his metaphors in the context of modern metaphor theory.[2]

1. See TJ to John Brazier, Aug. 24, 1819; LoA 1423. For abbreviations to source citations, see Appendix I.
2. A number of scholars have noted Jefferson's metaphors of the sea, but the most prominent of them could only say: "This farmer who loathed the sea often had recourse to nautical metaphors which would have come more appropriately from the mouth of an Adams of New England." Dumas Malone, *Jefferson and the Ordeal of Liberty,* 292. I have found only one scholar who makes any use of the metaphors to understand the man, and that scholar's theory, that Jefferson wrote metaphors in times of crisis, is only partially correct. Andrew Burstein, *The Inner Jefferson* (1995), 85-86, 161. My own early attempt at interpretation is *Jefferson and Nature* (1988), 114-15. (Complete information on works cited in the footnotes only by title and year may be found in the bibliography.)

A word should be said about the density of quotation in the essay. First, metaphors are brief and often carefully composed. An analysis of them, therefore, both invites and can accommodate verbatim examples. Second, many of the metaphors are instructive or thought-provoking. They are wonders of juxtaposition or beautiful creations with language. They deserve to be the objects of our attention as phrase, not paraphrase.

The appendixes that follow the essay collect all the metaphors that are mentioned in the text and a number of additional ones. Appendix I lists Jefferson's nautical metaphors in chronological order. Appendix II is a selection of Jefferson's non-nautical metaphors. Appendix III consists of nautical metaphors by other authors, divided according to whether they were written before or after Jefferson's death. All the appendixes contain full source citations and light annotations. They also serve as an index to all the metaphors that are mentioned in the essay.

* * * *

Jefferson lived within sight of the Appalachian Mountains, made his living from the land, looked to farming as the principal employment of other Americans, and was uncomfortable at sea. For these reasons his attachment to nautical figures of speech at first appears odd. But Jefferson cultivated his literary style through an education in the classics, where nautical imagery was pervasive and significant. Nautical imagery is central to the *Odyssey* and appears often in the *Iliad*. It is to be found in the Greek tragedians and, among the Romans, in the poetry of Horace and the philosophy of Lucretius. Unlike the ancients Jefferson did not write verse or drama, and his prose was written for political or personal ends, not cultural ones. Yet in his style he lived largely in the classical world. Since the great writers of that world employed nautical metaphors, it was reasonable for him to do so as well.

Style was hardly the whole man, however, and the sea was not only pervasive in Jefferson's classical education; it was the contemporary context necessary for his metaphors to be devised and to be effective. Indeed, the sea could hardly have been alien to a landed eighteenth-century Virginian. An Atlantic crossing accounted for the settlement of the North American colonies. Ocean commerce was required for much of the colonists' income, certainly that of Virginia tobacco growers, and for a good portion of their luxury items.[3] The sea was also at the center of much of Jefferson's public life from the time of independence until his retirement from the presidency. When the United States became independent, the country, as he later phrased it, was "kindly separated by nature and a wide ocean from the exterminating havoc of one quarter of the globe."[4] As minister to France and then as secretary of state he prepared studies on the nation's industries of the sea—whaling and cod fishing. As president he was obliged to consider, and constantly bothered about, the role of the navy for American defense and the international law of the sea.

Jefferson knew metaphors not only in practice. He also knew metaphors as the subject of rhetorical and aesthetic theory, even though he sometimes claimed to pay little attention to that theory. In the theory, metaphor was usually defined so as to distinguish it from nearby figures of speech that also make comparisons. The most common neighboring figure was, and still is, the simile. In the words of the first edition of the *Encyclopedia Britannica* (1771):

> Metaphor, in rhetoric, a trope, by which we put a strange word for a proper word, by reason of its resemblance to it; a simile or comparison intended to enforce or illustrate the thing we speak of, without the signs or forms of comparison.[5]

3. Concrete evidence of Virginia's sea-oriented economy and culture, if any were needed, appears in *Virginia Gazette Index,* Lester J. Cappon and Stella M. Duff, eds. (2 vols., 1950). Covering the leading newspaper of Virginia from 1736-1780, this index contains 32 three-column pages under "ships" and "shipwrecks," etc., more than any other category, and ahead of "British" (27 pages) and "horses" (15 pages). Further, Jefferson's library was stocked with contemporary literature, which contained numerous maritime references, as well as accounts of actual and imaginary sea voyages. For masterful studies of the voyages, see Philip Edwards, *Sea-Mark: The Metaphorical Voyage, Spenser to Milton* (1997) and *The Story of the Voyage: Sea Narratives in Eighteenth-Century English Literature* (1994). Neither contemporary seafaring nor contemporary literature, however, get to the source and significance of Jefferson's nautical metaphors.

4. First Inaugural Address, March 4, 1801. LoA 494.

5. American dictionaries, unlike the early *Britannica,* have always kept the metaphor and simile distinct, never explaining the second as a variety of the first. The examples given for one figure or the other, however, have often been nautical and, in their reference, sometimes classical. In the twentieth century,

Jefferson's nautical metaphors were true metaphors. They adhered to the classical definition and did not use the "like" of a simile. But Jefferson seems not to have paid attention to classical metaphor theory nor cared what his figure was called so long as it made a sharp comparison with his subject matter. Such indifference to rhetorical taxonomy has been justified by modern theory, which has mostly rejected a narrow understanding of metaphor as either beyond successful definition or of minimal aid in appreciating the intellectual or aesthetic qualities of a text. Moreover, since the late 19th century metaphor has leaped the bounds of literature, rhetoric and aesthetics, and has become an important subject of discussion in philosophy, philosophy of science, and throughout the social sciences.

Until a century or so ago, however, and certainly in Jefferson's mind, metaphor was strictly a rhetorical device, a "mere" figure of speech. Reflecting its Greek etymology, metaphor was a "carrying over" or, more colloquially, a kind of "stand for." To Jefferson a metaphor stood for something it did not state, carrying over the meaning of one word or phrase to the meaning of something else. In rhetorical theory—and in Jefferson's writing—the direction of a metaphor is normally from a concrete object to a more abstract idea. Following this pattern, the most common nautical metaphors in Western culture have been variations on the ocean of life and the ship of state. "What an ocean is life!" Jefferson wrote from Philadelphia to an old friend in Virginia whom he looked forward to seeing, "And how our barks get separated in beating through it!"[6]

In American history the ship of state is often best understood as the ship of the Constitution or the ship of the union, though the image and

---

Webster's was still illustrating metaphor with "a ship plows the sea" and *American Heritage Dictionary* with "sea of troubles." Nearer to Jefferson's time *Webster's* illustrated simile not only with a water image, but with classical orators: "Thus the eloquence of Demosthenes was like a rapid torrent, that of Cicero like a large stream that glides smoothly along with majestic tranquility" (1828 and 1848 editions). The synecdoche, another figure of speech common in classical authorities, by which a part stands for the whole, continues to be illustrated by nautical examples: "fifty sail for fifty ships" (*Webster's*), "ten sail for ten ships" (*Random House Dictionary*), and "hand for sailor" (*American Heritage*).

6. TJ to St. George Tucker, Sept. 10, 1793. Source information for Jefferson's metaphors may be found in Appendixes I and II.

the message long precede modern politics. "Hold on then like a good and faithful seaman," Jefferson wrote to an ally during a political crisis, "till our brother-sailors can rouse from their intoxication and right the vessel."[7] An ocean is not the abstract idea of life nor is a ship the same as a state. But in the right hands, the metaphor of the ocean *as* life and a ship *as* a state can become intellectually useful or aesthetically appealing. In such cases, they are metaphors that work, and in Jefferson's hands they always did.

Of course, more than a transfer of meaning must be involved for a metaphor to succeed. As theorists have always noted, a metaphor requires an objectively odd comparison—but not too odd. It brings together two words, groups of words or ideas that literally, linguistically, or logically have little or no connection with each other. In the phrase of John Quincy Adams, a metaphor involves a "strange association of words."[8] No dictionary would define ocean as life or a ship as the state, or the other way around. A metaphor depends on artistry, not science, and at metaphor Jefferson was an artist.

The oddness or strange association of terms in a metaphor must illuminate at least one of the two sides of the comparison, normally the more abstract one. If there is no illumination, dawning or blinding, then the metaphor does not work, or does not work well, and the two words have made an association that is either not strange enough, or the opposite—they ask for an association that is too strange to illuminate anything. Traditional canons of the metaphor other than the requirement of an appropriately "strange alliance," are essentially negative. Metaphors will fail if they are unrecognized, stale, or cliché, or if they tax or offend either our cognitive or our aesthetic faculties through figures that are strained, confusing, mixed, unduly complex, overextended or tasteless. As we will see, Jefferson's metaphors did not fail.

While there are many additional figures of speech in the classical repertoire, the metaphor is not only the most well-known of them, it is also the only one that is used to embrace other—even all other—figures of speech and concepts that transfer meanings. "Trope," which also covers a wide variety of transferred meanings, does not also specify a

7. TJ to William Branch Giles, Dec. 17, 1794.
8. *Lectures on Rhetoric and Oratory* (1810), 314. John Adams sent Jefferson a copy of his son's *Lectures* in 1812 to help effect a reconciliation between the old friends.

particular figure, nor is it a term widely used outside of literary studies.

In its wider sense, metaphor embraces terms of transferred meaning with classical origins: simile, synecdoche, metonymy, and dozens more that were organized by various logics and are known today only by specialists. Metaphor has covered concepts that are post-classical in origin: medieval personification, botanical signature, Elizabethan conceit, Emersonian correspondence. Metaphor may either be indistinguishable from, or become, proverb. Metaphor can refer to entire types of writing: parable, allegory, fable, myth, fairy tale. It may refer to transferred meaning in general: imagery, symbol, icon, model, paradigm, analogy.

There are, then, two quite different approaches to defining metaphor—the small and the large. Metaphor in its large reading encompasses the smaller definition. Metaphor in its large meaning takes in so much that all humans necessarily indulge in it, even if they have never heard of the word or consciously recognized or used the figure. Indeed, when metaphors can range from etymologies to world views there is obviously no way to avoid them. But Jefferson's nautical figures are an example of the small metaphor, a precise, isolatable figure of speech used for rhetorical or aesthetic effect. It is the central aim of this essay to discover, on the basis of Jefferson's practice, what can be learned about these smaller metaphors.[9]

9. Jefferson himself has been discussed under both the most liberal and the most specific understandings of metaphor, as can be seen in such titles as *The Jefferson Image in the American Mind* (1960), by Merrill Peterson, and "American Synecdoche: Thomas Jefferson as Image, Icon, Character, and Self" (1998), by Jan Lewis and Peter S. Onuf.

SECTION 2

SOURCES

JEFFERSON WAS QUALIFIED by his education and enthusiasm to be a professor of classics. His education in Greek and Latin began at a local "Latin school" to which his father sent him at the age of nine and became most intense at the next school he attended in the neighborhood. His classical education continued at the College of William and Mary in the early 1760s, where he heard lectures in rhetoric (which presumed a classical background) from William Small, the man who brought the Scottish Enlightenment to Virginia, and studied law under George Wythe, who was also a classical scholar.

From these studies followed a lifelong devotion to ancient languages and literature. Jefferson developed the habits of a philologist. His prose style, insofar as it can be labeled, became classical. Literature from Homer through the early Roman empire was always his favorite. He respected Aristotle in political theory and Epicurus (as represented by Lucretius) in cosmology and ethics. Tacitus set the standard in writing history. Filtered through the Italian Renaissance the ancients were his models for architecture. Whether considered in his own right or relative to his publicly active contemporaries, Jefferson had few peers either for depth or breadth in classical learning and none for the mark that an education in the classics left on his life.[1]

---

1. Letters Jefferson wrote in a single year when he was in his mid-seventies may represent the scope of his passion: TJ to John Adams, March 21, 1819; AJL.II.536 (pronunciation of ancient Greek); TJ to John Brazier, Aug. 24, 1819; LoA 1422 (the value of a classical education for Americans); TJ to William Short, Oct. 31, 1819; LoA 1430 (the philosophy of Epicurus); and TJ to John Adams, Dec. 10, 1819; AJL.II.548 (political lessons from the letters of

No procedure can prove conclusively that Jefferson's affinity for the nautical metaphor has its origin in his classical learning. But the irrefutable facts are that as to literary influence nothing held his attention and affection more than the writers of Greece and Rome, and that his nautical metaphors are entirely literary and never technical or time-bound. They require no knowledge of modern maritime practice on either his part or that of his readers.

Jefferson found more than images and a style in the classics. Where he found nautical figures of speech he also found ideas. The following passages from Homer ("the first of poets"),[2] from the Greek tragedians, and from Horace, Plato and Aristotle thus illustrate not only the nautical metaphors of these authors, but also the thinking that Jefferson absorbed from antiquity. Jefferson was never as profound and seldom as supple with his nautical metaphors as his ancient models. But an

---

Cicero). See in general the wise discussion by Louis B. Wright, "Thomas Jefferson and the Classics" (1943); the extensive survey by Karl Lehmann, *Thomas Jefferson: American Humanist* (1947), esp. 150-54 and "Index of Ancient Authors"; and the deep comparative study by Carl J. Richard, *The Classics and the Founders* (1994). For primary sources other than Jefferson's own writings, copious evidence of Jefferson's classical readings appears in E. Millicent Sowerby, *Catalogue of the Library of Thomas Jefferson* (5 vols., 1952-59) and in *Jefferson's Literary Commonplace Book* (1989), Douglas E. Wilson, ed. Andrew Burstein presents the Roman background for Jefferson as a letter writer in *The Inner Jefferson* (1995), 117-23.

In *Clear and Simple as the Truth: Writing Classic Prose* (1994), a treatment of prose style in history, philosophy, and language, Francis-Nöel Thomas and Mark Turner include Jefferson among their model classic stylists. Thomas and Turner are supported by Robert Dawidoff (who does not insist Jefferson wrote in a "classical" style) in "Man of Letters" (1986).

Unusually effective testimony to Jefferson as a classicist, as a writer in the classical style, and as a composer of nautical metaphors, is the eulogy to him by William Wirt. Among the most respected orators of his day, and well-trained in the classics himself, Wirt was also a close friend of Jefferson's and sought his advice on stylistic matters. Wirt's testimony, the more effective because it is unintentional, is scattered throughout his address in the form of classical quotations, references and allusions, observations on Jefferson's classical education and style, and elaborate nautical metaphors of his own. The eulogy is in *A Selection of Eulogies* (1826), 379-426. It also appears in incomplete but more convenient form in LB.XIII.ix-lvii.

2. TJ to John Waldo, Aug. 16, 1813; LoA 1296.

examination of these models throws light from an unexpected source on a number of his intellectual, cultural and personal views.

We begin with the *Iliad* and the *Odyssey*. Like the ancients and like ourselves, Jefferson had no reason to prefer the poetry of one epic of Homer over the other. But if we may attribute to the years when he first read Homer the temperament of his later years, he had strong reasons to prefer the *Odyssey*'s theme of homecoming over the *Iliad*'s theme of warfare. Thus when it comes to nautical images, we find him softening, if indirectly, the *Iliad*'s calamity of battle, and adapting, if modestly, the *Odyssey*'s homecoming scene on Ithaca.

In the *Iliad* Jefferson read sea similes about both the Greeks and the Trojans as their armies charged into battle. For the Greeks:

> As when a swell of sea on a sounding beach,
> urged wave on wave as the West Wind moves it on,
> lifts whitecaps first in the open sea, then later
> breaks on land with a great crash round the headlands,
> and curls in crests and spits the salt foam back,
> so wave on wave the Danaans' ranks kept marching on to war.[3]

For the Trojans:

> As when a great wave joins a swollen river
> at its mouth, and roars against its stream,
> and spits salt water spume against the headlands,
> so with a roar the Trojans came.

When the two armies joined in conflict Jefferson did not merely read a Homeric simile. He entered—he "commonplaced"—the simile into his commonplace book, the notebook where he recorded striking passages from his studies. He wrote it out first in the original and then in his own translation:

> As when rivers in winter spate running down from the mountains throw together at the meeting of streams the weight of their water out of the great springs behind in the hollow stream-bed, and far away in the mountains the shepherd hears the thunder; such, from the coming together of men, was the shock and the shouting.

Jefferson copied down these lines for more than their own sake, however. He was reminded of them by a passage from Ossian, with

---

3. Source information for nautical metaphors not by Jefferson may be found in Appendix III.

whose epic poetry he had become infatuated. This Celtic bard, who was discovered and "translated" by James McPherson in the 1760s, had purportedly written:

> As two dark streams from high rocks meet, and mix and roar on the plain; loud, rough, and dark in battle meet Lochlin and Innis-fail: chief mixed his strokes with chief, and man with man; steel clanging sounded on steel, helmets are cleft on high.

The similarity between Ossian and Homer, far from leading to any doubt in Jefferson's mind that McPherson, a real translator of the *Iliad,* had made up the Ossianic lines or even adapted them, only confirmed to Jefferson Ossian's Homeric greatness.

Homer's simile presumably also reminded Jefferson of the torrential streams that cascaded from the Blue Ridge Mountains. In fact it was the cascading and the shepherd who hears it, not the armies' "shock and shouting," that Jefferson concentrated on in his commonplacing. He omitted two preceding lines of carnage in Homer that would have elaborated Ossian's "loud, rough, and dark in battle." But he retained the figure of a distant inland shepherd that has no parallel in the Celtic verse. Thus, by artful but probably unconscious selection, Jefferson's metaphor revised both Ossian and Homer in order to focus on a longing for rural calm.

When we turn from the *Iliad* to the *Odyssey,* this is the archetype sea simile that Jefferson read:

> And as when the land appears welcome to men who are swimming,
> after Poseidon has smashed their strong-built ship on the open
> water, pounding it with the weight of wind and the heavy
> seas, and only a few escape the gray water landward
> by swimming, with a thick scurf of salt coated upon them,
> and gladly they set foot on the shore, escaping the evil;
> so welcome was her husband to her as she looked upon him,
> and she could not let him go from the embrace of her white arms.

Now listen to the metaphor of Jefferson as he yearns for Monticello during his trials as secretary of state:

> I look to that period [retirement] with the longing of a wave-worn mariner, who has at length the land in view, and shall count the days and hours which still lie between me and it.[4]

4. TJ to George Washington, Sept. 9, 1792.

And on reaching home after leaving the presidency:

> Safe in port myself, I shall look anxiously at my friends still buffeting the storm.[5]

There is no Homer in these lines, perhaps because there is no Penelope at Monticello—Martha Jefferson had died a decade before the first of the these metaphors was written. But the underlying sentiment and image are the same.

Jefferson read classical examples of the nautical metaphor not only in Homer but also in the Greek tragedians. Although the record of his knowledge of particular tragedies of Aeschylus, Sophocles, and Euripides is slight, he was familiar with the entire corpus and could not have missed the extensive nautical imagery in a number of the plays. An example from each of the tragedians illustrates what the dramatists contributed to his world of metaphor.

Uniquely among the Greek tragedies, Aeschylus's *The Persians* is based on an historical event rather than on Greek mythology. At first glance, therefore, it might seem of little interest to later ages. But the event was the victory of the Greeks over the Persians in the naval battle at Salamis, a victory that came both to symbolize and set the course of Western freedom over Eastern tyranny. The attraction to Jefferson of this theme is obvious, but it is the nautical imagery of the drama that contributed to his style.[6] *The Persians* contains so much detail about a sea battle that a great deal of its nautical imagery is necessarily literal rather than figurative. But it is in Aeschylus's separating out metaphor from description and then reintegrating them, that the reader discovers the dramatist's control of language. Jefferson's control of the language of metaphor is certainly masterful, but his metaphors are never as complex as those of Aeschylus.

Near the beginning of the play the chorus of Persian elders speaks of their country's heroes as a "great torrent [of] unconquerable billows of ocean." Soon afterward, the herald, who brings to the Persian queen the fateful news of Salamis, speaks of Persia as "wealth's great anchorage." He then narrates the battle with both a metaphor ("floods of Persians") and a simile:

---

5. TJ to Gen. John Armstrong, March 5, 1809.
6. Jefferson presumably also appreciated the play's sympathetic portrayal of a defeated foe. In the Declaration of Independence, in a very Greek figure of speech, the chiasmus, he wrote that Americans would hold the British, as they hold the rest of mankind, "enemies in war, in peace friends."

All who survived . . .
Like mackerel or some catch of fish,
Were stunned and slaughtered, boned with broken oars
And splintered wrecks.

The queen responds:

Alas, a sea of troubles breaks in waves
On the Persians and barbarian tribes.

The sea imagery of *The Persians* goes further. Aeschylus incorporates into the play an early variant of ship of state, the nautical metaphor Jefferson used most frequently and the most important nautical metaphor in the Western tradition.

In Greek, ship of state is a metaphor almost too easy to coin, because the same word, *kubernētēs,* means both helmsman of a ship and governor of a state. Thus the closest linguistic connection possible exists between ship and state in Greek, and anyone who knew this, including Jefferson, would have found the ship-of-state metaphor so natural as to be virtually built into the language. The English *governor,* although derived from *kubernētēs,* concerns politics only and not seafaring. In English, therefore, ship of state is a real metaphor, while the capaciousness of *kubernētēs* makes the Greek seem more like a permanent and serious pun.[7]

We find this natural connection at work in *The Persians* when the ghost of King Darius laments the defeat of his son Xerxes at Salamis and then introduces a variation on ship of state. Among the glorious line of Persian kings, Darius says, was one "whose reason was helmsman to his spirit." Once this heritage and the principle it represents are acknowledged, the plight of Xerxes is plain. In order to steer the state

---

7. Assuming the usual philological progression, the material, or maritime, meaning of *kubernētēs* preceded the more abstract, or political, meaning. Thus "the 'government' of a ship was the model from which the government of a nation was borrowed, not vice versa." Edward Jenks, *The Ship of State: The Essentials of Political Science* (1939), 23. But this assertion neglects the fact that to the Greeks the community being governed was not the abstraction of a state or nation, but the more intimate *polis,* which was far more concrete and "ship-like" than our "state"; and that a political leader is just as real a person as a ship's helmsman. In the circumstance, it seems as futile to assign priority in the origins of *kubernētēs* to seacraft or statecraft as to look for priority in the significance of the meanings of the word.

effectively a leader must first allow reason to steer his spirit, and Xerxes was conspicuously inferior to his ancestor. At Salamis he was a poor helmsman, both outwardly and literally, because he was not a good helmsman inwardly and figuratively.

The political lesson of Aeschylus's compact metaphor could not have been lost on Jefferson. Indeed, he said the same:

> Man, once surrendering his reason, has no remaining guard against absurdities the most monstrous, and like a ship without a rudder, is the sport of every wind.[8]

But note that Jefferson's figure is weaker than that of Aeschylus. His figure is not a true metaphor, but a simile, using "like." More, Aeschylus's is a metaphor that, by language and setting, intermixes philosophic meaning and attractiveness of phrasing; his figure must be thought about to be appreciated. Jefferson keeps meaning and metaphor apart; each element is taken in quickly and complete, and the reader moves on, enjoying the phrase but not likely to keep either the figure or its import in mind.

The case for the classics as the source of Jefferson's nautical metaphors continues with a consideration of Sophocles' *Antigone*. In contrast to *The Persians, Antigone* is set completely on land; its sea imagery is therefore entirely figurative and never literal. Nevertheless, as Robert F. Goheen's study of the play demonstrates, the drama is pervaded with images of the sea.[9] Two passages of Creon's on the ruler of a polis illustrate the range of this imagery. Jefferson presumably noticed these passages and absorbed them; or Western culture may have absorbed them for him. In either case, modified to fit his times and outlook, Jefferson employed comparable metaphors himself, if without the sophistication of the originals.

The first passage is Creon's extended working out of the ship of state. He has summoned the chorus of Theban elders to announce his edict that one nephew, Eteocles, who remained loyal and defended the city, is to be buried with honors, while his other nephew, Eteocles's brother, who sought to destroy the city, is to lie unburied on the battlefield, prey to birds and dogs. The nautical imagery is somewhat cryptic in English because the Greek does not contain any word for ship and the whole is spread out thinly over a number of lines. To an Athenian

8. TJ to James Smith, Dec. 8, 1822.
9. *The Imagery of Sophocles' Antigone* (1951), esp. 46-50.

audience, however, accustomed to the ship-of-state image and needing only one root word for both elements of the metaphor, this posed no problem. On the contrary, it displayed the skill of the playwright. Condensed, this is what Creon says:

> Gentlemen: as for our city's fortune,
> the gods have shaken her, when the great waves broke;
> but they have brought her through again to safety.

> A man with the task of guiding [steering] a whole city,
> if he does not reach for the best counsel for her,
> I judge the worst of any.

> It is the city which gives us our security. While she sails
> steady under us, friends will be ours for the making.

If we transfer the scene from ancient Greece to the United States at the time of Jefferson's assuming the presidency in 1801, and then imagine the framers of the Constitution as the gods, the guidance of Congress in place of the counsel of a prophet, and the Federalists in place of Creon, we can hear echoes of Sophocles in the nautical metaphors Jefferson employed at the time of his inaugural.[10] There is no reason to think that he consciously heard the echoes. The claim is rather that his deep grounding in the classics emerged in his own thoughts and style.

Creon's second nautical image comes at the end of *Antigone* and is not about the ship of state but about the voyage of life. When contrasted with a similar image of Jefferson's it illustrates a basic rule in understanding metaphors: Context is as crucial as text. With the wreckage of Thebes mounting around him because of his own intransigence, Creon cries out: "O harbor of Death, hard to cleanse. Why? Why do you destroy me?" How different this is from Jefferson, who wrote, even in a national crisis, that he was "content to be a passenger in our bark to the shore from which I am not distant."[11] The reasons for the difference between Creon's harbor and Jefferson's shore are not hard to find, but without recognizing these reasons neither metaphor has a meaning. Creon is in the prime of life; Jefferson is in old age. Creon is the active

10. First Inaugural Address, March 4, 1801; TJ to Lafayette, March 13, 1801; TJ to Nathaniel Niles, March 22, 1801; and TJ to Elbridge Gerry, March 29, 1801.

11. TJ to John Holmes, April 22, 1820.

ruler of a royal domain; Jefferson has long since retired from a republican presidency. Creon's world is the grim one of tragic fate; Jefferson's is the sanguine one of Epicureanism and the Enlightenment. Harbor and shore may bring them together literally, but the meanings of the two metaphors could hardly be further apart.

A connection between Jefferson and the nautical metaphors of Aeschylus and Sophocles is a matter of inferential reasoning. With regard to Euripides, however, the last of the Greek tragedians, Jefferson has left clear evidence. He entered nautical metaphors from Euripides' play *Orestes* into his commonplace book. Like most people who maintain such books Jefferson had no systematic aim in mind, but his interest seems to have been principally in the content rather than the style of his entries. Therefore, the dozen nautical metaphors scattered among the four hundred passages he copied out may be said to be there by accident, not design. This reinforces the view that he absorbed the nautical metaphor in the course of his reading rather than that he consciously studied it. In the case of *Orestes*, his entries are about friendship, a subject of importance throughout his life.

Here are three brief passages from the play. The first two were commonplaced by Jefferson (in Greek); the third has been added for purpose of discussion.

> A trusty comrade is a more cheering sight in trouble than a calm is to sailors.

> Great prosperity abideth not amongst mankind; but some power divine, shaking it to and fro like the sail of a swift galley, plunges it deep into the waves of grievous affliction, boisterous and deadly as the waves of the sea.

> As with sailing,
> so with politics: make your cloth too taut,
> and your ship will dip and keel, but slacken off
> and trim your sails, and things head up again.

The first passage, the simplest one, reflects the theme of friendship. It is spoken by the disconsolate Orestes when he spies his loyal friend Pylades (whom he addresses a few lines later as "helmsman"). The second passage, sung by the chorus of women of Argos, reflects a philosophy that Jefferson may have held when young and making commonplace entries, but by the time of the Revolution had abandoned in favor of Enlightenment optimism. Far from foreseeing Euripidean grief, Jefferson envisioned prosperity—at least in America—precisely in the midst, and even because, of the boisterous waves of the sea.[12] The third passage Jefferson did not enter into his commonplace book; indeed, he would never have adapted it for his own use. The reason is not that Euripides' speaker is imperceptive, but rather that he is too realistic. When Jefferson trimmed his metaphoric ship, it was for idealistic, republican purposes only.[13]

Jefferson's tastes in the classics inclined him towards the Greeks, not the Romans. But as an educated British colonial he was inevitably also a Latinist, at home with Horace, Virgil and Ovid, Cicero, Lucretius and Tacitus. Only Horace, however, concerns us here, and in particular a single poem of his, the ode "O navis"—"O ship." By far the most frequently cited of all classical sources for the ship of state, "O navis" may stand for the Latin origins of Jefferson's nautical metaphors.[14]

"O navis" is actually an allegory, which may be thought of as an extended and implied metaphor. The image throughout is of a ship of state, addressed by one who loves it. The ship has been severely damaged—in its keel and its mast, in its yardarms, sails and oars. Sailors would be foolish to rely on its merely painted prows or its noble lineage, or to pray to the gods for help. Instead, it must quickly come into harbor and avoid the winds and waves that would force it back to the treacherous sea.

What these images referred to when Horace wrote the ode is not

12. See TJ to Richard Rush, Oct. 20, 1820 and TJ to Lafayette, Dec. 26, 1820. The same language minus the wave appears in TJ to Philip Mazzei, April 24, 1796.

13. See TJ to Thomas Pinckney, May 29, 1797; and TJ to Robert R. Livingston, Dec. 24, 1800.

14. As is clear from the discussion of the tragedians, the origin of the ship-of-state metaphor is Greek, not Roman. But Horace, who admired the earliest Greek poet known to have used the metaphor, the sixth century lyricist, Alcaeus, has been considered the most important classical source for it from his own time to the present. Another nautical metaphor that Jefferson used, "in the same boat," has been traced to Roman times only. See Detmar Peil, " 'Im selben Boot' " (1986), 271. Evidence of Jefferson's fondness for Horace lies in a dozen entries in his commonplace book, numerous references in his letters, and in his library. His catalogue of 1815 shows four editions of Horace in Latin, two bilingual editions, and one in English. The discussion here has been aided by David H. Porter, *Horace's Poetic Journey* (1987), and notes in Charles E. Passage, *The Complete Works of Horace* (1983).

known. Like the ship of state in the Greek tragedies, Horace's figure also is more allusive than the metaphors written by Jefferson. Jefferson's metaphors are point-by-point comparisons with contemporary public affairs; they might require explication, but they do not remain enigmatic. Just as significant, Horace and Jefferson, though working with the same underlying image, hold opposite views about the ship of state and the dangers it faces. Horace writes in despair, Jefferson more commonly in eager anticipation: "I steer my bark with Hope in the Head, leaving Fear astern."[15] It is true that the temperament of Horace lies behind the potential shipwrecks that Jefferson sometimes sees for the French and American constitutions.[16] But unlike Horace, he remains confident that the American ship of state will survive the trials.

To say that Jefferson's nautical metaphors are not as complex as those of the ancients, nor as allusive, is also to say that they are not really philosophical. This is nowhere so evident as when we compare them with a well-known passage in Plato. Plato's nautical image is easy enough to apprehend; but it is not easy to comprehend. It appears in the central scene in *The Republic,* embedded in the argument that an ideal state requires that either philosophers become kings or kings become philosophers. Unlike any nautical metaphor of Jefferson's, Plato's metaphor is integral to persuading an audience of a philosophical position. It is a "required" metaphor.[17]

In his parable as argument Plato imagines a ship whose captain is both physically and educationally deficient for his job, and whose sailors, quarreling over who should take his place, claim that no special qualifications are needed. They praise, instead, "as a navigator, a pilot, a master of shipcraft, the man who is most cunning." In this situation, if a "true pilot" should turn up, he would be ridiculed, or, at the least,

15. TJ to John Adams, April 8, 1816.

16. TJ to La Rochefoucauld, April 30, 1790; TJ to James Madison, Dec. 28, 1794; TJ to James Madison, Jan. 1, 1797; TJ to Thomas Pinckney, May 29, 1797.

17. What Plato called his image is commonly translated as "parable," not metaphor. But "image" would seem to be more accurate, and for present purposes "metaphor" poses no problem. See the translation of Allan Bloom (1968), 167 and 462, n.5. As to the necessity of the nautical image for Plato's argument, the passage in *The Republic* should be contrasted with an analogous one in his *Statesman,* where he also invokes a nautical image, but without insisting that it is required in order to understand his philosophy.

ignored. The purpose of this image of chaos and cunning at sea is to prove that it takes innate talent and arduous training to rule a state well, and that if the state is ruled badly, the people will fasten on any doctrine that suits the moment and bring it to ruin.

To this story and its contribution to Plato's argument, Jefferson would have two kinds of response. The first would assert that metaphor has no place in philosophic argument. The second would attempt to refute the ship-state comparison on its own terms. But if Jefferson took this second route he would encounter a curious difficulty. He disapproved of Plato as a political theorist in part because Plato was no democrat. Yet Jefferson, who argued passionately on behalf of the right of the people to rule, was untiring in devising plans of education that acknowledge the central meaning of Plato's image—that those who possess innate talent for political leadership and are rigorously trained for it should be selected to rule. They are Jefferson's "natural aristocracy." Like Plato, Jefferson assumes that only certain people are suited to steer the ship of state, and that they must begin with reason. In addition he agreed with Plato that prudence was the trait of a true helmsman. "The prudence of the President," he wrote about Washington's presidency, "is an anchor of safety." Not surprisingly, he found a philosopher-ruler in James Madison.[18]

Jefferson's metaphors, in short, support rather than subvert the parable of Plato. Yet reason, prudence, rigorous training, and even the discovery of a philosopher-ruler cannot bring Jefferson close to Plato. Plato could never cross the gap to Jefferson's self-evident truths of equality, individual rights, the consent of the governed, and the right of revolution.

Jefferson's political philosopher among the Greeks was not Plato. It was Aristotle. Although in important respects Jefferson found him outdated, in the *Politics* Jefferson read seafaring imagery in the service of political theory that made sense to him. Aristotle's subject was not the well-trained captain compared with a philosopher-king, but good sailors compared with good citizens:

18. TJ to Nicholas Lewis, Feb. 9, 1791; TJ to James Madison, April 27, 1795 ("not another person in the U.S. who being placed at the helm of our affairs, my mind would be so completely at rest for the fortune of our political bark"). When Madison was president Jefferson wrote that "our ablest steersman [is at the] helm." TJ to John Melish, March 10, 1811. For Jefferson on a natural aristocracy, see TJ to John Adams, Oct. 28, 1813; LoA 1304.

Like the sailor, the citizen is a member of a community. Now, sailors have different functions, for one of them is a rower, another a pilot, and a third a look-out man. . . . They have all of them a common object, which is safety in navigation. Similarly, one citizen differs from another, but the salvation of the community is the common business of them all.

Aristotle's conclusion, that "the excellence of the citizen must be an excellence relative to the constitution," matched Jefferson's hope of training republican citizens for a republican government.

In Aristotle, Jefferson found more than a nautical metaphor that enhanced good political theory. He also found a discussion of metaphor itself. From Aristotle's discussion one may infer Jefferson's first hypothetical response to Plato, that metaphor is not philosophy and should not be employed in explaining it. Aristotle's treatment of metaphor implies that its proper settings are in poetry and in legal argument: that is, as an ornament for language and useful for persuading the public.

Jefferson agreed. He wrote of the Greeks and Romans that they "have left us the present models which exist of fine composition, whether we examine them as works of reason, or of style and fancy."[19] To learn style he advised law students to "read the orations of Demosthenes and Cicero [for] the correctness of [their] figures."[20] It is worth noting that he did not propose that students read Aristotle's *Poetics* or *Rhetoric,* where the metaphor was first examined, or the Romans who at far greater length classified, illustrated, and prescribed figures of speech. Although he had once dutifully studied these theorists himself, he went to ancient writers, and advised others to do so for models, not for precepts.[21]

19. TJ to Joseph Priestley, Jan. 27, 1800; LoA 1072.

20. TJ, enclosure to John Minor, Aug. 30, 1814; LoA 1560, 1561. Jefferson said he was updating a course of study of "near 50 years ago." This would place the original document (which has not been found) in the late 1760s, a few years after he had completed his own legal training and when he had been so engrossed in the classics.

21. For Aristotle, see *The Poetics,* chs. 21-23, 25; and *On Rhetoric,* bk. 3, chs. 2-12. The aridity of Aristotle's remarks, at least for Jefferson, may be seen in Aristotle's two examples of nautical metaphor from Homer, both of them poetically uninspiring.

The leading modern scholar of Greek metaphor, W. B. Stanford, is harsh on Aristotle. Cicero, however, with his "supreme mastery of terminology combined with his Latin precision of thought," Stanford praises as "an

By education and temperament Jefferson skipped over, indeed disdained, the masters of the Middle Ages. Yet if his antipathy to the theology and institutionalized religion of those centuries had not kept him from reading Augustine and Aquinas, he might have been stimulated by their discussions of metaphor theory, as he evidently was not by the theory of classical authors. For here metaphor theory (though not metaphor itself) served the cause of philosophy. Because Augustine's aim was a correct interpretation of Christian doctrine, he wrote what Jefferson never read but certainly believed: that it is imperative to distinguish between literal and figurative expressions. In Aquinas, on the other hand, Jefferson would have found the doctrine in which can be heard an echo of Plato on the "required" parable: that metaphor, far from being a mere figure of speech, was "both useful and necessary in representing divine truth."[22]

---

admirable interpreter of the rather untidy and free-and-easy doctrines of the Greeks," as well as for applying, if only "for a tantalizing instant," "a psychological and physiological criterion to the problem of metaphor's pleasure-giving faculty, just as he tries elsewhere to use anthropology to explain the origin of metaphor—two brilliant forecasts of modern methods." Stanford himself is enamored of the nautical metaphor, employing one at the beginning of his book ("Before I launch my frail bark upon the shifting currents of literacy criticism") and illustrating his own doctrine through an examination of "a ship ploughs the sea" from the viewpoints of a casual newspaper reader, a sailor, a farmer, and—this could be Jefferson—"the cultivated reader of literary works," who alone would understand the phrase as a true metaphor. *Greek Metaphor,* vii, 5, 35, 42, 101-2.

Among the Latin theorists of rhetoric other than Cicero, Jefferson presumably read in Quintilian (1st century A.D.) that metaphor was "by far the most beautiful of tropes," illustrating the assertion with Horace's "O navis." *Institutio Oratio,* VIII.6.4, VIII.6.44. Whatever respect Jefferson had for Quintilian, however, was not enough to consider him worth a modern edition: "We have Blair's and Adams's books which give us the rhetoric of our own language and that of a foreign and dead one will interest few readers." TJ to Wells and Lilly, April 1, 1818; LoA 1414. A phrase on metaphors in Longinus (3rd century) might also have caught Jefferson's eye: "The right time for their use is when the feelings roll on like a spring torrent." Gilbert, *Literary Criticism,* 182. But Longinus was no more a favorite classical author of Jefferson's than were theorists of rhetoric generally.

22. Augustine, *On Christian Doctrine,* bk. III. Aquinas is summarized in Shibles, *Metaphor* (1971), 30. An expansive study in the Thomistic tradition is

When Jefferson returned to metaphor of the contemporary era, that is, of the seventeenth and eighteenth centuries, he found figures that were both more showy and more introspective than those of antiquity. Nautical images themselves, however, had barely changed over the centuries, partly because seafaring had changed so little and partly because oceans were still considered to be under a form of theistic control (except that a Judeo-Christian God or a deistic providence had replaced the divinities of Greece and Rome).[23] Jefferson also found contemporary metaphor theory that made explicit what was presumably implicit in Aristotle: that metaphors had no place in philosophy.

We know that Jefferson was attracted to Shakespeare's nautical imagery in classical settings, because of his commonplacing from *Troilus & Cressida* and *Coriolanus.* If he had conceived of metaphor broadly enough to take in an entire play, he would have found it in *The Tempest,* which from its opening scene of shipwrecked mariners to Prospero's closing promise of "calm seas, auspicious gales" reminds its audience that it is set on an island at sea. Among the ways of thinking of *The Tempest* as a metaphor, however, Jefferson would probably have been particularly attentive to the island as a potential utopia.

The Tempest was no isolated model. Whether inspired by shipwreck or otherwise, several utopias of the era were set on islands that, as Jefferson said about America in his First Inaugural, were "kindly separated by . . . a wide ocean" from the havoc of the world. That islands were metaphoric homes for utopias, which themselves were

Stephen J. Brown, *The World of Imagery: Metaphor and Kindred Imagery* (1927).

23. Poems by Shakespeare, Marvell and Cowper in Appendix III illustrate the new nautical metaphor. In Sonnet 80, in seven consecutive lines, Shakespeare uses more than one image per line to help an inferior poet explain how he had been bested in love by a superior one: wide ocean, broad main, soundless deep, proud sail, saucy bark, boat, wrack'd, shallowest, afloat. An admirer of the sonnets, Jefferson would have been at home with the images, though incapable of making his own nearly as complex or personal. Andrew Marvell in "The Garden" writes of the mind as an ocean. While this is a simple, single image, Jefferson was never so introspective as to employ a metaphor in this way. Nor did Jefferson ever turn to a nautical metaphor to express a state of mind, the way William Cowper does in his metaphor of grief in "The Castaway." The poem retells a drowning at sea that had been recorded in a volume of exploration that was in Jefferson's library: George, Lord Anson, *Voyage Round the World* (1748).

metaphors for the perfect society, was one of the standard visions of progress in the early Enlightenment. Utopia was not a vision that Jefferson believed in, balanced as he was between the visionary and the practical. But as a political thinker he was familiar with imaginary worlds off at sea, most prominently Sir Francis Bacon's *New Atlantis* (1627) and James Harrington's *Commonwealth of Oceana* (1656).

Whatever the practice of the nautical metaphor of his own era meant for Jefferson, more important were the boundaries marked out by philosophers for a metaphor's proper use. One of the aims of the Baconian program for science, a program with which Jefferson wholly identified, was to protect science, or "natural knowledge," from other realms of human thought. In order to maintain the distinction between the realms, the language of science needed to be cleansed of what the earliest historian of the Royal Society labeled "the trick of Metaphors." Tropes and figures, explained Thomas Sprat,

> are in open defiance against Reason. . . . [T]hey give the mind a notion too changeable and bewitching to consist with right practice. Who can behold, without indignation, how many mists and uncertainties [they] have brought on our Knowledge. . . . [O]f all the Studies of men, nothing may be sooner obtain'd, than this vicious abundance of Phrase, this trick of Metaphors, this volubility of Tongue, which makes so great a noise in the World.[24]

This stricture is no doubt warranted in general, though Bacon himself more than permitted similes and metaphors ("similitudes and translation" in his language). He also widely practiced them. What he forbade in science were the "parables and tropes" of religion.[25]

A distinct anti-metaphor strain also appears in Hobbes and Locke, who reacted, as did Bacon, to the pervasiveness of superstition that passed for science, as well as to the exuberant use of metaphor in literature.[26] The development of Hobbes's views on metaphor provides

24. Sprat, *The History of the Royal Society of London for the Improving of Natural Knowledge* (1667), quoted in Wilbur Samuel Howell, *Logic and Rhetoric in England, 1500-1700* (1956), 389.

25. *Advancement of Learning,* bk. II, ch. XVII, sec. 10.

26. For a modern study that champions the efflorescence of metaphor of the time, see Marjorie Hope Nicolson, *The Breaking of the Circle: Studies in the Effect of the "New Science" Upon Seventeenth-Century Poetry* (1960). "George Herbert," Nicolson declares, "wrote the epitaph of the most charming

a particularly illuminating context for Jefferson's understanding of the figure. Always minded towards the classics, Hobbes translated Thucydides (1629), Aristotle's *Rhetoric* (1637?), and all of Homer (1673-76). His rather loose translation of Aristotle reflects his own early views on the "admirable variety and novelty of metaphors and similitudes."[27] But during his stay in Paris, 1640-51, Hobbes became absorbed in rationalism and returned to England to write *Leviathan,* in which he contends that a "cause of absurd conclusion" is

> the use of metaphors, tropes, and other rhetorical figures, instead of words proper; [that] in reckoning, and seeking of truth [i.e., in mathematics and philosophy], such speeches are not to be admitted; [and that] metaphors, and senseless and ambiguous words, are like *ignes fatui*; and reasoning upon them is wandering amongst unnumerable absurdities.[28]

These may seem curious assertions from the creator of one of the most potent metaphors in the history of political philosophy, and of the string of metaphors and submetaphors in the introduction to *Leviathan.* But Hobbes largely carries out his anti-metaphor program, and Jefferson, who had no use for *Leviathan* as political philosophy, was, in his delimited use of metaphor, in the Hobbesian tradition.

Above all, however, it was Locke's views on metaphor that influenced Jefferson. In his *Essay Concerning Human Understanding,*

---

poetry our language has ever known: 'Farewell, sweet phrases, lovely metaphors. . . . Lovely enchanting language.' " 46. For a study of poetic metaphor aligned with the old science in the works of the master of the metaphysical conceit, see Joseph Anthony Mazzeo, "Notes on John Donne's Alchemical Imagery" (1957). An example of the Baconian science cleansed of metaphor is William Harvey's *On the Circulation of the Blood* (1628). Yet one would not have predicted such cleansing on the basis of Harvey's dedication to Charles I: "The heart of animals is the sun of their microcosm. The King, in like manner, is the heart of the republic. The knowledge of his heart, therefore, will not be useless to a Prince, as embracing a kind of Divine example of his functions" (ellipses omitted). For a historical and philosophical discussion of "attraction" as a metaphorical formulation for gravitational force in Newton's *Principia* (1686), see J. M. Coetzee, "Newton and the Ideal of a Transparent Scientific Language" (1982).

27. Quoted without citation but presumably from the early Hobbes, in Brown, *The World of Imagery,* 111. See generally George Watson, "Hobbes and the Metaphysical Conceit" (1955).

28. *Leviathan,* pt. I, ch. 5.

Jefferson's epistemological bible, Locke warned against metaphor as deceptive and a cloud to the discovery of truth. But at the same time he realized that readers, including readers of his *Essay,* delighted in metaphor and so helped his argument along with metaphors of his own: in particular, according to a modern scholar, metaphors of the sea.[29] The ever-reasonable Locke writes of metaphor with the ambivalence the subject deserves. On the one hand he pronounces that "language is often abused by figurative speech," and holds, in the manner of Hobbes, that

> if we would speak of things as they are, we must allow that . . . all the artificial and figurative application of words eloquence hath invented, are for nothing else but to insinuate wrong ideas, move the passions, and thereby mislead the judgment; and so indeed are perfect cheats. . . . [T]hey are certainly, in all discourses that pretend to inform or instruct, wholly to be avoided; and where truth and knowledge are concerned, cannot but be thought a great fault, either of the language or person that makes use of them.

On the other hand, he recognizes that

> in discourses where we seek rather pleasure and delight than information and improvement, such ornaments . . . can scarce pass for faults. . . . And it is in vain to find fault with those arts of deceiving, wherein men find pleasure to be deceived. . . . [In metaphor and allusion] lies that entertainment and pleasantry of wit, which strikes so lively on the fancy, and therefore is so acceptable to all people, because its beauty appears at first sight, and there is required no labor of thought to examine what truth or reason there is in it.[30]

Like Jefferson, Locke risked being inconsistent. But Locke wrote the creed that is also Jefferson's. A clear distinction exists between the requirements for seeking truth and the requirements for public persuasion and literary beauty. It is a distinction that goes back to Aristotle. Jefferson is in the tradition of both the ancient thinker and the modern.[31]

29. Philip Vogt, "Seascape with Fog: Metaphor in Locke's *Essay"* (1993). For a different approach and partial reply to Vogt, see S. H. Clark, " 'The Whole Internal World his Own:' Locke and Metaphor Reconsidered" (1998).

30. *Essay Concerning Human Understanding,* bk. III, ch. X.

31. The most original European thinker on metaphor of the Enlightenment was Giambattista Vico. But Vico's anthropological-philological approach made

Nothing in eighteenth century philosophy improved on Locke's ideas about metaphor, but the figure remained important in literary criticism. Edmund Burke, following Locke, distinguished "clear expression [which] records the understanding" from "strong expression [which] belongs to the passions."[32] More pungently, David Hume wrote:

> Many of the beauties of poetry and even of eloquence are founded on falsehood and fiction, on hyperboles, metaphors, and an abuse or perversion of terms from their natural meaning. To check the sallies of the imagination, and to reduce every expression to geometrical truth and exactness, would be most contrary to the laws of criticism.[33]

In the periodicals of the time and in prominent treatises on rhetoric, Jefferson also read about theory of metaphor, along with the application of that theory to nautical figures of speech. In *The Spectator,* for instance, Joseph Addison wrote:

> There is not anything in the World, which may not be compared to several things, if considered in several distinct Lights; or, in other Words, the same thing may be expressed by different Metaphors. But the Mischief is, that an unskilful Author shall run these Metaphors so absurdly into one another, that there shall be no simile, no agreeable Picture, no apt Resemblance, but Confusion, Obscurity, and Noise.[34]

Beyond condemning ill-formed metaphors, Addison remarked that an object of the imagination could quite appropriately be used to illustrate different things. His example was the sea, which when calm could be

---

no impact on English and French thought, and Jefferson seems never to have heard of him. See Vico's *New Science,* bk. II, sec. II, ch. II; and also Isaiah Berlin, *Vico and Herder, Two Studies in the History of Ideas* (New York: Viking Press, 1976), 45-47.

32. *A Philosophical Enquiry into the Origin of our Ideas of the Sublime and Beautiful* (1756), J. T. Boulton, ed. (London, 1958), 175.

33. "Of the Standard of Taste" (1742) in *Essays: Moral, Political and Literary* (1777; repr. 1985), 231. Jefferson owned Hume's *Essays* as well as Burke's *Enquiry.*

34 *The Spectator* No. 595, Sept. 17, 1714. Jefferson owned a set of Addison and Steele's essays. An excellent statement of contemporary views on metaphor, which Jefferson also owned, is Sir Thomas Fitzosborne [William Melmoth], *Letters on Several Subjects* (1749; repr. 1971), "Letter LI," vol. 2, 44-59.

depicted as a "pleasing astonishment" and in a tempest as an "agreeable horrour."[35]

Later in the eighteenth century, thinkers of the Scottish Enlightenment, the intellectual movement Jefferson was most attached to, treated metaphor systematically and provided copious examples of what were considered good metaphors and poor ones. Lord Kames (Henry Home) and his protégé, Hugh Blair, added little to Locke or the ancients by way of theory, but they organized and confirmed the theory for modern readers. Both Kames and Blair recognize that metaphor may have an "extended sense" (metaphor as a figure of speech in general), and not only a "proper sense." But, guided by a taxonomic approach to literary criticism, they concentrate on the proper sense and therefore present metaphor in a way that perfectly fits both Jefferson's theoretical understanding and his practice. In addition, Blair, concurring in the anti-metaphor admonitions of the seventeenth century, is emphatic in holding that metaphors must be "dress, not character." When a writer reasons, he continues, "we look only for perspicuity; when he describes we expect embellishment."[36]

Treating the two together with respect to what secured their approval in practice, and what did not, we find a number of examples in Kames and Blair of nautical imagery. Kames, like Quintilian before him, points to Horace's "O navis" as a model of allegory.[37] Blair, more fashionably, quotes approvingly from a burlesque by Matthew Prior, a writer around the turn of the eighteenth century:

> Did I but purpose to embark with thee
> On the smooth surface of a summer's sea,
> While gentle zephyrs play with prosperous gales,
> And future's favor fills the swelling sails;
> But would forsake the ship, and make the shore,
> When the winds whistle, and the tempests roar?

As if sensing Jefferson among his readers, Blair also praises the works of Ossian as abounding

---

35. *The Spectator* No. 489, Sept. 20, 1712.

36. Blair, *Lectures,* 160, 161. For helpful information on the theory and practice of the time, with chapters on Locke, Burke, Kames, Blair and Jefferson's friend Joseph Priestley, see Michael G. Moran (ed.), *Eighteenth-Century British and American Rhetorics and Rhetoricians* (1994).

37. *Elements of Criticism* (6th ed. 1785), 278.

with beautiful and correct metaphors; such as that on a hero: "In peace thou art the gale of spring; in war, the mountain storm."[38]

Under the category "Figuring human life to be a voyage at sea," Kames presents Shakespeare's Brutus:

There is a tide in the affairs of men,
Which, taken at the flood, leads on to fortune;
Omitted, all the voyage of their life
Is bound in shallows and in miseries.
On such a full sea are we now afloat;
And we must take the current while it serves,
Or lose our ventures.

For his part, Blair is critical of a passage in Edward Young, one of Jefferson's favorite contemporary authors. Speaking of old age, Young says it should

Walk thoughtful on the silent, solemn shore
Of that vast ocean, it must sail so soon;
And put good works on board; and wait the wind
That shortly blows us into worlds unknown.

Blair comments: "The first two lines are uncommonly beautiful; . . . but when he continues, the metaphor . . . plainly becomes strained and sinks in dignity."[39]

Yet did Jefferson really pay attention to the particularized judgments of the critics, or even to the theory in back of those judgments? Both Kames and Blair fault as a mixed metaphor Hamlet's "to take arms against a sea of troubles."[40] This is a criticism of Shakespeare common to the times, but it might not have appealed to Jefferson, who was little burdened with aesthetic theory. He claimed to "despise artificial canons of criticism," holding that

38. Blair, *Lectures on Rhetoric,* 164.
39. Blair, 167. Jefferson recommended Young in his reading list of 1771 and quoted him fifteen years later in his "Thoughts on English Prosody." LoA 743, 600, 610, 611. For nautical metaphors in Jefferson's commonplace book by Young's contemporaries, see Appendix III under John Langhorne and James Thomson; and under George Villers for a parody on nautical metaphor in a play popular in Jefferson's time. For a parody metaphor in Samuel Richardson's *Clarissa,* condemned in the twentieth century as "overdone," see H. S. Fowler, *A Dictionary of Modern English Usage* (1926), 349.
40. Kames, 287; Blair, 167.

one should ask about a work of art "only whether it gives . . . pleasure, whether it is animating, interesting, attracting? If it is, it is good for those reasons."[41] Artificial canons of criticism might get in the way of exercising our innate faculty of taste, he held, just as over-training in ethics could be an impediment to exercising our innate sense of morality.[42]

But even if he said he was indifferent to it, Jefferson practiced what contemporary theory held. His own nautical metaphors met the most proper standards, never deviating from the classical pattern. At the same time, he did not require of others the style that he followed himself. He never came close to writing extended voyage-of-life metaphors, at bottom, no doubt, because he was not a poet. But he freely copied them from contemporary poetry into his commonplace book, such as this one, which takes us across the River Styx to the

> sacred shore,
> Beyond time's troubled sea, where never wave,
> Where never wind of passion or of guilt,
> Or suffering, or of sorrow, shall invade
> The calm, sound night of those who rest below.
> The weary are at peace; the small and great,
> Life's voiage ended, meet and mingle here.[43]

A second example of the baroque practice of others that Jefferson admired when young makes a surprising connection to one of his more

41. TJ to William Wirt, Nov. 12, 1816; F.X.61.

42. See TJ to John Waldo, Aug. 16, 1813; LoA 1295 (he was "more indebted for style to reading and memory" than to rules). On an innate sense of the beautiful, see TJ to Thomas Law, June 13, 1814; LoA 1336. See also TJ, "Thoughts on English Prosody" (1786); LoA 614 (anyone incapable of reading Homer without sensing the correct meter "is an unfavored son of nature to whom she has given a faculty fewer than to others"); and TJ to Maria Cosway, April 24, 1788; LoA 921 ("I am but a son of nature, loving what I see and feel, without being able to give a reason, nor caring much whether there be one"). On a natural sense of ethics, see TJ to Peter Carr, Aug. 10, 1787; LoA 901-02. Jefferson held that the moral and aesthetic senses are independent of each other, but maintained that the example of characters in good literature would lead to good behavior. See TJ to Robert Skipwith, Aug. 3, 1771; LoA 741 (in literature "everything is useful which contributes to fix the principles and practices of virtue"); and TJ to Peter Carr, cited above ("the writings of Sterne particularly form the best course of morality that ever was written").

43. David Mallet, "Excursion," LCB.132.

restrained metaphors many years later. The underlying theme is the same, the voyage of life. In 1771, under the title "Inscription for an African Slave," Jefferson copied out the following verses, which he intended for a pedestal "on the grave of a favorite and faithful servant" at Monticello:

Shores there are, bless'd shores for us remain,
And favor'd isles with golden fruitage crown's
Where tufted flow'rets paint the verdant plain,
Where ev'ry breeze shall med'cine every wound.

There the stern tyrant that embitters life
shall vainly suppliant, spread his asking hand;
There shall we view the billow's raging strife,
Aid the kind breast, and waft his boat to land.[44]

Though hardly personalized, these lines are compassionate, and they undoubtedly reflect Jefferson's views at the time. Yet it might have been uncomfortable for a slaveholder, whether sensitive or detached, to display verses, even in the guise of a nautical metaphor, that speak of healing wounds inflicted by a stern tyrant, and Jefferson never used them. But half a century later Jefferson hoped to stand aside from the national debate on slavery on the ground that he was "content to be a passenger in our bark to the shore from which I am not distant."[45] Like the deceased slave, though in more classical language, at the end of his life's voyage he was to be removed from "the billow's raging strife."

In contrast to most seventeenth and eighteenth century literature, which was so unlike his own practice, Jefferson must have been relieved to find the classically controlled nautical imagery of Milton, where he could see his own future style. Such imagery was true throughout "Lycidas," Milton's ode to a friend who had drowned at sea, and a poem that Jefferson presumably read. Nautical imagery also appeared in *Samson Agonistes,* which we know Jefferson read because he entered these lines in his commonplace book:

What Pilot so expert but needs must wreck,
Imbark'd with such a Steermate at the Helm?

As was customary, Jefferson commonplaced the lines not for the metaphor, but for the real life sentiment they conveyed. Milton was writing on the

44. The verses were misattributed to Jefferson for more than a century. See Appendix III for their source in William Shenstone.
45. TJ to John Holmes, April 22, 1820.

temptations of love, which was possibly Jefferson's own circumstance at the time. But when he began to fashion his own nautical figures a number of years later, and the context was politics rather than love, he did so in a similar style. It was a style derived from an education in the classics and confirmed by Milton, the most classically-minded of the moderns.

SECTION 3

JEFFERSON'S NAUTICAL METAPHORS

WHEN THE TIME CAME for Jefferson to write his own nautical metaphors, he was imbued with the classics as a model both for his style in general and for the nautical metaphor in particular. He was also familiar with classical metaphor theory. Although he barely commented on it, he practiced that part of the more recent theory that was critical of figures of speech for their potential to stand in the way of truth. He had read nautical imagery in the literature of his age. In light of this background it is not surprising that he employed nautical metaphors frequently, at the same time keeping them under close control. But however varied and stylistically appealing, his metaphors never carried or even enlarged upon his principal ideas. In this respect his nautical metaphors differed from many of the metaphors he had read. They also differed from the nautical metaphors of gifted writers and thinkers who came after him. And they differed from his own, often more telling, non-nautical metaphors.[1]

When Jefferson's nautical metaphors are examined individually, their meaning is sometimes not immediately clear. As a whole, however, they are not difficult to analyze, and the opening remarks of this section are drawn from an inspection of the entire group, printed in Appendix I.

1. Since a study of nautical metaphors by Jefferson's contemporaries does not exist, I can only report that while the practice was certainly common, no one else seems to have used the metaphors with Jefferson's frequency or consciousness of style. As might be expected, John Adams is especially unconstrained in devising his. Examples from Adams and several other writers of the time, including satirical verse from the partisan press (*Aurora* and *Echo*), are printed in Appendix III.

When viewed chronologically, we find that the metaphors are not spread evenly over Jefferson's writings. At times they are prolific, at other times scarce. The years of greatest use correspond with the turbulent decade of establishing the national government, 1789-98. They peak thereafter on three occasions approximately a decade apart: when he entered the presidency in 1801, when he retired from it in 1809, and when he commented on the "Missouri Question" in 1819-20. The metaphors in these concentrated years account for more than half the entire list. Interestingly, these years are not identical to the times when, in his public duties, Jefferson is especially concerned with the sea—not when he is writing on fisheries, establishing maritime law, dealing with pirates or impressment, building up the navy, or carrying out a trade embargo against England. This reinforces the view that his nautical metaphors are strictly matters of style or reflections of temperament. Classical both in their restrained language and non-nautical choice of occasions, Jefferson's metaphors are kept in their place. A glance at the list also reveals a range of recipients, with Jefferson's political ally and eventual neighbor, James Monroe, far in the lead.

A reading of the nautical metaphors for purposes of classifying them by type finds Jefferson faithful to the main branches of the classical tradition: ship of state and voyage of life. But his voyage-of-life metaphors are often as political as his ship-of-state figures because the voyage of life that he preferred was frequently obstructed by the demands of serving on the ship of state. Jefferson also uses a cousin of ship of state that is social, though not necessarily political: We're all in the same boat. This metaphor he employs not in private correspondence but in appeals to larger audiences.[2] An exception to the classical sources of Jefferson's nautical metaphors are several on political whales, minnows, and fishing. No matter which variety of the metaphor he deploys, we find a good deal of passivity in Jefferson's expression. He is a mere passenger aboard the ship of state and on the voyage of life.

No examples of nautical metaphors appear in Jefferson's writings before the 1780s (when, admittedly, there is rather little material to consult). At the time of independence one finds his colleagues in Phila-

2. See TJ to the County Lieutenants of Berkeley and Frederick, Feb. 16, 1781; and TJ, Draft of the Kentucky Resolutions, Oct. 1798.

delphia using such metaphors (Washington and Adams), but it may be that Jefferson's interest in the figure was only kindled a few years later, when he was governor of Virginia. At that time he read a nautical metaphor in a letter from his closest friend from college days, John Page. Eager to leave office in the middle of his term, Jefferson had proposed that Page succeed him. But his friend, who had already resigned as lieutenant governor, thought the idea perverse. It was not himself, Page said, but Jefferson who demonstrated the "skill to steer us through the storm" and who should not "leave the helm" in favor of someone who had just "quitted the ship . . . unable to hand a rope or keep the deck, even in a calm. It [Jefferson's idea] will never do."[3]

Not long after hearing from Page, Jefferson began his own career with nautical metaphors. His early ones make reference to constitutional principles that few quarreled with. A bicameral legislature was necessary to prevent shipwreck; trial by jury was an anchor.[4] Soon, however, he began to fear for the republican principles of the Revolution as long as the nation was directed by an anti-republican faction of Federalists. He criticized Congress for resting on its oars, though later reluctantly agreed that republicans must do the same, letting the bark drift so long as George Washington remained at the watch.[5] At the same time he encouraged political allies to hold on "till our brother-sailors [in Congress] can rouse from their intoxication & right the vessel." More dramatically, he pled with them to help avoid shipwreck.[6] To a French acquaintance, on the other hand, he wrote reassuringly: "We too have our aristocrats and monocrats, and as they float on the surface, they shew much, though they weigh little."[7]

3. John Page to TJ, Oct. 20, 1780.

4. TJ to La Rochefoucauld, April 3, 1790; TJ to Thomas Paine, July 11, 1789. For a numbingly long nautical metaphor on the floor of Congress at the time, see James Jackson in Appendix III. Another Congressman, Fisher Ames, devised an arresting "proportional metaphor" in which a monarchy is to a merchantman as a republic is to a raft. Jefferson was never as verbose as Jackson or as clever as Ames.

5. TJ to James Monroe, June 20, 1790; TJ to James Monroe, June 12, 1796; TJ to Archibald Stuart, Jan. 4, 1797; TJ to Nicholas Lewis, Feb. 9, 1791; TJ to George Washington, May 23, 1792.

6. TJ to William Branch Giles, Dec. 17, 1794; TJ to James Madison, Dec. 28, 1794.

7. TJ to Jean Pierre Brissot de Warville, May 8, 1793.

While Jefferson himself was longing for and eventually enjoying the port of Monticello after resigning as secretary of state, he urged others to continue at the helm, or take it, or in some way come to the aid of the public vessel.[8] As the political crisis of the late 1790s worsened, he witnessed waves agitating the vessel and discovered in the American union (by which he meant the federated states, not the national government) a "common bottom" and "the last anchor of our hope."[9]

Jefferson's nautical metaphors on foreign affairs were nearly as common as those on domestic politics, beginning with his service in Europe in the mid-1780s. He described the French government as engaged in throwing out a barrel for political whales, and a dispute over the West Indian trade as a furious tempest.[10] As secretary of state he was more generous, finding France to be the sheet anchor of the United States.[11] Several years later he held that John Adams and the Federalists would have to steer clear of European difficulties. He criticized American merchants for lying on their oars and the public generally for only slowly coming to recognize the port (England) towards which their leaders were steering. More humiliating, the United States was being

8. TJ to George Washington, May 23, 1792; TJ to James Madison, April 17, 1795; TJ to Edward Rutledge, Nov. 30, 1795. On Jefferson's departure from Washington's cabinet in January 1794, General Horatio Gates, a friend from Revolutionary days, chastised him: "If the best Seamen abandon the Ship in a Storm, she must Founder; and if all Human means are neglected, Providence will not Care for the Vessel; She must Perish!" Gates to TJ, Jan. 5, 1794. Jefferson's "right of retirement," which he applied selectively to himself, was related to a "right never to serve," which he had applied during the Revolution to his friend, the scientist David Rittenhouse: "Nobody can conceive that nature ever intended to throw away a Newton upon the occupations of a crown." TJ to David Rittenhouse, July 19, 1778; LoA 763. Much earlier, Benjamin Franklin had used a nautical metaphor to argue just the opposite: "Had Newton been Pilot but of a single common Ship, the finest of his Discoveries would scarce have excus'd or atton'd for his abandoning the Helm one Hour in the Time of Danger." Franklin to Cadwallader Colden, Oct. 11, 1750.

9. TJ to Thomas Pinckney, May 29, 1797; Draft of the Kentucky Resolutions, Oct. 1798; TJ to Elbridge Gerry, May 13, 1797.

10. TJ to Richard Henry Lee, Feb. 7, 1785; TJ to Elbridge Gerry, May 11, 1785.

11. TJ to William Short, March 15, 1791; TJ to William Short, Jan. 3, 1793. A sheet anchor is one which can be depended on in emergencies.

treated as a fish flouncing on the hook of a dexterous British angler.[12]

In the mid-1790s, reporting discontent in upcountry Virginia over the treaty that John Jay had negotiated with England, Jefferson was so carried away with a nautical metaphor that when he finally checked himself, he did so with a rare remark—it does not amount to a reflection—about his own style:

> Our part of the country is in considerable fermentation. . . . They say that while all hands were below deck mending sails, splicing ropes, and every one at his own business, & the captain in his cabin attending to his log book & chart, a rogue of a pilot has run them into an enemy's port. But metaphor apart, there is much dissatisfaction with Mr. Jay & his treaty.[13]

For such a lengthy figure, this is not a metaphor that contains much substance. Rather, as with most of his nautical metaphors, Jefferson seems simply, if stylishly, to be enjoying himself. Mending sails and splicing ropes have no external referents, but merely confirm the scene. "Below deck . . . attending [their] own business" suggests that Americans were either not taking their civic obligations seriously or were quite properly engaged in non-political activities. Captain Washington is concerned with the long view, while Helmsman Jay has steered into the English port. Except for its length and his self-consciousness on emerging from it, this is a typical nautical figure for Jefferson, noticeable and agreeable as epistolary style but contributing little if any meaning to his subject.

Far different are an extraordinary series of nautical metaphors, ten of them, that surround Jefferson's election as president in 1800. This series, which is worth reading verbatim, has a life of its own. It begins with what amounts to a rehearsal metaphor in December 1800, continues with three figures in the Inaugural address itself on March 4, 1801, climaxes two days later in one of his most beautiful examples, plateaus with half a dozen variations through the rest of March, and drops off with a pointed but less than beautiful one in early May. If we ignore their dramatic arc, the story line is this. The Constitution, or the American nation, is an indestructible vessel, an Argosie with tough sides. Trimmed to a federalist (or Federalist) tack and steered into a storm, she almost shipwrecked. But though her rigging was crippled

12. TJ to James Madison, Dec. 17, 1796; TJ to James Madison, June 1, 1797; TJ to Arthur Campbell, Sept. 1, 1797; TJ to Aaron Burr, June 17, 1797.
13. TJ to Mann Page, Aug. 30, 1795.

and many good men had abandoned deck, the vessel can now safely moor on the rock of national character and be steered on her natural, republican course, proving the skill of her builders by the smoothness of her motion.

This 1800-1801 collection is notable for two reasons. First, for an image that fundamentally does not vary, Jefferson is remarkably unrepetitive in his expression of it. The collection thereby testifies to Jefferson's mature ingenuity with the figure. Second, since the subject matter of the metaphors, the "Revolution of 1800," does not change, the series offers an unusual opportunity, a kind of controlled experiment, to examine how, even in metaphor, Jefferson fashioned his language to fit his audience. In the examination that follows we see this in the distinction between Jefferson's public and private utterance, in the historical significance of his writing to a colleague from the revolutionary era, and the philosophical orientation of his metaphor in a letter to a scientist and theologian.

The Inaugural address is arguably Jefferson's finest state paper, its only competition being the Declaration of Independence, a document whose contents were much less his own. The Inaugural has two aims. The first is to lay out Jeffersonian principles of government. The second is to bring the country together after an intensely partisan presidential election. In the course of carrying out the second aim Jefferson writes the most prominent nautical metaphors of the occasion. He is speaking to a Congress that, through a constitutional flaw in the electoral college system, has just barely elected him. Now, on behalf of the new administration, he appeals to Congress "for that guidance and support which may enable us to steer with safety the vessel in which we are all embarked amidst the conflicting elements of a troubled world." A few sentences later he explains how the safety of the vessel came to be at risk:

> During the throes and convulsions of the ancient world, during the agonizing spasms of infuriated man, seeking through blood and slaughter his long-lost liberty, it was not wonderful that the agitations of the billows should reach even this distant and peaceful shore.

Ultimately, he asks for the "preservation of the general government in its whole constitutional vigor, as the sheet anchor of our peace at home and safety abroad."

The nautical metaphors in the Inaugural are unmistakable, but they are sparser and less imaginative than in his private correspondence at the time. It is as if Jefferson were conscious that his stylistic hallmark needed to be restrained in public in order to keep the audience focused on his political goals. Compare this version of the Inaugural metaphor in a letter to Lafayette, a week after the address:

> The convulsion of Europe shook even us to our centre. A few hardy spirits stood firm to their post, and the ship has breasted the storm. . . . I will only add that the storm we have passed through proves our vessel indestructible.[14]

But even in their less dramatic public form, Jefferson's metaphors serve their purpose. In the Inaugural both their style and their reference to foreign affairs draw attention away from the domestic fight for the presidency. Jefferson's light touch with the ship-of-state metaphor also speaks to the classical education of his congressional audience, regardless of party.

The reconciliation aim of the Inaugural is best known through the phrase "We are all republicans; we are all federalists." The phrase is a tricky one, but it is certainly the principles of republicanism and federalism that Jefferson is talking about, not political parties. On the other hand, in his private correspondence of 1801 he wrote only to Republicans or republicans and so did not mind being partisan as well as principled. This is the case with his letters to John Dickinson and Joseph Priestley.

Dickinson, the first person to whom he wrote with a nautical metaphor after the inauguration, was a good choice for several reasons. He was the most prominent political thinker from the revolutionary era to whom Jefferson could write—John Adams, just defeated for the presidency, having become an ineligible correspondent. By virtue of his role in the Continental Congresses of the 1770s and 1780s Dickinson was perhaps the nation's best example of an earlier patriot-conciliator, precisely the kind of person Jefferson now hoped to be. Although the two men had taken different approaches to the break with Great Britain, they had worked together at the time. Dickinson had written a widely circulated early critique of English policy in "Letters from a Farmer in Pennsylvania to the Inhabitants of the British Colonies" (1767). In 1775 he had joined with Jefferson in composing the "Declaration of the Causes of Taking Up Arms," a prelude to the Declaration of Independence

---

14. TJ to Lafayette, March 13, 1801.

(which out of conservative principle Dickinson declined to sign). When the break with England came Dickinson joined the revolutionaries, helped draft the Articles of Confederation, participated in the Philadelphia convention, and signed the Constitution—whose ratification he urged in letters signed with the classical tag of the cautious Roman general, Fabius. These were services to the United States that Jefferson could not forget.

This is what Jefferson wrote to his old friend:

> The storm through which we have passed, has been tremendous indeed. The tough sides of our Argosie have been thoroughly tried. Her strength has stood the waves into which she was steered, with a view to sink her. We shall put her on her republican tack, & she will show by the beauty of her motion the skill of her builders.[15]

Dickinson was one of Jefferson's fellow builders of the Argosie—of the new nation and its principles. But "Argosie" more than added a familiar touch to a correspondent who was steeped in the classics. Jefferson had devised an image that went beyond the metaphors in the Inaugural. The tough sides of the Argosie were the republican and federal principles of the Constitution, a rephrasing of the Inaugural's "We are all republicans; we are all federalists."

Jefferson's letter to Joseph Priestley was less overtly political than the one to Dickinson. Its unusual nautical image is incorporated into a philosophic and scientific meditation that is intended to suit the mind of its recipient, a scientist, a deist and, because of his sympathies with the French Revolution, an exile from England. Priestley could hardly have been more unlike Dickinson, his almost exact contemporary. Priestley lived by Reason. The prudent Dickinson had famously declared, "Experience must be our only guide. Reason may mislead us." That Jefferson was on warm terms with both men is a tribute to an intellect well balanced between Reason and Experience. This is what he wrote his philosopher-scientist acquaintance:

> As the storm is now subsiding, and the horizon becoming serene, it is pleasant to consider the phenomenon with attention. . . . [T]his whole chapter in the history of man is new. The great extent of our Republic is new. Its sparse habitation is new. The mighty wave of public opinion

---

15. TJ to John Dickinson, March 6, 1801. The next sentence begins, "Figure apart . . . ." Aside from the letter to Mann Page quoted above, this is the only example found of Jefferson's alluding to his penchant for metaphor.

which has rolled over it is new. But the most pleasing novelty is, its so quickly subsiding over such an extent of surface to its true level again.[16]

In this passage, instead of looking to the past, as he had in the metaphor to Dickinson, or speaking of the immediate present, as in the metaphors of the Inaugural, Jefferson speculates on the future and asks what is distinctive about the United States in world history. The scientific phenomenon to be examined is the political storm that preceded his becoming president. The waves of that storm quickly subsided because the American chapter in the history of man was new: in the country's extent, its habitation, and, Jefferson implied, its political principles. A wave of public opinion in America could quickly subside to its true, republican level because the surface of the nation was so broad. In suggesting this benefit, Jefferson was, if opaquely, bringing federalism into his metaphor, too, not only republicanism, for it was a federal, or extensive republic, that theorists of the Constitution asserted would ameliorate the political tumult associated with the small republics of European history.

Whether Jefferson intended or Priestley understood the metaphor in this way we cannot say. But in the context of his nautical metaphors of 1801 and in view of his principles in politics and practice at metaphor, a republican/federal interpretation of the metaphor to Priestley is as plausible as in the case of the metaphor to Dickinson. Each is tailored to its recipient. Both metaphors continue the Inaugural theme that occasioned them, "We are all republicans; we are all federalists."

After the display of 1801, Jefferson wrote few nautical metaphors while he was president. When he resumed his habit at the end of his second administration, the features and mood of his images had changed. He is now desperate to leave the sea of politics for the haven of Monticello. Anticipating retirement within a year, he already speaks of having reached the harbor, trusting that his successor will begin on a calmer sea than he did because the vessel is in the hands of its friends. He repeats the sentiment several months after he has left office.[17] In March 1809, safe in port at last, he looks on those still buffeting the storm with anxiety but not with envy.[18] The storm he was referring to was the fury in New England and New York

16. TJ to Joseph Priestley, March 21, 1801.
17. TJ to James Monroe, March 10, 1808; TJ to Richard M. Johnson, March 10, 1808; TJ to Charles Pinckney, Aug. 29, 1809.
18. TJ to Dupont de Nemours, March 2, 1809; TJ to Gen. John Armstrong, March 5, 1809.

directed at the embargo laws of 1807-09. Instead of forcing the British to abandon the impressment of American sailors and the French to abandon the confiscation of American goods, the embargo had led to the collapse of the nation's maritime commerce and the repeal of the legislation with the support of northern Republicans. Jefferson said these consequences were not the fault of American policy but of British intransigence. He agreed that a fog had arisen in the east (disaffected and defecting Republicans), but warned that dangerous rocks and shoals remained (the British).[19]

At this juncture, 1809, we may let the language of others describe the situation. About Jefferson's successor, John Adams wrote:

> I pity poor Madison. He comes to the helm in such a storm as I have seen in the Gulph Stream, or rather such as I had to encounter in the government in 1797. Mine was the worst however, because he has a great Majority of the officers and Men attached to him and I had all the officers and half the Crew always ready to throw me overboard.[20]

But about Jefferson, a visitor to Monticello reported:

> He has passed through the tempestuous sea of political life, has been enveloped in clouds of calumny, the storms of faction . . . and often threatened with a wreck, of happiness and fame. But these things are now all passed away, and like the mountain on which he stands, fogs and mists and storms gather and rage below, while he enjoys unclouded sunshine.[21]

Jefferson himself told correspondents that he had such confidence in the new watchmen at the helm, led by their ablest steersman (Madison), that he slept secure in knowledge that the ship was sound.[22]

Of course Jefferson could not avert his mind's eye from politics for long, and public affairs drew his attention throughout retirement. Nothing remotely exercised him as much as the threat posed in 1820 by the Missouri Question, a phrase standing for the admission of Missouri to the union as slave or free and for the status of slavery in the territories. Slavery had been the torment of Jefferson's life, but the possibility that it would be a rock that shattered the union, drove him to despair. As he wrote John Adams at the beginning of the congressional debate on Missouri's admission, many political questions "are occurrences which like waves in a storm will pass

19. TJ to Governor Robert Wright of Maryland, April 3, 1809.
20. John Adams to Benjamin Rush, March 4, 1809.
21. Margaret Bayard Smith, Aug. 1, 1809.
22. TJ to William Duane, Aug. 12, 1810; TJ to John Melish, March 10, 1811.

under the ship." But this one? It "is a breaker on which we lose the Missouri country by revolt, and what more, God only knows."[23]

The "breaker" figure here is the most anguished of several in Jefferson's letters on the Missouri Question. In other letters, two of his figures are as striking, but more positive. One depicts Missouri simply as a wave on the boisterous sea of liberty.[24] Another belongs to his small group of whaling images.[25]

But a final metaphor in the series deserves special attention. It represents not Missouri and the ship of state, but Jefferson himself on the voyage of life—and in the mode that he favored, that of a passive passenger on that voyage. He was, he said about the crisis over slavery, "content to be a passenger in our bark to the shore from which I am not distant."[26] But this metaphor is then swallowed up almost immediately by two non-nautical metaphors, about the fate of the union and the fate of slavery. The second of them, "we have the wolf by the ear," is perhaps the most memorable metaphor he ever penned. Nautical metaphors had met their match.

By their nature, ship-of-state and voyage-of-life metaphors appear in different settings. The first refer to public affairs, the second to an individual in his private capacity. But as the voyage-of-life figure in the letter about slavery suggests, and as may be recalled from Jefferson's plans half a century earlier to use a voyage metaphor for his "Inscription for an African Slave," Jefferson lived so much in the public world that nautical metaphors that normally belonged in the private world could not avoid public implications.[27] Renewing his friendship with John Adams in 1812,

23. TJ to John Adams, Dec. 10, 1819. Jefferson was seldom given to invoking God, but slavery had occasioned it as early as 1785, in *Notes on the State of Virginia:* "I tremble for my country [Virginia] when I reflect that God is just." LoA 289.

24. TJ to Richard Rush, Oct. 20, 1820; TJ to Lafayette, Dec. 26, 1820.

25. TJ to Charles Pinckney, Sept. 30, 1820.

26. TJ to John Holmes, April 22, 1820; see also TJ to Thomas Ritchie, Dec. 25, 1820 ("an inert passenger"); TJ to Samuel Kercheval, July 12, 1816 ("resign myself as a passenger"); and TJ to Francis Hopkinson, June 13, 1790 ("only a passenger").

27. Insofar as voyage-of-life metaphors are personal they may also sound, or at least murmur, a religious tone. Whether a religious tone is faint or clear in Jefferson's metaphors, however, depends as much on who is listening as on the words of the metaphors themselves. In text or context, Jefferson's voyage-of-life metaphors have nothing about them that is explicitly Christian, and can

Jefferson opens with a nautical metaphor that is both public and personal:

> Laboring always at the same oar, with some wave ever ahead threatening to overwhelm us and yet passing harmless under our bark, we knew not how, we rode through the storm with heart and hand, and made a happy port.[28]

Even at the end, his voyage-of-life metaphors are not completely private in their reference, for Jefferson never lost touch with the scene of his life's main work. In 1824 he blended the two metaphors in writing to an old acquaintance: "I resign myself cheerfully to the managers of the ship, and the more contentedly, as I am near the end of my voyage."[29] Combining public and private realms through nautical metaphor in a different way in the last year of his life, Jefferson returned to the classics of his youth, this time to Greek legend. Appropriately, the image appears in his final letter to John Adams. Now, imagining a near Homeric setting, he asks Adams to receive his grandson, who was visiting New England:

> Like other young people, he wishes to be able, in the winter nights of old age, to recount to those around him what he has heard and learnt of the Heroic age preceding his birth and which of the Argonauts particularly he was in time to have seen. . . . Theirs are the Halcyon calms succeeding the storm which our Argosy had so stoutly weathered.[30]

Nothing more Jeffersonian could have closed the record of one of the great friendships in American history.

---

more reasonably be read as derived from the classical tradition. A perspicacious essay on Jefferson's religious outlook is Paul K. Conkin, "The Religious Pilgrimage of Thomas Jefferson." But I do not believe with Conkin that Jefferson was "always confident of life after death" (20), even if some of his voyage-of-life metaphors can be interpreted to support the claim. Rather, I find Conkin's assertion about Jefferson undermined by his own persuasive discussion of the classical influences on Jefferson, both Stoic and Epicurean.

28. TJ to John Adams, Jan. 21, 1812.
29. TJ to Edward Livingston, April 4, 1824.
30. TJ to John Adams, March 25, 1826.

SECTION 4

JEFFERSON'S NON-NAUTICAL METAPHORS

IN THIS SECTION we learn about Jefferson's nautical metaphors by contrasting them with his metaphors on other subjects. His metaphors about the sea are by far the more numerous, and his non-nautical metaphors do not challenge them as a distinctive feature of his writing. But the non-nautical metaphors embrace many subjects and are often more striking, more extended, or more passionately felt than the nautical ones. Significantly, unlike any of his nautical metaphors, Jefferson's non-nautical metaphors are at times philosophical.

Table I outlines Jefferson's metaphors in their entirety. The table is organized according to what is helpful for discussion rather than according to a consistent logic (always a dubious endeavor when it comes to metaphors). The table shows at a glance the wide array of topics that prompted Jefferson's metaphorical creativity. Anyone familiar with Jefferson's writings will recognize many of the examples but may still be surprised at their scope. The table also provides graphic evidence of the significance of metaphor in general as an element of Jefferson's style.

Jefferson's Metaphors

Nautical
ship of state
voyage of life
all in the same boat
whales

Mechanical
the atmosphere: rebellion is like a storm
the planetary system: American federalism
    (a) approaches perfection
    (b) contains a wandering star

Organic
liberty:
    (a) achieving it is worth rivers of blood
    (b) its tree is nourished by blood
women: flowers
old age:
    (a) an overripe fruit
    (b) a solitary tree without limbs
worthless money: leaves
the spread of settlers: leaves
political opponents: they plant thorns and sow tares
Federalist judicial offices: parasite limb
education: like cultivating a wild plant
genius: sowing its seeds

Domestic
removing a boiling pot from the fire: adjourning Congress
chimneys carry off smoke: newspapers vent political fury
weaving: unraveling error from the web of life
family: Indians
plowman: decides a moral case as well as a professor
firebell in the night: a fright in public affairs
wolf by the ear: a potentially fatal dilemma (slavery)

Two further observations are suggested by the table directly. The first is that Jefferson, who had a leaning toward pacifism, also maintained that violence was inevitable, and in the achievement of liberty was even desirable. Typically sanguine, he could also be sanguinary. With either acute foresight or misjudgment of the moment, he predicted the French Revolution five years before the storming of the Bastille. Writing from Paris in 1784, he observed:

> The lamp of war is kindled here, not to be extinguished but by torrents of blood.[1]

The heady years in France occasioned a comparable response to Shays' Rebellion, the uprising of farmers in western Massachusetts in 1787:

> The tree of liberty must be refreshed from time to time, with the blood of patriots and tyrants. It is its natural manure.[2]

In old age he returned to the image, still a perfect Jacobin. For mankind to attain representative government, he wrote,

> rivers of blood must yet flow, and years of desolation pass over. Yet the object is worth [it] for what inheritance so valuable can man leave to his posterity?[3]

A second observation from the table is that, in an apparent lapse of stylistic sense, Jefferson employed metaphors so simple as to risk being banal. Look at some of his domestic metaphors: money as worthless as leaves, a pot removed from a boiling fire, a chimney that carries off smoke. But to examine these metaphors in their contexts is to prove the observation of banality misleading. Like most of their nautical cousins the domestic metaphors are sheer ornament. And like the nautical ones they are rescued from banality by careful selection, phrasing, and placement. Consider: "I did not receive the money till it was not worth oak leaves."[4] Appropriately, this refers to a payment for the sale of lands. "Oak" saves the metaphor from undue generality (as in "not worth leaves") and specifies the most common forest tree at Monticello. The compactness and elegance of the phrasing hones the figure. (Jefferson does not write: "worth as little as oak leaves" or the simile, "was like oak leaves.") An even more ordinary figure, also well

1. TJ to James Madison, Nov. 11, 1784.
2. TJ to William Stephens Smith, Nov. 13, 1787.
3. TJ to John Adams, Sept. 4, 1823.
4. TJ to Alexander McCaul, April 19, 1786.

chosen and perfectly placed, similarly shows what Jefferson could accomplish. In a letter on the congressional storm over the XYZ Affair of 1798 he wrote to Madison: "To separate [adjourn] Congress now, will be withdrawing the fire from under a boiling pot."[5] In an unusually long letter this metaphor not only makes a dramatic contrast to the unadorned style of the preceding paragraphs, it aptly summarizes Jefferson's description of explosive politics and his recommendation regarding how to deal with the situation.

Among the points Table I cannot demonstrate is that a single letter may contain more than one metaphor. Such occasions occur when Jefferson is especially exercised, whether in love or in politics, and when, in old age, he writes with the ease of friendship. The most extended and complex example of his use of metaphor is his amatory "Dialogue Between my Head and my Heart," composed for Maria Cosway when he was in France. Two classical schools of philosophy—Stoicism, the "head" in the dialogue, and Epicureanism, the "heart"—confront one another without ever being named. This pair of silent metaphors is carried out through a number of sub-metaphors (among them a nautical one).

For compactness of metaphors nothing matches Jefferson's letter in 1820 on the Missouri Compromise:

> I had for a long time [been] content to be a passenger in our bark to the shore from which I am not distant. But this momentous question, like a fire bell in the night, awakened and filled me with terror. I considered it at once as the knell of the union. It is hushed, indeed, for the moment. But this is a reprieve only, not a final sentence. . . . [A]s it is, we have the wolf by the ear, and we can neither hold him, nor safely let him go.[6]

Here Jefferson achieves his rhetorical power with three metaphors that accompany the growing drama of the argument: (i) a calm opening with a nautical metaphor—"content to be a passenger in our bark"; (ii) a dramatic interruption—"fire bell in the night"; and (iii) a dangerously unstable future—"we have the wolf by the ear." A lesser writer might have used more metaphors or found an overarching image whose variants could be applied to the stages of the argument. But in either of those cases, instead of enhancing the meaning, metaphor would have taken it over. The passage, especially its last sentence, is an inspiration of image, truth and meter. It is a fused achievement in meaning and style, its cadence heightening its impact.

5. TJ to James Madison, June 21, 1798.
6. TJ to John Holmes, April 22, 1820.

For a moment, Jefferson is a writer in the tradition of the Greek tragedians. In an 1823 letter to John Adams it is the ruminative Jefferson who produces a string of metaphors. He begins by noting the "hoary winter of age" and the "friendly hand of death." He ends with arresting references to the efforts of enemies "to plant thorns on the pillow of age [and] sow tares between friends." In between is a another metaphor, one that displays a more complex psychology than Jefferson commonly acknowledged, even if behind that psychology lies a simple view of the nature of truth:

> [A]ll men who have attended to the workings of the human mind, who have seen the false colors under which passion sometimes dresses the actions of others, have seen also those passions subsiding with time and reflection, dissipating, like mists before the rising sun, and restoring to us the sight of all things in their true shape and colors.[7]

Among Jefferson's revelatory metaphors which speak more than their gracefully composed language seems to say and actually tell us something about his thinking, are those about women and Indians. These metaphors reflect distinctions that he made among mankind, regardless that he held all people morally equal. In addition, the metaphors on women and Indians speak directly to audiences who are expected to learn the lessons the metaphors express, whether the expression is poetic or admonitory.

Jefferson respected the intelligence of a number of women, such as Abigail Adams and his elder daughter, Martha. But he did not doubt that by nature women belonged in the home, whether as managers of a complex household or bearing and raising children. Women did not belong in the public realm. This is the lesson of a botanical metaphor that Jefferson wrote to his eldest granddaughter, who had just given birth to his first great-grandchild:

> The flowers come forth like the belles of the day, have their short reign of beauty and splendor, and retire like them to the more interesting office of reproducing their like.[8]

Although stylishly phrased by a horticulturalist, the metaphor is an assertion, if an implied one, about the place of women. It is not a mere epistolary decoration.

With respect to Indians, Jefferson's primary metaphor is the family. This is a metaphor simpler to visualize and less poetic than flowers that

7. TJ to John Adams, Oct. 12, 1823.
8. TJ to Anne Randolph Bankhead, May 26, 1811.

come forth like the belles of the day. It is less visual but more visceral than ship of state. But in its simplicity, and in the feelings it can evoke, lies its power.

As Jefferson uses it, the family consists of a father from the outside—English, French, Spanish or American—and native Americans on the inside. Disregarding facts, as metaphors must, the father, who is white, has either red children or children who are both red and white. The place of the Indians in the family changes over time. As governor of Virginia and early in his presidency, Jefferson considers Indians his brothers, presumably the equal of whites. Eventually, although they remain his brothers, Indians also become his children (while white settlers become children of the states).[9]

The family may be a simple model, admitting of only a few words and relations among words; but in Jefferson's hands it becomes a tangle of images in the service of politics. It transfers the patriarchal model of society from one that is internal to white society to one that describes the relationship between whites and Indians. It seems a benign metaphor, but stands for white political domination, only slightly masked. It provides an easy vocabulary for moralizing: "My children, this is wrong and must not be." And since Jefferson presumed that the language of family suited all people, the metaphor is a reasonable way to converse across cultures.[10]

Because the family metaphor can accomplish so much, it might seem a good candidate for a "master metaphor," one that is universally available and can describe, if not determine, an entire worldview. But perhaps because it is concrete and appears uncomplex, and because it offers no obvious point of comparison with any other master metaphor, the family metaphor has not been considered among the master metaphors in Western history. Rather, as suggested by Table I, the leading master metaphors in Western history have been the mechanical and the organic. As such, they deserve a place in an analysis of Jefferson's world of metaphor. In that world, Jefferson draws his mechanical metaphors from natural philosophy, in particular from

9. TJ to Brother John Baptist De Coigne, June 1781, LoA 551; to Brother Handsome Lake, Nov. 3, 1802, LoA 555; To the Brothers of the Choctaw Nation, Dec. 17, 1803, LoA 558; to the Chiefs of the Cherokee Nation, Jan. 10, 1806, LoA 561; to the Wolf and People of the Mandan Nation, Dec. 30, 1806, LoA 564.

10. TJ to the Wolf, ibid. For the complex context of Jefferson and the family metaphor see Jan Lewis, "'The Blessings of Domestic Society': Thomas Jefferson's Family and the Transformation of American Politics" (1993) and especially the references cited there; and Lucia Stanton, "'Those Who Labor for My Happiness': Thomas Jefferson and His Slaves" (1993).

meteorology and astronomy. He finds his organic metaphors in natural history, mainly botany.[11]

In the era that formed Jefferson's intellectual and cultural outlook, the dominant master metaphor was the machine. Evidence for this lies in the leading images of the time in the study of God, the study of nature, and the study of man. In religion, Jefferson's God, the God of deism and of reason, was analogized to a watchmaker, the creator of the most intricate man-made machine. In science, the most successful subject of study was the solar system, the celestial machine that was explained through Newtonian mechanics and demonstrated by the planetarium, such as the one designed by Jefferson's friend David Rittenhouse. In the study of man, the mechanical metaphor was represented by the social contract, according to which society derives from the voluntary consent of atomistic individuals, as if comprising a machine of separable and equal parts. A good constitution governing organized society included checks and balances and was also formed on the model of a machine. In international affairs the mechanical metaphor was represented by the balance of power.

Now consider the organic metaphor in Jefferson's world, once more with glances at the study of God, man, and nature. Whatever re-sources existed in Western religion for an organic metaphor, they would have had no appeal to the deistic Jefferson. In the study of man there are many more resources, but the central one of these, "the body politic," was incompatible with a belief in a society composed of equal, self-standing individuals. Only the realm of nature provides Jefferson with examples of the organic metaphor.

If mechanical metaphors bring together so many of Jefferson's important beliefs, however, why, in Table I, do they not appear to cover the bulk of the metaphors that he actually wrote? Two reasons may be proposed. The first is that there needn't be any connection between one's greater, or master, metaphor and one's smaller, everyday metaphors. The everyday observations that enter into one's writing style may not be what count in one's intellectual assumptions. The Jefferson who coins non-nautical metaphors is the farmer and naturalist living in piedmont Virginia, not

---

11. For a philosophical study of master metaphors emphasizing the mechanical and organic, see Stephen C. Pepper, *World Hypotheses: A Study in Evidence* (1942). In literary theory, M. H. Abrams examines the shift from the mechanical view of the eighteenth century to the organic of the nineteenth. *The Mirror and the Lamp* (1953), ch. 7.

Jefferson the intellectual and cosmopolitan. At Monticello he looks around and sees the organic world, not the more mechanical world of the city.

The second reason is that to be fair to the purpose of this study as well as to the protean character of metaphor, Table I avoids labeling every example as either mechanical or organic and places nautical metaphors outside of the mechanical/organic logic. A consequence of this is that we discover that nautical metaphors may be either mechanical or organic. We then find that in Jefferson's hands the nautical metaphors are entirely mechanical, consisting of artful permutations of several dozen independent components, words about the sea and seafaring. Should it be thought that this is the nature of nautical metaphors, we need only consider the nautical metaphors of other writers. Recall that Plato's maritime parable in the *Republic* depicted a functioning (or rather non-functioning) organic community. In Jefferson's day organic nautical metaphors were also readily available. The poetry of Philip Freneau, his political ally (and an experienced seaman), is dense with organic nautical metaphor. According to a modern interpreter, Freneau's sea, unlike Jefferson's, is not the mere background for isolated mechanical metaphors, but rather is organic, a primal force of nature or a stage on which other organic forces play themselves out.[12] The nautical metaphors of Thoreau, as we shall see in the next section, are also not composed of interchangeable parts in the fashion of Jefferson.

Regardless of the category to which Jefferson's non-nautical metaphors belong, whether mechanical, organic or domestic, they, unlike his nautical ones, come without a classical pedigree. It is this background outside the classics that distinguishes the non-nautical metaphors as a group. They are drawn from contemporary life and fall into no standard pattern. Although they are as aesthetically pleasing as their nautical cousins, they are often more serious and stimulate thinking about the real world objects of their language.

Jefferson invokes the mechanical universe as an analogy to important social phenomena: storms to violence and the planetary system to the federal system of government. His storm metaphors were composed in response to Shays' Rebellion:

12. Richard C. Vitzthum, *Land and Sea: The Lyric Poetry of Philip Freneau* (1978), 14. Vitzthum's comment on Freneau's use of metaphor is telling: "Although terms like 'trope' and 'metaphor' were in common use, they denoted something very different from Freneau's method. Figurative language was used either ornamentally or to evoke precise mental pictures." 16.

I hold it that a little rebellion now and then is a good thing, and as necessary in the political world as storms in the physical.

I like a little rebellion now and then. It is like a storm in the atmosphere.[13]

These lines raise several questions. First, if a rebellion is a good thing and at the same time a necessary one, has Jefferson not glided between the "is" and the "ought," between the realm of natural fact—the storms—and the realm of human judgment—that a rebellion is a good thing? He probably has, for philosophically he accepted ethical naturalism, according to which nature provides the standard for human choice. The literary quality of the metaphor may leave unrecognized the fact that it states a philosophical position.

Second, how important is it that the storm be a small one and not a big one, that social change come from a small rebellion rather than a full-throated revolution? Shays' Rebellion merely pricked the rulers of Massachusetts, and they reformed. The rebellion did not, to use Jefferson's original wording for the Declaration of Independence, "expunge . . . former systems of government." Only a "little storm" is needed by farmers to nourish their crops; a violent storm damages them. To Jefferson, analogously, it is not a revolution but rather a little rebellion that would nourish a general attention to public affairs, while a revolution would destroy the bonds of civic society. To test this line of analysis further, consider that the usefulness of a storm to the citizen, as to a farmer, depends not only on the strength of the storm, but also on whether the individual is living in the right regime to begin with. If the underlying political or physiographical regime is not right, an ordinary storm cannot make it so.

A final question raised by the storm-rebellion metaphor returns us to the distinction between the two master metaphors. A storm is a mechanical metaphor. Is Jefferson's choice of a mechanical image appropriate for his purpose, or would an organic image have worked just as well? The answer is that Jefferson chose correctly. The sharp blows and social discontinuities entailed by rebellion and revolution can hardly be presented in an organic image, an image that assumes gradual change, whether as growth or decay. It would be difficult to wage revolution under a master metaphor that depends on evolution, and Jefferson did not try. His treatment of rebellion as a storm is thus a logical result in metaphor of living under a mechanical worldview.

13. TJ to James Madison, Jan. 30, 1787; TJ to Abigail Adams, Feb. 22, 1787.

Jefferson's second prominent mechanical metaphor that is not also a nautical metaphor compares American federalism to the planetary system. The metaphor appears in two forms. The first, written to a political ally in 1798, is glittering in its analogy and radiates unclouded optimism about the future of the Constitution. The second, to a British acquaintance during the War of 1812, is unusually complicated in its references and is a worried report on the current operation of the Constitution.

In the 1798 metaphor Jefferson displays a poetic feeling about the Constitution not inferior to that of his nautical metaphors of 1800-1801. But here he is both more elaborate and more precise:

> I dare say that in time all these [the state governments] as well as their central government, like the planets revolving round their common sun, acting and acted upon according to their respective weights and distances, will produce that beautiful equilibrium on which our Constitution is founded, and which I believe it will exhibit to the world in a degree of perfection, unexampled but in the planetary system itself.[14]

One would have to create a single metaphor from the finest of Jefferson's nautical metaphors to equal this one. But even if the nautical and planetary metaphors are equally arresting images of the Constitution, they differ sharply in their cultural origins and constitutional implications. The nautical image dates to classical antiquity; the planetary image requires the post-Copernican Enlightenment. At the same time, and reflecting these different origins, the planetary system, having been created by nature's god, provides a metaphor of perfection for the federal system, while the ship of state, having been created by humans, yields a metaphor of probable imperfection in a republican government.

The second form of Jefferson's planetary metaphor does not deny that the planetary system is perfect. But because the positions of human observers can change, we might not always recognize the perfection. Jefferson composed a complicated metaphor in this vein several years after retiring from the presidency. Written to a British geographer, the metaphor

---

14. TJ to Peregrine Fitzhugh, Feb. 23, 1798. It may be doubted that Jefferson would have written about the Constitution's "degree of perfection" several months later, when the Alien and Sedition Acts had been passed and he was engaged in preparing the Kentucky Resolutions in opposition to them. Yet perhaps it is precisely the coming role of the states in successfully restraining the national government that Jefferson had in mind in writing about federal-planetary perfection.

has two centers and so, appropriate to its image, may be thought of as an ellipse. The first center is an explanation why he will be unable to prepare a revised edition of *Notes on the State of Virginia*. That book, he writes, was "nothing more than the measure of a shadow," referring to Virginia in the dim past of the mid-1780s, and that shadow was "lengthening as the sun advances." Someone else, he says, will be required to develop a more modern system "for calculating the course and motion of this member of our federal system."

The other center of this metaphor, a metaphor that is in more than one sense elliptical, is the resurgence of High Federalism in New England—Jefferson might have called it False Federalism—as a consequence of the War of 1812. For this center Jefferson depicts a previously unknown set of constitutional and planetary relations. He writes that Virginia,

> every day, is adding new and strange matter [to the federal system]. That of reducing, by impulse instead of attraction, a sister planet [Massachusetts] into its orbit, will be as new in our political as in the planetary system. The operation, however, will be painful rather than difficult. The sound part of our wandering star will probably by its own internal energies, keep the unsound within its course.[15]

This is the explication: All planets (the states) are wandering stars, but one of them (Massachusetts), under the influence of Federalists, has wandered off orbit, and it will take another planet (Virginia), rather than the sun (the national government), to influence the wanderer's return to the planetary-constitutional system—at least if the sounder part of the off-orbit state doesn't accomplish this itself.

In its complexity the wandering star metaphor was a risk. But here as elsewhere Jefferson kept his metaphor under control. He did not suggest inexact parallels or go on too long. With his nautical metaphors he avoided risk because the metaphor, molded in antiquity, had been refined through long practice. But Jefferson was restrained with most of his non-nautical metaphors, as well, even if the one on the wandering star required an unusual recipient to understand it.

One of Jefferson's non-nautical metaphors, however, breaks his normal bounds and takes a far greater risk. This one appears in a public paper, the Rockfish Gap Report of 1818, proposing the establishment of the University of Virginia. In the report Jefferson justifies formal education by means of a

15. TJ to John Melish, Dec. 10, 1814.

metaphor that is integral to his idea. The question he asks is, Why educate? Here is the answer of an experienced horticulturalist who believes in progress and is an artist of analogy:

> We should be far . . . from the discouraging persuasion that man is fixed, by the law of his nature, at a given point; that his improvement is a chimera, and the hope delusive of rendering ourselves wiser, happier or better than our forefathers were. As well might it be urged that the wild and uncultivated tree, hitherto yielding sour and bitter fruit only, can never be made to yield better; yet we know that the grafting art implants a new tree on the savage stock, producing what is most estimable both in kind and degree. Education, in like manner, engrafts a new man on the native stock, and improves what in his nature was vicious and perverse into qualities of virtue and social worth.[16]

Among Jefferson's metaphors this passage is a rarity. To say that education engrafts a new man on native stock is more than verbal decoration. It is an idea that gives his argument an unexpected surge of meaning.

Formally, Jefferson has written not a metaphor but a simile: "as well might it be urged" and "in like manner." But in carrying out his simile, with its virtual Homeric proportions, he prompts us to ask not whether his analogy is beautiful, but whether it is true. *Is* education like the art of grafting, or, to back up, *are* humans in some way like plants? Or, even more broadly—and this brings us at the same time to ask about the core of analogical reasoning—isn't all nature interconnected?[17] Jefferson's implied answer to the question of interconnectedness is at least "probably." Therefore his answers to the other questions are yes, education is possibly like the art of grafting, and yes, in some way humans are like plants. These answers explain why, in contrast to virtually all his other metaphors, we are prompted to think deeply about the lines in the Rockfish Gap Report.

The grafting metaphor is provocative about more than education. It also provokes us to think about Jefferson and the idea of progress. Immediately following the grafting analogy Jefferson pursues the idea:

16. Report of the Commissioners for the University of Virginia (Rockfish Gap Report), Aug. 4, 1818. For an earlier interpretation of these lines, see Miller, *Jefferson and Nature*, 80-81.

17. As if in practice for the passage in the Rockfish Gap Report, Jefferson had once written, albeit in a decorative context: "If plants have sensibility, as the analogy of their organization with ours seems to indicate . . . ." TJ to Mrs. Samuel H. Smith, March 6, 1809.

And it cannot be but that each generation succeeding to the knowledge acquired by all those who preceded it, adding to it their own acquisitions and discoveries, and handing the mass down for successive and constant accumulation, must advance the knowledge and well-being of mankind, not *infinitely*, as some have said, but *indefinitely*, and to a term which no one can fix and foresee. Indeed, we need look back half a century, to see times which many now living remember well, and see the wonderful advances in the sciences and arts which have been made within that period.

This is unquestionably Jefferson's mature view: progress certainly, but progress only indefinitely, not infinitely. Phrased differently, progress is an advancement towards perfection that can never reach its goal.

Few thinkers worth examining are completely consistent throughout their lives, and Jefferson's thinking about progress is certainly not unchanging. Even less worth studying would be the collection of a man's metaphors that seemed always to mean the same thing, for thinking in metaphor, like speaking in proverbs, is by nature a plastic exercise. But the variability of Jefferson's ideas and metaphors on progress present in compact form a cross-section of Enlightenment thought on the subject. One discovers Jefferson's metaphors on progress oriented by turns towards perfectibility, realistic hope, and discouragement. It is a range of orientation that may be found among both his nautical and non-nautical metaphors.

Among his nautical metaphors, Jeffersonian optimism appears when his faith in the Constitution is at its height, at the time of his first Inaugural:

I hope we shall now be able to steer [the republic] in her natural course, and show by the smoothness of her motion the skill with which she has been formed for it.

His middle ground is reflected in the acceptance of the troubles that a republic inevitably encounters: "The boisterous sea of liberty is never without a wave." Discouragement appears in one of his metaphors of shipwreck: "[T]he Missouri question is a breaker on which we lose the Missouri country by revolt, and what more, God only knows."[18]

It is in his non-nautical metaphors, however, that Jefferson most memorably displays the range of his thought on progress. Lengthy metaphors have already been discussed that represent optimism and realism. Optimism was illustrated by a mechanical metaphor: The federal union "will exhibit to the world a degree of perfection, unexampled but in the planetary system

18. TJ to Gen. James Warren, March 21, 1801; TJ to Richard Rush, Oct. 20, 1820; TJ to John Adams, Dec. 10, 1819.

itself." Realism was illustrated by an organic metaphor, the one on grafting and education in the Rockfish Gap Report.[19] It remains for a humble domestic metaphor to represent pessimism:

> Error is the stuff of which the web of life is woven, and he who lives longest and wisest is only able to weave out the more of it.[20]

While a number of Jefferson's metaphors reflect the life of the mind and Jefferson's yearning to live it, with this one we can say that he created a motto for himself. The weaving metaphor is a motto for the pursuit not of happiness or fame, profit or power, but a motto for the pursuit of knowledge and wisdom.[21]

Jefferson's nautical metaphors are numerous and they provide unfailing evidence of the man as a stylist. But as this section has shown, they are of less intellectual interest and effect than his non-nautical metaphors. Why? Contrary to what might be supposed, it is the classical and therefore intellectual origins of the nautical metaphors that seem responsible. This derivation becomes derivativeness and comes to confine them to the role of embellishment. Yet because they were there from the beginning, in the years when he was learning what metaphors were and what they could accomplish, they came to play a crucial role throughout his life. They enabled the non-nautical metaphors, when they finally appeared, to be adventuresome and engage the mind. Jefferson became practiced at nautical metaphors and never ceased to enjoy inventing them; but he also never strayed from the pleasing route where they began. When he went beyond his classical education, even as he held onto his classical style, his mind's eye saw the opportunity for metaphor of greater meaning, and for that he no longer looked to the sea.

19. For other metaphors on "realistic" progress see TJ to Samuel Kercheval, July 12, 1816; LoA 1401 (a man should not be required to wear the coat that fitted him when a boy); and TJ to Benjamin Rush, Jan. 16, 1811; LoA 1236 (construing Jefferson's heroes, Bacon, Newton and Locke, to stand for progress).

20. TJ to Chastellux, Oct. 1786. I am grateful to David Spadafora for leading me to think about this metaphor in connection with Jefferson's ideas on progress.

21. In the margin of his copy of *Notes on the State of Virginia* Jefferson phrased the idea without metaphor: "A patient pursuit of facts, and cautious combination and comparison of them is the drudgery to which man is subjected by his Maker, if he wishes to attain sure knowledge." *Notes on Virginia*, William Peden, ed., 277, n. 104.

SECTION 5

NAUTICAL METAPHORS SINCE JEFFERSON'S DEATH IN 1826

ON JEFFERSON'S DEATH, eulogists who were sensitive to his style carried the nautical metaphor forward. They often did so in joint memorials to Jefferson and John Adams, who had died on the same day. Beginning with the metaphors of these eulogists and examining a selection of examples since, this section brings the nautical metaphor in American life and letters up to the present. Paying special attention to examples that can be fairly related to Jefferson, the examination further helps to set his own nautical metaphors in their time, to appreciate their place in his style and confirm their congruence with his temperament.

William Wirt, serving his tenth year as attorney general, delivered the nation's most prominent eulogy to Jefferson and Adams. In his address to a joint session of Congress, Wirt made Virginia and Massachusetts metaphors for the two men and proceeded from there. In the seventeenth century, he declaimed, Massachusetts "had been buffeting with the storm" while Virginia was "resting on a halcyon sea." But in Philadelphia in 1776,

> stroke for stroke they breasted the angry surge [against declaring independence], and threw it aside . . . until they reached shore.

A quarter century later, on becoming president, Jefferson "had the good fortune to find or to make a smoother sea" than Adams had met with. The Virginian "continued at the helm for eight years."

In another eulogy, a Congressman from Maine, Peleg Sprague, said of the role of the two statesmen in the Revolution:

But when the storm rages, and all feel that they are embarked together upon the waves . . . none but the strong hand, and the firm heart, and the unblenched eye, can hold the helm and direct the course.

Edward Everett, then a Congressman from Massachusetts as well as professor of Greek at Harvard, held Jefferson and Adams among the men, who,

when the wisest and most sagacious were needed to steer the newly launched vessel through the broken waves of the unknown sea, sat calm and unshaken at the helm.

And according to Daniel Webster, the death of Jefferson and Adams left America

like the mariner whom the currents of the ocean and the winds carry along till he sees the stars which have directed his course and lighted his pathless way descended, one by one, beneath the rising horizon.

These nautical metaphors are more florid than any Jefferson coined. To use his own word about classical style, they are not as chaste as his. Otherwise, however, the eulogists are like him, painting simple, concrete pictures of the seafaring world.

But Wirt goes further. Jefferson and Adams, he says, had become apostles of liberty who

rested not until they had . . . given such an impulse to the great ocean of mind, that they saw the waves rolling on the farthest shore.

An "ocean of mind" is not Jeffersonian. It is abstract language, difficult to visualize. Further, although the idea had appeared in seventeenth century British poetry (see Andrew Marvell in Appendix III), and thus provided Jefferson with a possible precedent, his own metaphors are never psychological. His nautical metaphors are also seldom instructive, as is the full passage in Wirt. Wirt's eulogy may thus be considered a hinge between Jefferson's pictorial, non-intellectual style of nautical metaphor and a wider scope for the metaphor's use.

Pictorial metaphors can of course be instructive. But they are the more instructive the more complex the thought, and the thinking behind Jefferson's nautical metaphors is seldom complex. They do not even go so far as to make comparisons. Contrast the use of *headland* by Jefferson, who is reacting to press accounts of current affairs, with the use of the word by Justice Joseph Story of the Supreme Court, who raises a problem in legal theory. Jefferson's image and idea are appealing enough:

> A truth now and then projecting into the ocean of newspaper lies, serves like head-lands to correct our course.[1]

But by a comparison of images and with no loss of pictorial quality, Story accomplishes far more:

> When I examine a question, I go from headland to headland, from case to case. [Chief Justice] Marshall has a compass, puts out to sea, and goes directly to his result.

In this metaphor of proportionality we learn about two jurists and at the same time about two methods of deciding cases. Jefferson's nautical metaphors were never so sophisticated. (For a metaphor of proportionality contemporary with Jefferson, see Fisher Ames in Appendix III.)

In the generation following Jefferson's death, it was men like Wirt, Story, and Webster, all of them professionals in constitutional law, who coined nautical metaphors about public affairs. With respect to the thought they conveyed they were greater practitioners of the metaphor than Jefferson. A modern study of Webster's rhetoric permits a convenient, extended comparison with Jefferson. The education of the two men was similar. Both were grounded in the classics and well read in Locke's *Essay on Understanding* and in the Scottish school on rhetoric and criticism (Hugh Blair and Lord Kames).[2] But Webster studied at the beginning of the romantic era. His rhetoric tended toward the orotund; his mode was the oration. His style was not "rational and chaste" nor, as to nautical metaphors, characteristically expressed in private correspondence.

A single nautical metaphor of Webster's reflects a background similar to Jefferson's but produces profoundly different results. Here is Webster in 1850 on the topic Jefferson most feared, the possible breakup of the United States over slavery:

> The imprisoned winds are let loose. The East, the North, and the stormy South combine to throw the whole sea into commotion, to toss its billows to the skies, and disclose its profoundest depths.

1. TJ to James Monroe, Jan. 1, 1815.
2. Paul D. Erickson, *The Poetry of Events: Daniel Webster's Rhetoric of the Constitution and Union* (1986), 13, 42-43.

Webster's accomplishment in these lines cannot be discovered on a simple reading. But Jefferson, though probably not most of Webster's audience, would have recognized it as an adaptation of a passage in Homer: As Poseidon let loose imprisoned winds in order to shipwreck Odysseus, so slavery has loosed the winds of sectionalism that may wreck the United States. The genius of Webster is to go beyond his classical source and devise from non-metaphoric language in Homer an apt metaphoric, modern version of the original. This is Homer:

> He spoke, and pulled the clouds together, in both hands gripping
> the trident, and staggered the sea, and let loose all the storm-blasts
> of all the winds together . . . .
> East Wind and South Wind clashed together, and the bitter blown
>   West Wind
> and the North Wind born in the bright air rolled up a heavy sea.[3]

Webster's is only one of a remarkable collection of nautical metaphors that attempted to cope with the great crisis of the time—really with the multiple crises of Union, slavery and the Constitution. Crisis is a disruption of ordinary life which language often helps us understand and sometimes overcome. Whether as reasoning or as metaphor, language could not prevent the Civil War, but nautical metaphors of the era may be seen as attempts to do so.

One of the metaphors of crisis appeared in poetry and became far more famous than the learned and allusive one in the speech by Webster. Composed by another New Englander steeped in the classics, it is Longfellow's "The Building of the Ship," written in 1849. Most of Longfellow's poem narrates the construction of a ship by a builder whose daughter is to wed the son of the vessel's owner. A stanza on the sources of the ship's timber introduces the public theme:

> Cedar of Maine and Georgia pine
> Here together shall combine.
> A goodly frame, and a goodly fame,
> And the UNION be her name!

---

3. In the complete rendition of his metaphor Webster seems to be comparing himself to Odysseus, except that he would rather drown than survive the wreck. See Appendix III for the full metaphor, as well as other nautical metaphors by Webster.

When the ship is completed and the wedding held, the minister's sermon refers obliquely to the political crisis. However, near the end of the poem, Longfellow is unambiguous in both content and tone. The last section of "The Building of the Ship" is an ode that begins with perhaps the most famous couplet in nineteenth-century American poetry:

> Thou, too, sail on, O Ship of State!
> Sail on, O UNION, strong and great!

In private correspondence Jefferson had looked back to the founding of the American ship of state and wrote of the "skill of her builders." Longfellow, with poetic room to maneuver, is more expansive:

> We know what Master laid thy keel,
> What Workmen wrought thy ribs of steel,
> Who made each mast, and sail, and rope,
> What anvils rang, what hammers beat,
> In what a forge and what a heat
> Were shaped the anchors of thy hope!

The politics of their times led Jefferson and Longfellow to view different sides of the ship of state. Jefferson's metaphors looked to the nation's "republican tack," Longfellow's to the ship as a union. Yet both men found their original image in antiquity. Longfellow, indeed, seems consciously to have adapted Horace's "O navis," to a modern purpose.[4]

The oratory of Webster and the poetry of Longfellow mark the end of the era of nautical metaphors derived from a classical education. The remaining metaphors on the mid-nineteenth century crisis are home-grown. They come from Frederick Douglass, Abraham Lincoln, and Walt Whitman.

4. The odes of Longfellow and Horace, nearly the same length, are crucially different in temper, as was pointed out by a contemporary critic who contrasted Longfellow's "spirited, hopeful lines" to Horace's "timid, tremulous" ones. *The Poetical Works of Longfellow* (1893; repr. 1975), 98.

The opening lines of Longfellow's ode, including the famous couplet, found employment in an international crisis many decades later. In early 1941 President Roosevelt wrote them out for Winston Churchill. Churchill, who later said that "these splendid lines were an inspiration," replied to Roosevelt: "I shall have [them] framed as a souvenir of these tremendous days and as a mark of our friendly relations which have built up under all the stresses." Churchill, *The Grand Alliance* (Boston: Houghton Mifflin, 1950), 25-28.

Not unexpectedly, Frederick Douglass shifts the focus from the crisis over the union to the crisis over slavery. In a sense, he returns to the subject of Jefferson's nautical metaphors on the nature of republicanism. But Douglass is concerned not with distinguishing a republic from other forms of government, but with the right of black Americans to membership in a republican society. Here he reports on his soliloquy when, held in slavery, he looked out over the Chesapeake Bay:

> I have often, in the deep stillness of a summer's Sabbath, stood all alone upon the lofty banks of that noble bay, and traced . . . the countless number of sails moving off to the mighty ocean. . . . I would pour out my soul's complaint, in my rude way, with an apostrophe to the moving multitude of ships: —
> "You are loosened from your moorings, and are free; I am fast in my chains, and am a slave! You move merrily before the gentle gale, and I sadly before the bloody whip! You are freedom's swift-winged angels, that fly around the world; I am confined in bands of iron! O that I were free!"[5]

As uninclined as Jefferson was to find artistic talent in African-Americans, he could not have failed to recognize the force of these lines.

Douglass found sources for his classically-sounding metaphor not in the classics themselves, as Jefferson had, but in his own life, both in his private experience on the shores of the Chesapeake and in his public experience as an American. For his public experience he understandably turned to the era of liberty, that is, to the era of Jefferson. Indeed, because the following passage comes from a July Fourth speech, Douglass is able to allude to, perhaps draw directly on, Jefferson himself. The passage comes from "The Meaning of July Fourth for the Negro," a speech Douglass delivered (to whites) in Rochester, New York, in 1852:

---

5. *Narrative of the Life of Frederick Douglass* (1845). Should a reader overlook this passage in Douglass's autobiography, William Lloyd Garrison, in his preface, points to it as the "most thrilling" in the book, and rephrases it: "receding vessels as they flew with their white wings . . . animated by the living spirit of freedom." For nautical metaphors about slavery much more home-grown than Douglass's, one can go to Negro spirituals, in which to cross the River Jordan or join Noah in the ark is to gain freedom. For titles of several of these spirituals, see Appendix III.

As the sheet anchor takes a firmer hold, when the ship is tossed by the storm, so did the cause of your fathers grow stronger as it breasted the chilling blasts of kingly displeasure. . . . [But now] from the round top of your ship of state, dark and threatening clouds may be seen. Heavy billows, like mountains in the distance, disclose to the leeward huge forms of flinty rocks! That blot drawn, that chain broken, and all is lost. Cling to this day—cling to it, and to its principles, with the grasp of a storm-tossed mariner to a spar at midnight.

Jefferson's ship of state, the Constitution, had been threatened by slavery in 1820. Douglass's ship of state, the Declaration of Independence, is threatened by slavery even more in the 1850s.

Whether the American crisis was about union or about republicanism, the Missouri Compromise and the Compromise of 1850 both failed. So, too, did the Kansas-Nebraska Act of 1854, which Abraham Lincoln, in a compact image, asserted had replaced freedom with slavery as "the very figure-head of the ship of state." This is only one of a number of nautical metaphors by Lincoln, and an examination of the group provides a small but convincing illustration why his rhetoric as a whole is unmatched in presidential history. Further, because his nautical metaphors are so effective in conveying his meaning, they necessarily invite a contrast with the ornamental nautical metaphors of Jefferson.

Jefferson, it may be recalled, came into office glowing with confidence, his Federalist foes either vanquished or won over. In both private correspondence and his inaugural he painted the victory of a republican constitution in classical style. But he never embedded the metaphors in his argument, or his argument in metaphor. Lincoln, on the other hand, that great admirer of Jeffersonian principles, was utterly different. For him, a storyteller rather than a classical scholar, and speaking in public rather than writing in private, nautical metaphors became a living means of stating his position. This is true from his first deployment of the metaphor in October 1854, mentioned above, until his last, a decade later. Although Lincoln's nautical metaphors are far fewer than Jefferson's, their pertinence and pungency leave Jefferson's looking tame and mannered.

The nautical metaphors in Lincoln's remarks in early 1861, as he traveled from Springfield to Washington for his inauguration, form a remarkable series. Listen to him appealing to audiences in Ohio who had voted for his opponent in the presidential election:

Mr. Lincoln shook hands with [a supporter of Stephen A. Douglas] and said if he and the other friends of Mr. Douglas would assist in keeping the ship of state afloat, that perhaps Mr. Douglas might be selected to pilot it sometime in the future. . . . If all do not join now to save the good old ship of the Union this voyage, nobody will have a chance to pilot her on another voyage.

Listen to him making the argument for Union in New York:

> I understand a ship to be made for the carrying and preservation of the cargo, and so long as the ship can be saved with the cargo, it should never be abandoned. This Union should likewise never be abandoned unless it fails and the possibility of its preservation shall cease to exist without throwing the passengers and cargo overboard.

When Lincoln opens this second example with "I understand," it is not the phrase of an insecure Midwesterner speaking in the nation's largest port city. Rather, it reflects that portion of his rhetoric that belongs to his folk-style. A classicist might have entered into the metaphor with the spare "A ship is made for the carrying." While the metaphor itself is unexceptional, it is reasonably Jeffersonian in image and completely Jeffersonian in its unionist and, more softly, republican sentiment. But to begin with "I understand" signals a metaphor that is intended to make an argument, not merely to adorn one.

In his first inaugural, Lincoln continues the series, alluding to the age of Jefferson with a classical image: "I am . . . for the old ship, and the chart of the old pilots." In the summer of 1862, he uses a nautical metaphor with cold vehemence to criticize complaining Union loyalists in Louisiana:

> They are to touch neither a sail nor a pump, but to be merely passengers—deadheads at that—to be carried snug and dry, throughout the storm, and safely landed right side up.

Finally, in October 1864, when the Union was on its way to victory and Lincoln was anticipating re-election, he returns to the theme of his trip to Washington four years earlier:

> I shall do my utmost that whoever is to hold the helm for the next voyage shall start with the best possible chance to save the ship.[6]

6. For a study contrasting the richness of Lincoln's figurative language with the stultifying rhetoric of the highly educated Jefferson Davis, see James M. McPherson, "How Lincoln Won the War with Metaphors" (1990). A provocative psychological interpretation is Kenneth L. Leetz, "Abraham Lincoln, Psychotherapist to the Nation: The Use of Metaphors" (1997).

Lincoln saved the ship; and he died. The final example of nautical metaphor from the Civil War era, therefore, is appropriately Walt Whitman's ode on Lincoln's death, "O Captain! My Captain!" Two of the three stanzas in Whitman's ode are entirely metaphor—ship, port, keel, vessel, anchor'd, shores—and all of them end with the Captain on the deck "fallen cold and dead." Further, like Longfellow's "sail on, O Ship of State" and Douglass's apostrophe to the ships of freedom, Whitman's ode addresses its subject directly, a Latinate practice (as in Horace's "O navis") that the more restrained Jefferson never employed.

The writers of the Civil War era surveyed here reflect differences in social outlook that also reflect a division within Jefferson himself. The earliest of them—the two New Englanders, Webster and Longfellow—are the heirs of Jefferson as classicist and aristocrat. The later writers—Douglass, Lincoln, and Whitman—are influenced by the age of Jackson and belong to Jefferson's modern democratic legacy. Within the democratic legacy, Douglass wrote in a classical style, Lincoln never did, and Whitman was capable of both styles, as is shown by a contrast of his formal "O Captain!" with his immeasurably greater elegy to Lincoln, "When lilacs last in the dooryard bloom'd." But in "When Lilacs," Whitman not only returned to his democratic free verse; like Jefferson before him, he turned to non-nautical metaphors when he had more profound ideas to express.

Jefferson would not have been surprised that the classically derived metaphor, second nature to him, had become less capable of bearing literary weight. By the end of his life he was resigned to, and in some ways even satisfied with, the loss of the classics as the touchstone of education. This was partly because ancient political theory, lacking the concept of representative government, was inadequate to modern times. It was partly because other fields of study had increased their cultural worth and justifiably took time away from Greek and Latin. But two European thinkers who wrote about American government in the generation following Jefferson's death continued the classical tradition of the nautical metaphor, albeit with dramatically different results. They were Thomas Babington Macaulay and Alexis de Tocqueville.

In a letter of 1857 to a biographer of Jefferson who had hoped for more sympathetic comments, Lord Macaulay criticized Jeffersonian democracy. In the course of his critique he penned a catchy phrase that has not left the language: "Your constitution is all sail and no anchor."

Unlike Jefferson's metaphors, Macaulay's image is meant to convey an argument: that in America there is no restraint on constitutional change. For two reasons, however, Macaulay's phrase has caused nothing but confusion. In the first place, and this is only slightly his fault, Macaulay wrote "constitution," a word that in England refers to a nation's fundamental political practices. He did not write "Constitution," which in America is the written charter of the federal government. But the distinction between "constitution" and "Constitution" has been lost on most Americans as well as in every American printing of Macaulay's metaphor. Over and over we read: "Your Constitution is all sail and no anchor." This simple orthographic difference has led to absurd interpretations of the phrase.

Second, as applied to the American Constitution, Macaulay's metaphor is simply wrong. Many people in the founding era, including Jefferson, expected the Constitution to be an anchor, not a sail. Yet the most potent criticism of the Constitution since then, sometimes from Jefferson himself, has been just the reverse, that the Constitution has been altogether too much anchor, a drag on political progress and without enough sail to keep up with changing needs. Macaulay's phrase, cited time and again, has been repeated because of the prominence of its author and the cleverness of its image. But unlike the nautical metaphors of Jefferson, it makes no sense.

How different from Macaulay are the nautical metaphors of Tocqueville. Here we have acuteness of insight without any ambiguity in meaning. In two metaphors on the Constitution, Tocqueville speaks of natural limits on the makers of the law and on the law's interpreters. As to the first, he writes that a lawgiver

> is like a man steering his route over the sea. He, too, can control the ship that bears him, but he cannot change its structure, create winds, or prevent the ocean stirring beneath him.

As to the second, he writes that federal judges

> must know how to understand the spirit of the age, to confront those obstacles that can be overcome, and to steer out of the current when the tide threatens to carry them away.

Jefferson would not have penned these metaphors. This is not because he was incapable of the complexity of thought embedded in them; in fact, he would have agreed with Tocqueville that political culture draws the contours of what legislators enact and what judges decide. Rather, the language is not Jefferson's because it hands so much meaning over to metaphor. As precise as Jefferson in his choice of words, Tocqueville is able to serve political sociology with nautical metaphors unconfined by classical disposition and Lockean caution.[7]

At the time that foreign observers were writing nautical metaphors about American politics that were stylistically akin to Jefferson's, American men of letters, the Transcendentalists, developed a theory and practice of metaphor that were distinctly unJeffersonian. Through Emerson, Transcendentalism presents a theory of metaphor in which Jefferson could never have concurred. Through Thoreau, Transcendentalism exhibits a practice of nautical metaphor far removed from Jefferson's plain style. Moreover, Thoreau's metaphors are often philosophy, not filigree.

Everything that Jefferson found wrong with the anti-materialism of Plato he would have found wrong with Transcendentalism. Never doubting the existence of an objective nature, he would have been infuriated by Emerson's assertion that "the whole of nature is a metaphor of the human mind." To elaborate his meaning and emphasize the seriousness of his assertion, Emerson surrounds "metaphor" with a phalanx of its relatives: allegory, analogy, correspondence, emblem, fable, image, parable, proverb, sign, symbol. The absence of "simile" from this group is presumably deliberate, for simile would have been the most technical term on a list that was meant to be decidedly nontechnical. Emerson elaborated "nature is a metaphor" with "man is an analogist" and "good writing and brilliant discourse are perpetual allegories." How alien these ideas are to those of the classically constrained Jefferson.[8]

No one among the Transcendentalists has proved better than Thoreau that man is an analogist: he left for posterity a body of writing

7. What Tocqueville says about the decline of the classics in America would, like his nautical metaphors, have also made sense to Jefferson. He maintained that the writings of the ancients, "always admirably careful and skillful in detail," were not needed in a democracy, whose "continual restlessness" led to "endless change in language." Among the consequences of these facts he found that "the rules of style are almost destroyed" and that the bombastic style of American poetry and oratory was "prodigal of metaphors at every opportunity." *Democracy in America,* vol. 2, pt. I, chs. 15, 16, 18 (quotations from 476, 478, 480, 488).

8. Emerson, "Nature" (1836), in *Five Essays on Man and Nature,* Robert E. Spiller, ed. (Arlington Heights, Ill.: AHM Publishing, 1954), 16, 13, 15.

that Emerson might have considered perpetual allegory. However much Jefferson would have challenged Emerson's philosophy of metaphor, he could not have helped but be interested in, if not amazed by, Thoreau's practice. We draw only on *Walden,* in which metaphors of the sea reinforce the book's examination of a life in solitude and the inner self.[9]

One of his metaphors helps Thoreau distance himself physically from the outside world. Jefferson would have had little trouble following him home from Concord, and, with effort, might have been able to analogize his own intellectual pursuits at Monticello with Thoreau's philosophizing in his Walden cabin:

> It was very pleasant, when I staid late in town, to launch myself into the night, especially if it was dark and tempestuous, and set sail from some bright village parlor or lecture room . . . for my snug harbor in the woods, having made all tight without and withdrawn under hatches with a merry crew of thoughts, leaving only my outer man at the helm.

> I had withdrawn so far within the great ocean of solitude, into which the rivers of society empty, that for the most part, so far as my needs were concerned, only the finest sediment was deposited around me. Beside, there were wafted to me evidences of unexplored and uncultivated continents on the other side.

But there are two crucial differences between Thoreau and Jefferson. First, Thoreau's metaphors are part of his philosophy; as in Plato, they are a way of understanding truth, while Jefferson's metaphors stand apart from his thoughts. Second, Jefferson simply could not have accepted most of Thoreau's ideas, such as this one:

> What I have observed of the pond is no less true in ethics. It is the law of average. . . . [D]raw lines through the length and breadth of the aggregate of a man's particular daily behaviors and waves of life into his coves and inlets, and where they intersect will be the height or depth of his character. . . . [A]n inclination in the shore in which a thought was harbored becomes an individual lake, cut off from the ocean, wherein the thought secures its own conditions, changes, perhaps, from salt to fresh, becomes a sweet sea, dead sea, or a marsh.

9. For a stimulating general discussion see Willard H. Bonner, *Harp on the Shore: Thoreau and the Sea* (1985). Bonner's chapter "World as Symbol" carries out a journal entry of Thoreau's: "He is the richest who has most use for nature as raw material for tropes and symbols with which to describe his life." 38.

Or consider Thoreau's claim that

> we are such poor navigators that our thoughts, for the most part, stand off
> and on upon a harborless coast, are conversant only with the bights of the
> bays of poesy, or steer for the public ports of entry, and go into the dry
> docks of science.

To Jefferson, this would have been unacceptable. As metaphor it was
wrong because an idea was so intertwined with the imagination. As to
the metaphor's idea, it was an affront to one who relished the bays of
classical poetry, could not stay away from public affairs, and considered
the dry docks of science his workshop.

Thoreau's nautical metaphors are like Jefferson's at least in the
sense that, in not many words, something is said about the sea in order
to speak about something else. But the mid-nineteenth century is an
appropriate moment to look at three kinds of nautical metaphors that,
although not meeting this common understanding of a metaphor, add to
marking the boundaries of the traditions of metaphor in which Jefferson
and Thoreau both wrote. These kinds of metaphor are sea literature as a
genre, the metaphor in art, and the metaphor that has migrated from the
ocean to the land.

For two reasons, stories and novels whose settings are the sea have little
place in this study. On the one hand, these works may be seen as metaphor
in their entirety and are therefore completely unlike Jefferson and his use of
the "small" metaphor. On the other hand, if literature of the sea does contain
discrete metaphors, they are likely to be applied to the sea or seafaring,
whether fashioned from maritime or from non-maritime language. Neither
of these alternatives is like Jefferson's nautical metaphors. *Moby-Dick,* for
instance, set almost entirely at sea, is no exception to this reasoning, and the
entire work can be conceived as "standing for" something other than a
whaling voyage. Indeed, in its larger symbols it is not obvious whether
seafaring or land-living is the more illuminated. But this monument of
American sea literature contains two examples of small metaphors that are
derived from the land, applied to the sea and, most pertinently, can be
associated directly with Jefferson.

Melville and his novels are not an obvious home for Jefferson. Melville
knew the sea and Jefferson did not. In *Moby-Dick* he worked with materials
that are hardly Jeffersonian: a sea made treacherous by the God of the Old
Testament and a community of men divided into classes and intent on the
capture of a beast of the sea. Yet unJeffersonian though the work is as a

whole, *Moby-Dick* contains figures of speech that refer to terrestrial phenomena of lifelong interest to Jefferson. These are "looming" and the Natural Bridge of Virginia.[10]

When Jefferson writes about looming he takes the word from the sea in its factual sense and applies it to the land:

> The seamen call it *looming*. Philosophy [science] is as yet in the rear of the seamen, for so far from having accounted for it, she has not given it a name. Its principal effect is to make distant objects appear larger, in opposition to the general law of vision, by which they are diminished. . . . I am little acquainted with the phenomenon as it shows itself at sea; but at Monticello it is familiar.

When Jefferson writes about the Natural Bridge, he begins with science and concludes with rhapsody: "So beautiful an arch . . . springing, as it were, up to heaven."

In the cases of both looming and the Natural Bridge, Melville revises Jefferson, if he does not reverse him. In *Moby-Dick* he writes about looming in its figurative sense—on top of which he adds that loomings are, like metaphors, conceits. They are "the wild conceits," says Ishmael, "that swayed me to my purpose." Chief among Ishmael's conceits were the "endless processions of the whale, and midmost of them all, one grand hooded phantom, like a snow hill in the air." Near the end of the novel, when the midmost of the loomings becomes visible and Captain Ahab spies the whale, Melville draws on Jefferson to depict the scene:

> [S]oon the fore part of him slowly rose from the water; for an instant his whole marbleized body formed a high arch, like Virginia's Natural Bridge.

Thus contrary to anything Jefferson could have expected, his descriptions of phenomena on land were converted into images at sea. Melville has given us what may be thought of as nautical back metaphors to Jefferson.

Because of its allusions to Jefferson, *Moby-Dick* is a special case. But sea literature after Melville deserves mention because it views the

---

10. "Loomings" is the title of the first chapter of *Moby-Dick* (the word does not appear in the chapter itself). The Natural Bridge is referred to in a chapter near the end, "The Chase—First Day." In *Notes on the State of Virginia,* looming and the Natural Bridge are the subjects of the last paragraphs of the chapters "Climate" and "Cascades." LoA 207-08, 148-49. Melville also quotes "Thomas Jefferson's Memorial to the French Minister in 1788" in his collection of "Extracts" preceding the narrative.

sea itself so differently from the sea as viewed by Jefferson. The reason is the impact of Darwinism.

Jefferson would have found Darwinism as repugnant as Transcendentalism. Evolution and extinction of species were not in his scientific world. The seeming randomness of individual life was incompatible with his political vision. Nature as a malign force was unsuited to his philosophic disposition. But these Darwinist differences came to characterize American literature of the sea, as in Stephen Crane's "The Open Boat" and stories by Jack London. Scholars have also pointed to literature in which religious faith, suffering under Darwinist doubts, is renewed at sea.[11]

A different boundary to Jefferson's metaphors is the pictorial or visual metaphor. Metaphors of all kinds are traditionally pictorial in the sense that at least one term can be the subject of a representational picture. But what is meant here is a metaphor without words, or a metaphor for which words are secondary. It is a metaphor that must be seen. It is nautical iconography. In antiquity a trident stands for the god of the sea, a ship on a coin stands for the Roman empire, a rudder for governance. In Jefferson's time the ratification of the Constitution was celebrated by parades that included a ship of state, complete with sails and sailor boys. Shortly after ratification, a political cartoon, an obvious vehicle for the nautical metaphor, criticized the new government for maintaining its headquarters in Philadelphia when Washington, D.C., was under construction. The cartoon shows a devil luring a ship into rocky rapids over the caption "Con-g-ss Embark'd on board the Ship Constitution of America."[12]

---

11. In *Sea Brothers,* Bert Bender writes: "[N]o writer [after Melville] could depict the ocean reality without focusing on the mechanism of evolution by natural selection or, more important, attempting to interpret its implications for the human community." p. x. For a general discussion, consult the chapters by Bender and Robert B. Stein in Springer, ed., *America and the Sea* (1995).

For important fiction of the late nineteenth century that is not Darwinian but can be interpreted through nautical metaphor, one may turn to Henry James, whose psychological sensitivity is also not Jeffersonian. James' *The Patagonia* (1888), largely set at sea, yields frequent metaphors for society. A study that explores the nautical metaphor in several James novels, is Greg W. Zacharias, "The Marine Metaphor, Henry James, and the Moral Center of *The Awkward Age*" (1990).

12. [Library of Congress], *Thomas Jefferson: Genius of Liberty* (2000), 62.

In the nineteenth century, the voyage of life, the other prominent theme of nautical metaphor, was depicted in a series of paintings by the Hudson River School artist Thomas Cole. Completed in 1840, Cole's "Voyage of Life" series is vaguely Christian and therefore unJeffersonian; but it is an allegorical maritime voyage set in American nature and in that way in the tradition of Jefferson. The case of entire seascapes as pictorial nautical metaphors, however, differs from the example of Cole. As in the case of maritime literature, seascapes, such as those by Winslow Homer or Fitz Hugh Lane, may represent themes beyond their ostensible subjects. But then we deal with critical interpretation of whole works and not with isolatable metaphors of the Jeffersonian sort.

The culmination of the visual nautical metaphor in the nineteenth century is a massive sculpture erected in 1893 for the Chicago World's Fair. Named *The Barge of State; or, The Triumph of Columbia*, the sculpture breaks with ship-of-state tradition, but on Lake Michigan perhaps a barge amounts to a ship. Drawn by sea-horses of Commerce, the barge has Fame at the prow, Time at the helm, and Arts and Industries at the oars. The creator of this monumental metaphor, Frederick William MacMonnies, was among the most prominent American sculptors of his time.[13]

By the time *The Barge of State* sat at sculptural anchor on the shores of the Prairie State, a third kind of nonstandard nautical metaphor had long since been in print. This is the inland nautical metaphor. In Jefferson's time the metaphor was still undeveloped, but it had been applied to the Blue Ridge Mountains by Jefferson's acquaintance, the Quaker botanist William Bartram, and by an enraptured visitor to Monticello, Jefferson's friend, Margaret Bayard Smith. Shortly after Jefferson's death the inland metaphor moved west, matured, and the prairies became a sea of grass.

To speak today of the prairie as a sea of grass borders on the trite, but in the nineteenth century, when the image was written for people who did not know the interior of the continent, it was serious description. The

13. Information on *The Barge of State* may be found in Laura V. McKay, *The Dream City, A Portfolio of Photographic Views of the World's Columbian Exposition* (St. Louis, 1893), and Neil Harris, et al., *Grand Illusions: Chicago's World's Fair of 1893* (Chicago: Chicago Historical Society, 1993). An up-to-date visual nautical metaphor is the computer game *The USS Ship of State*, in which a submarine commander is a "metaphor for the President." <http://web.wizvax.net/dlegg/State.html>; 11/20/99. A stained glass window in a modern American church imagines the body of Christ as a slave ship during the middle passage. *New York Times*, Feb. 9, 2001, A14.

connotation of the metaphor depended partly on reality: which prairie was being depicted, the season of the year, and recent experience with weather and pests. It depended partly on hope: what was expected of the grasslands as farmland. In 1827, James Fenimore Cooper, a sometime Jeffersonian who was experienced at sea, described the trans-Mississippi prairie (which he never visited) as "not unlike the ocean," where "swell appeared after swell, and island succeeded island." William Cullen Bryant, an ardent Jeffersonian who visited Illinois, wrote in "The Prairies" (1834):

> Lo! they stretch,
> In airy undulations, far away,
> As if the ocean, in his gentlest swell,
> Stood still, with all his rounded billows fixed,
> And motionless forever.

J. H. Buckingham, a Boston journalist travelling in Illinois in the 1840s with Congressman Abraham Lincoln, reported:

> For miles we saw nothing but a vast prairie of what can compare to nothing else but the ocean itself. The tall grass, interspersed occasionally with fields of corn, looked like the deep sea; it seemed as if we were out of sight of land, for no house, no barn, no tree was visible, and the horizon presented the rolling of waves in the afar-off distance. There were all sorts of flowers—as if the sun were shining upon the gay and dancing waters.

Appealing images like these were common before the mid-nineteenth century. But a few decades later, while Easterners were still hearing about "amber waves of grain" (the poem "America, the Beautiful" was written in 1893), actual settlers on the plains were encountering blizzards, locusts and loneliness. Their experience produced a different class of nautical metaphors.

The finest example of the new inland nautical metaphor is O. E. Rölvaag's saga of Norwegian immigrants on the great plains, *Giants in the Earth* (1927). The novel is simultaneously about a recollected literal sea and a lived figurative one. From its opening, when the track left by prairie schooners "was like the wake of a boat—except that instead of widening out astern it closed in again," to the end, when the temperaments of the settlers are compared to boats back in Norway, the novel may be read as a chain of metaphor. In a dramatic link between the sea of water and the sea of grass, the protagonist is caught in a blizzard with his oxen hitched to a wagon:

The boat that he steered was behaving very badly; it wouldn't answer to the helm; it didn't ride the swell like a sea-worthy craft. . . . The oxen gave a tremendous plunge . . . and off they careered into the heart of the storm. Per Hansa felt as if he were sliding down one huge wave after another; the boat was scudding now with terrific speed!

Rölvaag's immigrants, like Jefferson's America, had embarked on the boisterous sea of liberty. But what a difference context makes for the meaning of a metaphor.[14]

When we take leave of sea literature, metaphors-without-words, and the inland metaphor and return to the kind of nautical metaphor that Jefferson wrote, we find no reduction in its occurrence and, perhaps against literary odds, a continuation in its variety. A sampler from around 1900 displays the political uses to which the nautical metaphor could be put. Frightened by populism, an American legal scholar seconded Macaulay's line that the Constitution had too much sail and not enough anchor in his assertion that the judiciary was the only

breakwater against the haste and the passions of the people—against the tumultuous ocean of democracy.

Defending a Jeffersonian position, Henry George urged his followers not to think

that after the stormy seas and head gales of all the ages, *our* ship has at last struck the trade winds of time.

At the time of the Spanish-American War, a Senator looked to Jefferson to plead the anti-imperialist case:

I ask you to keep in the old channels, and to keep off the old rocks laid down in the old charts, and to follow the old sailing orders that all the old captains of other days have obeyed, to take your bearings, as of old . . . and not from this meteoric light of empire.

William Jennings Bryan said of his hero:

The ship of state may be intrusted to pilots during fair weather; but, in

14. I was led to *Giants in the Earth* by Emilio De Grazia, "The Great Plain: Rölvaag's New World Sea" (1986). De Grazia sums up Rölvaag's novels as expressing the immigrants' "frustrated attempts . . . to keep the sea metaphorically alive." 245. Other examples of looking back to a metaphorical prairie of the nineteenth century are Conrad Richter's *The Sea of Grass* (1936) and Pare Lorentz's documentary film *The Plow That Broke the Plains* (1935).

hours of storm, the people turn to the Sage of Monticello, the greatest of the world's constructive statesmen.

And in a flight of erudition which Jefferson was capable of but which he would not have taken, Woodrow Wilson explained political liberty by a lengthy analogy that included a boat "skimming the water with light foot."[15] In the twentieth century the nautical metaphor has been adapted to fiction, perhaps more often and possibly more successfully when the fiction is traditional in technique or when it looks to the past. In the midwestern Gopher Prairie of Sinclair Lewis's *Main Street* (1920),

> Miss Sherwin's trying to repair the holes in this barnacle-covered ship of a town by keeping busy bailing out the water. And Pollock tries to repair it by reading poetry to the crew! Me, I want to yank it up on the ways, and fire the poor bum of a shoe-maker that built it so it sails crooked, and have it rebuilt right, from the keel up.

In an historical recreation of an Appalachian community by Romulus Linney, a minister named Sales (sails) encounters a heathen church custodian named Starns (stern). In a scene in the sanctuary,

> three elderly ladies of the church, trim frigates in full sail under breezes of joy and innocence, moored themselves around Starns and attempted his conversion.[16]

15. The American legal scholar is John F. Dillon; the senator is George F. Hoar of Massachusetts. Additional nautical metaphors from the era, also in Appendix III, come from Booker T. Washington at the Atlanta Exposition of 1895 ("cast down your bucket where you are") and George Engelmann, president of the American Gynecological Society, on the "sexual storms" of the American girl (1900). Illustrating the invincibility of a cliché at the height of American imperial seapower, an entire book was published under the title *The Ship of State* (1903). It is a collection of articles for young people written by "Those at the Helm," who included Theodore Roosevelt when he was governor of New York. Michael Kammen finds that, in the manner of Macaulay's critique of the "constitution" as "all sail," *anchor* came into vogue as a metaphor for the Constitution in the second half of the nineteenth century. *A Machine That Would Go of Itself* (1986), 17.

16. *Heathen Valley* (1962). Louis MacNeice's poem "Homage to Wren (a memory of 1941)," written around the same time as Linney's novel, also uses a ship-church analogy to recreate a historical event. For further nautical metaphors in fiction set in the past, see J. P. Marquand and Gore Vidal in Appendix III.

John Updike has pertinently distinguished literary criticism from literature:

> Writing criticism is to writing fiction and poetry as hugging the shore is to sailing in the open sea. At sea, we have that beautiful blankness all around, a cold bright wind, and the occasional thrill of a gleaming dolphin-back or the synchronized leap of silverfish; hugging the shore, one can always come about and draw even closer to land with another nine-point quotation.

Outside of literature, a procession of nautical metaphors continues to march through American public life: by or about Presidents Franklin D. Roosevelt, Eisenhower, Johnson, Nixon, Carter, George Bush, Clinton, and George W. Bush; by politicians Spiro Agnew, Mike Mansfield, and Trent Lott; by jurists William Brennan, William O. Douglas, and Learned Hand (see also under "Supreme Court"); by diplomats Ralph Bunche, Philip C. Jessup, and Edward R. Stettinius; by economists John Kenneth Galbraith, Wassily Leontief, William Nordhaus, and David Rockefeller; by sociologist David Riesman; and by population pessimist Garrett Hardin. It would be invidious to single out any of these often striking and sometimes beautiful metaphors for quotation here. But a small collection of nautical metaphors on civil rights illustrates how much can be said through the same basic image.

We begin in 1955, shortly after segregated public schools were declared unconstitutional by the Supreme Court and shortly before the wave of independence began in Africa. In that year the chief executive of the NAACP wrote:

> All the peoples of the world are in the same boat now. Today that vessel is unseaworthy because we have not yet mastered the science of living together. Through a major leak caused by color prejudice the waters of hate are rushing in. Our survival may depend on how swiftly and expertly that leak is caulked.

In 1957, when the waters of hate rushed into Little Rock, it was not the international but the personal-domestic vessel that came to the mind of President Eisenhower in a letter to a friend:

> Possibly I am something like a ship which, buffeted and pounded by wind and wave, is still afloat and manages in spite of frequent tacks and turnings to stay generally along its plotted course and continue to make some, even if slow and painful, headway.

In 1959, winds and waves still pounding the ship, a congressional committee heard testimony on behalf of corrective legislation:

> [In civil rights] neither the Congress nor the executive branch has taken the lead or even acted to implement the pioneering work of the courts, usually looked upon as the keel, rudder, and sea anchor of our system of government. Lacking sail or propeller, the courts, though unaided by the other two branches of Government, have managed to hold a steady forward course in the great currents of change that sweep the world.

A decade later, an aide to President Nixon, unpersuaded that the United States had continued a steady forward course domestically, and unconcerned about America in the currents of global change, advised:

> The ship of integration is going down; it is not our ship . . . and we cannot salvage it; and we should not be aboard.

This advice was countered in the Civil Rights Movement by an artfully devised metaphor that has become a proverb and combines truth with trope: "We may have come on different ships, but we're all in the same boat now." Using at least twenty different nautical terms, these several passages express urgency, resignation, analysis, abandonment and plain talk about America's racial problems, all through metaphor. However uncomfortable Jefferson would have been with the subject matter of these metaphors, he would have been at home with the range of terms and not surprised by the range of views they could express.[17]

The nautical metaphors presented above come in Jefferson's wake. All of them are by Americans or, in the case of Tocqueville and Macaulay, about America. Just how American they are is suggested by a small selection of modern examples from abroad. It is hard to make sense in an American context, for instance, of the double simile, often attributed to Mao Zedong, for the Communist conquest of China, "The people are like water and the army is like fish." Americans would understand but presumably find unacceptable Lech Walesa's justification for changing his style of leadership when the Solidarity Movement overthrew communism in Poland: "Can you fully democratically steer a ship through a stormy sea?" In *An Enemy*

---

17. See "Civil Rights" in Appendix III for sources of this paragraph.

of the People Henrik Ibsen converts Walesa's rhetorical question into dialogue:

> *Billing:* Society is like a ship: every man must put his hand to the helm.
> *Horster:* That may be all right on shore; but at sea it wouldn't do at all.

The first line here apparently refutes Walesa's anti-democratic nautical metaphor. The second line accepts it, but only when one is actually, and not figuratively, on the ocean. For that reason, the effect to American ears of the two lines together is more agreeable than Walesa's formulation. When we turn to England, with traditions Americans understand, we finally find a metaphor that Jefferson would have appreciated completely, in Robert Bolt's *A Man for All Seasons*:

> What Englishman can behold without Awe
> the Canvas and the Rigging of the Law!

This limited survey, moving from China to Poland to Scandinavia to England, suggests that the nearer the culture is to America, the more Jeffersonian are its nautical metaphors.

Back in the United States, we may conclude our post-Jefferson tour of nautical metaphors with examples from two pairs of American historians, the Jefferson scholars Dumas Malone and Merrill D. Peterson, and the intellectual and maritime historians David A. Hollinger and Samuel Eliot Morison.

The contrast between Malone and Peterson, both writing in 1970, reflects the difference between their magisterial biographies of Jefferson. Halfway through Malone's six-volume study, one finds "The Captain and His Mates" as the title of a chapter on Jefferson and his cabinet in 1801. Opening the chapter, Malone comments pleasantly on Jefferson and the nautical metaphor, quotes Jefferson's "best-remembered nautical expression" (to John Dickinson in 1801) and one of eight years later (to Dupont de Nemours). Malone continues the figure on his own ("perils of the voyage"), and concludes self-consciously with "metaphors aside" (an unacknowledged adaptation of Jefferson in his letter to Dickinson).

By contrast, Merrill Peterson does not talk about Jefferson's metaphors. Nor does he quote them, invent a Jeffersonian moment to make one up, or allude to his own authorial style. Instead, he straightforwardly incorporates a nautical metaphor into his narrative at a place where it is substantively appropriate. Summarizing the Embargo of 1807, Peterson writes:

> Jefferson, for all the freight of idealism, had always steered a close-reefed political craft. The voyage of the embargo was under full sail, and the helmsman's single-minded commitment to the principle, with the rational hope it embodied, obscured his view of the navigational hazards. . . . The result was drift.

Although their styles of metaphor differ, the two biographers write in the Jeffersonian tradition. Like Jefferson's metaphors, theirs are uncomplicated and mildly learned adornments suited to the occasions for which they are employed.[18] The nautical metaphors of the other historians are also effective. David Hollinger's, in an article on William James, is mannered, almost unbelievable in its length (175 words, more than 10 percent of them nautical terms) and, because it is the last paragraph of an essay, bears the entire weight of the preceding argument. For all this, however, if one has followed Hollinger's argument, his is a metaphor that works.

The metaphor used by Samuel Eliot Morison is, in the first place, not his own but taken from Oliver Wendell Holmes, Sr. Further, the Morison-Holmes metaphor is not dropped into a narrative, as with Malone and Peterson, nor is it the culmination of an argument, as with Hollinger. It is an epigram to Morison's *Oxford History of the American People* (1965):

> I find the great thing in this world is not so much where we stand, as in what direction we are moving. . . . We must sail sometimes with the wind and sometimes against it,—but we must sail, and not drift, nor lie at anchor.

This is an epigram that befits a maritime historian and appropriately precedes a saga that sails along for more than a thousand pages. Holmes's metaphor is also suited to be an epigram, for it is not intended to enrich description but to prompt reflection and provide a moral. Yet look at it again and note the ellipsis. The ellipsis, which is Morison's, amends the tone of the original. Holmes did not begin the second sentence with, "We must sail." He began it: "To reach the port of heaven, we must sail." By omitting the words "to reach the port

18. For another historian's nautical metaphor about Jefferson, see Dixon Wecter in Appendix III.

of heaven," the modern historian erased any trace of religion in the original. But though the secularization may be misleading with respect to Holmes, it is true to Morison's book and perhaps his readers. It is also true to Jefferson.

JEFFERSON, THE NAUTICAL METAPHOR AND MODERN METAPHOR THEORY

THE ORIGINAL HOME of nautical metaphors in the classics was still standing when Jefferson received his education. The culture in which he lived allowed him to scatter the metaphor throughout a correspondence to an audience that could appreciate his classical embellishment and Latinate style. But by the time of his death, classical education was in decline, and the environments that had given life to his metaphors did not last much longer. Today, if they have not become cliché, nautical metaphors often seem dated or affected, especially if they are written in the fashion of Jefferson. Yet the practice of the nautical metaphor persists, and when the metaphors are used in moderation or with ingenuity, the practice persists in reasonably good health.

Metaphor in general flourishes more than ever. Indeed it has reached a state that was unimaginable in Jefferson's time. One reason for this is the pace of technological change, especially in communications, typified by the computer. New technology requires new language, and new language, often drawn from older language, is frequently metaphoric. In addition, because the new technology is so pervasive in communications, it has permitted the easy dissemination of the language of any community to an unlimited audience, no matter how the community is defined. This means that everyone has access to what amounts to new languages, and therefore to new sources of metaphor.

The needs and opportunities of the new languages for metaphor have inevitably led to confusion, some of it deliberate, as people attempt to communicate and at times avoid communicating across the new dialects. Moreover, the technological developments and the communication they permit are so rapid, that many of the dialects, old as well as new, become unstable. It is this instability in language, which Tocqueville long ago noticed as characteristic of American democracy, that leads to both difficulty in communication and the growth of intentional as well as unintentional metaphor. Speaking in metaphor—"metaphor talk"—develops in the languages of sports and entertainment, computers and finance; in the jargon of the professions, the slang of teenagers, and the code words of politics; in nonstandard English, the proliferating non-English languages in America, and the interaction of those languages with what, with some license, is considered standard English. The language of all these lingoes is metaphor in the making.

Specialized languages and dialects of English have always existed, of course. They were of great interest to Jefferson. But in Jefferson's time they were languages spoken by relatively stable communities, or they evolved more gradually than today; in any case, outsiders had less reason to know them. Technology has brought more dialects into being, sped up their creation, hastened their obsolescence, and required many people who are not native speakers to pay attention to them. In this situation, anyone's metaphors are everyone's metaphors, whether or not they are understood. Jefferson declared he was "no friend to what is called *Purism* but a zealous one to *Neology*."[1] But his classical style could hardly have accommodated the modern neologistic explosion and the metaphors that have accompanied it. It is equally certain that his mind could not accommodate—indeed no one's mind can accommodate—all the novelties and therefore the novel metaphors, of modern English.

The second reason why metaphor, if not the nautical metaphor, flourishes today is that intellectuals have abandoned the Baconian cautions on its use. Metaphors are no longer considered to interfere with the progress of science and therefore best confined to a decorative art. On the contrary, metaphors are now often thought of as indispensable to the progress of science, or embedded in it regardless of progress. The anti-metaphor temper that Jefferson inherited from the seventeenth century has been reversed, and today virtually every intellectual field takes metaphor seriously and studies it in one form or another. Indeed, much of cognitive science, the study of how we think, has fastened directly on our thinking through metaphor. Just why

---

1. TJ to John Waldo, Aug. 16, 1813; LoA 1295.

and how this has come about is difficult to say with confidence, but we may point to sources in psychology, anthropology, and rhetoric.[2]

In psychology three rather different avenues have contributed to modern metaphors: physiological psychology, therapeutic psychology, and social psychology.[3] In physiological psychology, in a chapter on "association" in his *Principles of Psychology* (1890), William James writes about a law, "not yet well understood," that explains how one thought follows the next. He illustrates these "thought relations" through six metaphors, every one of them nautical.[4] In therapeutic psychology, there is on the one hand a scientific vocabulary, beginning with Freud, that because it draws on words of everyday language for a specialized purpose may be said to be based on metaphor. On the other hand, therapy itself may be considered an effort by the therapist either to find metaphors in a patient's world of dreams that, interpreted, match the scientific vocabulary, or, by proposing or eliciting metaphors, to help the patient's self-understanding and therefore his healing by leading him from his original characterization of a situation to a different perspective on it. Finally, in social psychology one may find origins of modern metaphor studies in discussions of advertising and mass marketing, and in the study of the language of mass politics. The study of the metaphors of political language, a sub-branch of social and political psychology, began with the propaganda surrounding World War I; it continued in the study of the language that developed under the totalitarian regimes that grew out of the war, and in the private language that developed in response to the Nazi and Communist regimes.

In anthropology, the potential for the expansion of metaphor studies may be found in theories that take in so much social life—structuralism and functionalism—that the theories themselves seem to be metaphors for

---

2. For a penetrating discussion of the appropriate place of metaphor in the social sciences that leaves clues to the origins of its modern expansion, see Alexander Gerschenkron, "Figures of Speech in Social Sciences" (1974). Gerschenkron, whose account of metaphor ranges from literature to mathematics, is judicious in discussing the use of metaphor in economics (his own field) and harsh, but not unwarrantedly so, on metaphor in politics, particularly the metaphor of the state as an organism.

3. The unrivaled scholarship in the field is David E. Leary, ed., *Metaphors in the History of Psychology* (1990). Leary's introductory essay, with its accompanying list of more than 700 references, is an intellectual history of the metaphor in general with only a modest emphasis on psychology.

4. *Principles of Psychology,* ch. XIV (Great Books Edition, 380).

concrete social facts; or in studies of social facts that use the approach of symbolic anthropology, according to which custom and ritual are interpreted as standing for something else, and are thus a kind of metaphor. In a pertinent modern example, Jonathan Raban cites the theory of Claude Lévi-Strauss when writing about the Kwakiutl Indians of Alaska:

> The ship-of-state metaphor, usually rather a fancy notion, applied with peculiar literalness to the culture of the Northwest Indians, for whom the imperiled canoe was both a daily fact and, in their myths and stories, a figurative means of defining their society. The great protective web of customs, rules, and rituals that the coastal Indians spun around themselves was a navigational system, designed to keep the canoe of the family and village from drifting over the lip of the maelstrom.[5]

Because metaphor theory began in rhetoric it is no surprise that rhetoric should contribute to its modern expansion. If one publication can be named as having set off the expansion it is I. A. Richards' *The Philosophy of Rhetoric,* which appeared in 1936 and gave impetus to metaphor studies that has scarcely abated. A bibliographer of the phenomenon, which he calls "metaphormania," offers no theory of the relationship between rhetoric and everything else, except to say that both are phenomena of "communications systems." But he is in a good position to confirm what has happened:

> From the points of view of psychology, psychiatry, philosophy, linguistics, literary criticism, sociology, economics, anthropology, and even biology and medicine, we are trying to see a phenomenon so deep in our communications systems that we are usually unaware of it. We are calling it *metaphor,* a term borrowed from rhetoric, an older science.[6]

5. *A Passage to Juneau: A Sea and Its Meanings* (1999), 37. In general, see James W. Fernandez, ed., *Beyond Metaphor: The Theory of Tropes in Anthropology* (1991); the most relevant essays in this book are the broad-gauged, somewhat excited introduction by Fernandez and the exhilarating but meticulous comparative study by Terence Turner, " 'We are Parrots,' 'Twins Are Birds': Play of Tropes as Operational Structure."

6. Jean-Pierre van Noppen, in the preface to *Metaphor II: A Classified Bibliography of Publications, 1985-1990,* 1, 3. The three substantial bibliographies on metaphor published between 1971 and 1990 contain approximately 11,000 entries. The first of them, the work of Warren A. Shibles, takes the subject back to classical antiquity. The second and third volumes, compiled by van Noppen and others, cover only the 1970s and 1980s.

Accepting the origins of modern studies of metaphor in psychology, anthropology, and rhetoric, what follows here are remarks on the use of metaphor in several other disciplines. These remarks, eclectic and only illustrative, demonstrate how various the conscious concern with metaphor has become and how expanded and far distant we are from the time of Jefferson. The disciplines are literature and language studies; political science and law; philosophy; and science.

It is inevitable that metaphor continues as a subject in literature and language studies. Since there is no choice but to have metaphor in literature, it is understandable that literary analysis is the largest modern field to concern itself with metaphor. Wallace Stevens speaks to the point in "The Motive for Metaphor," a poem that indicates why in literature as in life we shrink from the hardness of "The A B C of being."[7]

Since all that has been said in this essay has assumed that metaphor is a universal concept, a word should be devoted to the challenge of comparative linguistics. Because the word *metaphor* and its associated ideas originated in Western languages, to study what someone may call metaphor outside of those languages requires unusual care.[8] Because metaphors cannot be

7. *Collected Poems* (New York: Knopf, 1954), 288. The best single source for interpretations of the sea in American literature, and with the best bibliography, is Springer, ed., *America and the Sea* (1995). Anna-Teresa Tyminieniecka, ed., *Poetics of the Elements in the Human Condition: The Sea* (1985) is a collection of essays in world literature (none on an American topic) prepared from the perspective of Husserlian phenomenology. Nautical metaphors both small and large are a constant theme in both of these books. Paul Ricoeur, *The Rule of Metaphor* (1977) is the most imposing modern treatment of metaphor in rhetoric and philosophy, from the Greeks to the present. A careful examination of the gap between literary criticism and metaphor theory is Phillip Stambovsky, *The Depictive Image: Metaphor and Literary Experience* (1988). In cognitive linguistics, George Lakoff and Mark Johnson's influential *Metaphors We Live By* (1980) holds that metaphor is at the core of all understanding. A major study in psycholinguistics, much of its material drawn from literature and including sections on metaphor in art, law, politics and science, is Raymond W. Gibbs, Jr., *The Poetics of Mind: Figurative Thought, Language, and Understanding* (1994). In semiotics, see Umberto Eco's dense, historically grounded encyclopedia article, translated as "The Scandal of Metaphor" (1984).

8. For a study profoundly sensitive to the problem of metaphor in a non-Western context, see Michelle Yeh, "Metaphor and *bi:* Western and Chinese Poetics" (1987). A stimulating and accessible essay that is largely on metaphor

understood apart from understanding the context in which they appear, translating metaphors is never without its problems, even across languages that share a heritage in the concept of metaphor. These problems are seldom completely solvable.[9]

In political science, several writers have given sustained attention to metaphor. One maintains that modern political science, no matter how scientific it may seem (the example is behavioralism), is as bound up with metaphor as was classical political theory. Metaphor, he says,

> is necessary to political knowledge . . . because the meaning or reality of the political world transcends what is given to observations. . . . [T]he observable is only a sign of the political—a sign that indicates the existence of political things through association or illuminates their meaning through likeness.

Another political theorist, apparently echoing this view, enters into his discussion with the analysis of a poem, the central lines of which are a nautical metaphor. The point of the poem and its role in his discussion seems to be that for human beings, words constitute reality, that without words we could have neither reality nor poetry, and that metaphors in poetry or elsewhere are thus a natural and probably inevitable means of understanding

---

and based on Chinese as a written language rather than on a particular idea in literary theory is Ernest Fenellosa, "The Chinese Written Character as a Medium for Poetry" (1920). A specialized article that includes nautical metaphors as the West understands them, but is not concerned about transferring the idea of metaphor across language and culture, is Whalen Lai, "Cha'an Metaphors: Waves, Water, Mirror, Lamp" (1979). A fascinating collection of Chinese metaphors that includes a number about the sea is C. A. S. Williams, *A Manual of Chinese Metaphor* (1920). Williams's collection indirectly proves how unlike metaphors in the West are from what a Western scholar calls metaphors in Chinese. For a debate over metaphor in Chinese poetry, see the articles by Yu and Bokenkamp listed in the bibliography.

A study of metaphor in language which is neither spoken nor written yields remarkable insights. In *Language from the Body: Iconicity and Metaphor in American Sign Language* (2001), Sarah F. Taub finds that because signed languages are "spoken" in space rather than in sound or in writing, these language have a different—she would argue a greater—potential for "iconic expression of a broad range of basic conceptual structures (e.g., shapes, movements, locations, human actions)." 3.

9. A convincing and beautifully composed treatment is Gregory Rabassa, "No Two Snowflakes Are Alike: Translation as Metaphor" (1989).

the world, including the political world. A third political philosopher, finding political education analogous to seamanship, summarizes his argument in a long nautical metaphor. A final author takes metaphor as a "bridge between the study of language and the study of politics" and applies this principle in international relations. His conclusion is that "metaphor appears to play a particular role at moments when the international environment has to be reconceptualized."[10]

In the law, metaphor appears in legal fictions, by means of which, just as with metaphors, a person says one thing and means something else. For instance, the law allows a ship to be sued on the fiction that a ship is a person. Although legal fictions as such have been roundly criticized, the law is typically extended by transferring an idea from one circumstance to another; that is, the law is extended through metaphor.[11] A different meaning of metaphor in the law has been proposed by a scholar who has studied Jefferson as a jurist. John T. Noonan fastens on "mask" as a metaphor to stand for that dimension of the law that "suppress[es] the humanity" of the law's participants. Noonan asserts that Jefferson and his law teacher George Wythe participated in suppressing their own humanity and the humanity of slaves through "their management of metaphor."[12]

10. The political scientists are Eugene F. Miller, in "Metaphor and Political Knowledge" (1979), 169; Fred R. Dallmayr, "The Rule of Metaphor," in *Language and Politics* (1983), 148 (the poem Dallmayr analyzes is Stefan George's "The Word," which was chosen both because of its subject and the fact that Martin Heidegger had given a lecture on it); Michael Oakeschott in "Political Education" (1962); and Paul A. Chilton, *Security Metaphors: Cold War Discourse from Containment to Common House* (1996), 413. A study in economics to which Chilton's book bears comparison for its blend of rhetorical theory and applied social science is Philip Eubanks, *A War of Words in the Discourse of Trade: The Rhetorical Constitution of Metaphor* (2000). Eubanks examines "trade is war" in light of metaphor theory. See also Otto Santa Ana, *Brown Tide Rising: Metaphors of Latinos in Contemporary American Public Discourse* (Austin: Univ. of Texas Press, 2002); in addition to "brown tide rising," the book reports on a "sea of brown faces," "great waves of immigration," and "foreigners flooding the country."

11. Legal fictions were criticized as early as Jeremy Bentham. A classic modern critique is Felix S. Cohen, "Transcendental Nonsense and the Functional Approach" (1935). The philosophical basis for the idea of fictions, in law and elsewhere, which could as well be a basis for a philosophy of metaphor, is Hans Vaihinger, *The Philosophy of "As If"* (1924).

12. *Persons and Masks of the Law* (1976), 20, 60-61.

As we have seen, philosophers since ancient Greece have used metaphors both to embellish and to establish their arguments. The practices have continued. Thus we find philosophers who make excursions into imagery that is unrelated to argument and thinkers who make the concept of metaphor a part of their philosophical understanding. We may let Kant and C S. Peirce represent the first group and Nietzsche and Hannah Arendt the second.

In Kant's inimitable portrayal, the "territory of pure understanding" is an island,

> the land of truth—enchanting name!—surrounded by a wide and stormy ocean, the native home of illusion, where many a fog bank and many a swiftly melting iceberg give the deceptive appearance of farther shores, deluding the adventurous seafarer ever anew with empty hopes, and engaging him in enterprises which he can never abandon and yet is unable to carry to completion.[13]

A century later, C. S. Peirce used a nautical metaphor to justify studying "the guiding principles of reasoning:"

> Let a man venture into an unfamiliar field, or where his results are not continually checked by experience, and . . . he is like a ship on the open sea, with no one on board who understands the rules of navigation.

However, Peirce also flaunted a nautical metaphor to make an antimetaphorical point worthy of Bacon:

> If we desire to rescue the good ship Philosophy for the service of Science from the hands of lawless rovers of the sea of literature, we shall do well to keep [one set of terms apart from another].[14]

Among modern philosophers who have written about metaphor as a concept, none is as provocative and provoking as Nietzsche. In "On Truth

---

13. *Critique of Pure Reason* (1781). Newton, one of Jefferson's heroes, reverses Kant and finds truth to be not an island, but the ocean. In a figure from near the end of his life he is reported to have said: "I seem to have been only a boy playing on the seashore, and diverting myself in now and then finding a smoother pebble or a prettier shell than ordinary, whilst the great ocean of truth lay all undiscovered before me." With a twist available only in poetry, Newton's image has been de-metaphorized by William Butler Yeats, who writes of a boy who carried to a friend "Not such as are in Newton's metaphor, / But actual shells of Rosses' lovely shore."

14. From "The Fixation of Belief" (1877) and "Issues of Pragmaticism" (1905).

and Lies in a Nonmoral Sense" Nietzsche compresses into a brief essay, unpublished in his lifetime, his general view of the pervasiveness and necessity of illusion, as well as a means of understanding illusion, in the "fundamental human drive . . . toward the formation of metaphors":

> What then is truth? A movable host of metaphors, metonymies, and anthropomorphisms: in short, a sum of human relations which have been poetically and rhetorically intensified, transferred, and embellished, and which, after long usage, seem to people to be fixed, canonical and binding. . . . [In society] to be truthful means to employ the usual metaphors.[15]

Just how unlike Nietzsche and Jefferson were (or how perceptive Nietzsche was about Jefferson's world) is shown by the fact that Nietzsche's "first metaphor" was Jefferson's first truth: the Lucretian-Lockean doctrine of sensationism, according to which knowledge depends on what we sense. To Nietzsche it is impossible for us truly to know what we sense, because knowledge comes in the form of language, and language is necessarily metaphoric. To Jefferson we must know what we sense, or at least learn something that is true by use of our senses, since to sense is to know, while metaphor is an element of rhetoric and poetry only, which are not part of "knowing" in the same meaning.

A less radical approach to truth through metaphor is that of Hannah Arendt. Arendt is concerned not about two kinds of meaning, literal and figurative, which she says dissolve into each other, but two kinds of apperception, inward and outward, which are kept apart, even though also united, by metaphor:

> The metaphor, bridging the abyss between inward and invisible mental activities and the world of appearances, was certainly the greatest gift language could bestow on thinking and hence on philosophy.[16]

Arendt then exemplifies "bridging the abyss" with a nautical metaphor (a simile) from the *Iliad*, because "metaphor is poetic rather than philosophical

15. *Philosophy and Truth: Selections from Nietzsche's Notebooks of the early 1870's* (1979), ed. and trans. Daniel Breazeale, 89. See also Breazeale's introduction, xxxiii-xxxiv; Paul Cantor, "Friedrich Nietzsche: The Use and Abuse of Metaphor" (1982; "the interplay between literal and figurative meanings becomes a basic principle in Nietzsche's understanding of man's historical development," 73); and Sarah Kofman, *Nietzsche and Metaphor* (1993).

16. *The Life of the Mind; Vol. I: Thinking* (1977), 104; see also 110 and 123.

in origin" and it is Homer who was "the discoverer of this originally poetic tool":

> So the Trojans held their night watches. Meanwhile immortal
> Panic, companion of cold Terror, gripped the Achaians
> as all their best were stricken with grief that passes endurance.
> As two winds rise to shake the sea where the fish swarm, Boreas
> and Zephyros, north wind and west, that blow from Thraceward,
> suddenly descending, and the darkened water is gathered
> to crests, and far across the salt water scatters the seaweed;
> so the heart in the breast of each Achaian was troubled.

Arendt's explication of Homer: "Think of the storms that you know so well . . . and you will know about grief and fear."[17] It is hard to believe that Jefferson, who would have been familiar with this simile on panic, terror and winds, would disagree with the explication—even though he himself would never write a nautical metaphor that contained such a burden of meaning.[18]

As the philosophers imply, to invite metaphor into one's thinking is to risk confidence in the nature of fact. Therefore, when we turn to science, which is ordinarily concerned fulltime with facts and with theory that can be derived from facts, the talk of metaphor can be positively dangerous. This is certainly the case from the standpoint of Jefferson, for the basic assignment of his life as a scientist was to understand "the system of things in which we are placed."[19] In carrying out this assignment the worst possibilities would be that either the things or the system didn't exist, and, as Nietzsche urged, that perhaps both had been replaced by metaphor. Without going that far, we take up three approaches to the relation of metaphor to science: studies in traditional fields of science; the metaphoric use of science to explain human history; and metaphor in philosophies of the history of science and the scientific process.

17. Ibid., 106.
18. Additional modern works on metaphor and philosophy include a pellucid and encompassing study, Jerry H. Gill, *Wittgenstein and Metaphor* (1996); a tentative proposal, A. T. Nuyen, "The Kantian Theory of Metaphor" (1989); an innovative scanning of approaches to philosophy, Richard Rorty, "Philosophy as Science, as Metaphor, and as Politics" (1991); and Walker Percy, "Metaphor as Mistake" (1958), an Arendt-like attempt to find metaphor uniting truth (philosophy and science) with poetry by considering it analogical in contrast to its being either logical or nonlogical.
19. TJ, Autobiography (1821), LoA 4.

Metaphor has taken many paths in studies of standard scientific disciplines. Because metaphor is a cultural contrivance, these studies have no choice but to connect science to culture. They cannot be studies internal to science only. One path examines the efforts of great scientists to *avoid* metaphor in explaining their theories, or at least to avoid metaphor that risks being misleading or causing controversy. Studies of Newton on attraction and Darwin on natural selection show how difficult if not impossible this task is.[20] Another path in a traditional scientific discipline looks at competing metaphors in the establishment of an entire field. The example here is alternative images of time in geology.[21] A most unsettling path examines a field not *through* metaphor, but *as* metaphor. A physicist has written of space, time, matter, and number as "cardinal metaphors" in order to find the "meaning, value, and purpose of human existence."[22] An inter-disciplinary path in biology and linguistics shows how a metaphor, the branching of a tree, became standard in the methodology of classification.[23] A final path studies metaphors in an applied science—medicine—and finds disastrous social consequences in their use.[24]

The metaphoric use of science to explain human history is perhaps best represented by an extremist, Henry Adams, not the least because he is an obvious candidate for Jefferson's interest. The great-grandson of John Adams, Henry Adams had learned foreign affairs from the inside, under his father, the American minister to England in the 1860s. On his return to the

20. J. M. Coetzee, "Newton and the Ideal of a Transparent Scientific Language" (1982) and Robert M. Young, "Darwin's Metaphor: Does Nature Select?" (1971).
21. Stephen Jay Gould, *Time's Arrow, Time's Circle: Myth and Metaphor in the Discovery of Geological Time* (1987), esp. 10-16 and 191-208.
22. Roger S. Jones, *Physics as Metaphor* (1982), ix.
23. Henry M. Hoenigswald and Linda F. Wiener, eds., *Biological Metaphor and Cladistic Classification* (1987).
24. Susan Sontag, *Illness as Metaphor* (1977) and *AIDS and Its Metaphors* (1989). Sontag does not at all object to metaphor as such, but holds that "the most truthful way of regarding illness—and the healthiest way of being ill—is one most purified of, most resistant to, metaphoric thinking." *Illness*, 3; cf. *AIDS*, 5. *Illness* is about cancer and tuberculosis and is very much a study in literature. *AIDS* begins with Lucretius and ends with a polemic against military metaphor and "total" metaphors, whether applied to AIDS or anything else. 7, 85-95.

United States he tried journalism in Washington (see Appendix III for his nautical metaphor on President Grant). After that he wrote on Anglo-Saxon law, a subject dear to Jefferson's historical and ideological heart; Albert Gallatin, Jefferson's brilliant Secretary of the Treasury; and John Randolph, the uncompromising Virginian politician and Jefferson's frequent nemesis. He culminated his scholarly life with a nine-volume *History of the United States During the Administrations of Jefferson and Madison* (1889-91) that combined historical detachment and a sense of personal intimacy that can never be repeated.

Near the end of his *History,* Adams found the United States "a single homogeneous society" set on a permanent democratic course and fixed enough to no longer need its story told in a heroic and dramatic fashion. Instead, its history was ready for scientific laws.[25] In his search for these laws, which he recorded in the final chapters of *The Education of Henry Adams* (1907), he carried over existing laws of science to his own field—literally. What might have remained metaphor became fact. What did remain metaphor often became nautical metaphor.

Adams recalled exploring "the shores of Multiplicity," but soon realized that "even within these narrow seas the navigator [Adams] lost his bearings and followed the winds as they blew." He then read Karl Pearson's *Grammar of Science* (1892), only to find that the author had left "science adrift on a sensual raft in the midst of supersensual chaos." But Adams had at last found himself—"on the raft, personally and economically concerned with its drift." From that moment he turned to science in the hope of understanding the drift of the raft and discovering the laws of history.

Adams conceded that "images are not arguments" but, like Locke, he also knew that images are what the mind craves. Therefore, by the end of *The Education* and in two papers written around the same time he made no apology for attempting the literal application of several laws of mechanics to the past, and therefore to the future. As he wrote of his search for a formula that would explain the American declaration of war on Spain in 1898:

> If Kepler and Newton could take liberties with the sun and the moon an obscure person in a remote wilderness like La Fayette Square could take liberties with Congress, and venture to multiply half its attraction into the square of its time.

25. *History of the United States during the Administrations of Jefferson and Madison* (1931 repr.), vol. IX, ch. x, 222.

Adams reported that "all his associates in history condemned [this] attempt as futile and almost immoral." Jefferson (and John Adams) would have condemned the attempt, too.[26]

Nothing seems further from the liberties Henry Adams took with metaphor than the argument of T. S. Kuhn based on "paradigm." But paradigm is a cousin of metaphor, and that justifies a look at Kuhn's *Structure of Scientific Revolutions* (1962) and a contrast of that work in the history of science with Adams's effort toward a science of history. Kuhn turns Adams completely around. While Adams had aimed for certainty in history and claimed to have found it in science, Kuhn discovered uncertainty in science and demonstrated how this was the result of history. Kuhn's paradigm is a model—a kind of metaphor—within which "normal science" operates and which is revised (a "paradigm shift") when there is a successful scientific revolution.[27]

An element in Kuhn's success and Adams's failure is the difference between paradigm well perceived and metaphor misperceived. A paradigm is a pattern or model that, in principle, all can agree on, and that, when carefully considered, is accepted as true. It also bounds a field of inquiry and is an idea found by looking around or (etymologically) looking to the side. A metaphor strictly considered is a proposal to the imagination that is not meant to secure cognitive assent or be accepted as true. It deliberately and temporarily yokes two

26. *The Education of Henry Adams,* 449, 452-53, 376. Adams's two papers are "The Phase Rule Applied to History" (1909; printed posthumously), and "Letter to American Teachers of History" (1910). An important study is Joseph Mindel, "Uses of Metaphor: Henry Adams and the Symbols of Science" (1965).

27. Kuhn's uses of "paradigm" are clarified in a postscript to the second edition of *The Structure of Scientific Revolutions* (1969). A helpful essay is David A. Hollinger, "T. S. Kuhn's Theory of Science and Its Implications for History" (1973).

For an admirable study in the philosophy of science that is explicitly tied to metaphor, see W. H. Leatherdale, *The Role of Analogy, Model and Metaphor in Science* (1974). Leatherdale reaches metaphor after examining analogy ("a more fundamental and simple concept") and model, which he considers a species of analogy. 1, 42. He tucks in a digressive chapter on metaphor in seventeenth century science and provides an excellent classified bibliography. Roy Dreistadt, "An Analysis of the Use of Analogies and Metaphors in Science" (1968), contains an impressive collection of metaphors from prominent scientists in many fields.

different things together and is found by looking to the outside or (etymologically) by carrying over. Paradigm and metaphor also differ in that paradigm is a model that can so thoroughly enclose our thought that we are seldom aware of using it, while a standard metaphor must ordinarily be noticed. Thus Kuhn first had to develop the idea of a paradigm in science and then demonstrate that the idea helped explain the history of particular sciences, while Adams relied on the well-known idea of metaphor, first by implicitly holding that science is a usable metaphor for history and then by explicitly attempting to apply scientific concepts to explain human history. The ideas of paradigm and standard metaphor may be mediated, however, by the notion of a master metaphor. Like a paradigm, a master metaphor is seldom noticed by its practitioners. Like a standard metaphor a master metaphor really requires that one thing stand for something else. Kuhn uses one kind of broad metaphor, the paradigm, far more appropriately than Adams used another kind, a metaphor narrowly conceived.

Kuhn's *Structure,* although a self-contained essay in the philosophy of the history of science, was published as a part of an ambitious project, the *International Encyclopedia of Unified Science,* whose editor-in-chief was Otto Neurath, an energetic polymath. The premise of Neurath's project was that although certainty of knowledge is an illusion, science, including the social sciences and humanities, could be unified by an objective language and a common set of methodological principles. One of Neurath's own contributions to these principles, however, is formulated in language that is by no means objective. He proposes a philosophy of the scientific process, if not a philosophy of the process of human existence, through a metaphor. The metaphor is known as Neurath's Boat.[28]

Neurath's Boat is not a literary decoration. It is a metaphor (actually a simile) that is meant to instruct and persuade. In slightly varying language, the metaphor appears in Neurath's writing several times. This is one of the versions:

> We are like sailors who must reconstruct their ship on the open sea but are never able to start afresh from the bottom. Where a beam is taken away a new one must at once be put there, and for this the rest of the ship is used as support. In this way, by using old beams and driftwood, the ship can be shaped entirely anew, but only by gradual reconstruction.

28. The following discussion is drawn from Nancy Cartwright, et al., *Otto Neurath: Philosophy Between Science and Politics* (1996), 89-166.

What does this metaphor mean? "We" is everyman. The ship is the world as we experience and understand it, and both the world and our understanding of it change. Yet neither the world nor our understanding of it changes in a single moment, but only gradually. When one element of experience or one concept of understanding becomes inadequate to the whole, it must, like a defective beam of a boat, be replaced. Or a concept has been abandoned or an experience forgotten and so the defective beam is thrown overboard and the ship is modified by an absolute loss. Missing from Neurath is the possibility that the sea itself might change. Neither is there any sight of land; or a mention, beyond sailors, of who is on board and their relation to each another. We concentrate on a physical ship out on a permanent sea. But from this image we learn a theory of scientific method and perhaps of human existence.

Jefferson would presumably have found Neurath's metaphor ingenious for its purpose. But he would have been displeased with the philosophy behind it. In Neurath, Jefferson's permanent "system of things in which we are placed" undergoes constant change; yet there is no hint of human progress. Moreover, Jefferson was too science-minded in the traditional, Baconian way to let facts be submerged in, emerge from, or be explained by a figure of speech. Theories should be built from facts, but facts could not stand for anything but themselves.

While Jefferson the philosopher and scientist stands outside metaphoric territory, Jefferson the American might have ventured in, for defining America was the intellectual task of his life and this was not a task that could be left to science. Rather, as he realized, if perhaps only subconsciously, it was a task of intellectual imagination and one that could include the use of metaphor. He would therefore presumably have noticed two modern interpreters of America who make metaphor central to their work. They are Annette Kolodny, who analyzes American attitudes toward the land under the phrase "Metaphor as Experience and History," and Daniel T. Rodgers, who traces metaphors through American political history.

The origin of Kolodny's work has a Jeffersonian cast to it, even if what she does with metaphor does not. *The Lay of the Land: Metaphor as Experience and History in American Life and Letters* (1975) originated in a "growing distress at what we have done to our continent." The aim of her book is to awaken America from environmental disregard and thereby help ameliorate the nation's environmental degradation. At this point Kolodny leaves the Jeffersonian trail and pursues her aim by examining "the ways in which language provides clues to the underlying motivations behind action." To find clues and motivations she treats language psychologically while searching for a master metaphor at work in American history. The distinctly unJeffersonian result is her discovery that a "central metaphor of American pastoral experience" is "land-as-woman." The American landscape, she asserts, has been experienced "as the female principle of gratification itself, comprising all the qualities that Mother, Mistress, and Virgin traditionally represent for men." Today, she continues, Americans are (or through her can become) conscious of this central metaphor of their experience and so have the choice "whether to allow our responses to this continent to continue in the service of outmoded and demonstrably dangerous image patterns" or to place our " 'yearnings for paradise' at the disposal of potentially healthier" systems. She concludes with an echo of Neurath's boat:

> [This may] be man's ultimate creative act: to pick and choose among the image systems available to him at any one time and to make of them, periodically, a new reality.

Unexpectedly, and despite her method and particular conclusion, in this sentence one also hears an echo of Jefferson, whose creativity lay precisely in participating in choosing an image system for America, in particular an image system of liberty.[29]

A dozen years after Kolodny, Daniel T. Rodgers published *Contested Truths: Keywords in American Politics Since Independence.* Equally intent on examining the interrelation between words and acts, and on drawing lessons from language, Rodgers presents American history as a series of overlapping contests for the definition and control of political terms. These are the "keywords" of his title. Throughout the book Rodgers calls his keywords metaphors: utility, natural rights, the people, government, the state, interests, and freedom. Yet these words are no more metaphors as Jefferson understood the term than is Kolodny's land-as-woman image. None of Rodgers's keywords are meant to evoke concrete images, nor, unlike metaphor, is there anywhere a logical strangeness of a relation between two ideas. Nevertheless, Rodgers's justification for calling his keywords metaphors is that "they create those pictures in our heads which make the structures of authority tolerable and understandable." It is therefore not difficult to

---

29. Kolodny, *The Lay of the Land* (1975), ix, 150, 158-60. A sophisticated study in European history based in metaphor is Antoine de Baecque, *The Body Politic: Corporeal Metaphor in Revolutionary France, 1770-1800* (1997).

think of the keywords collectively as the language tools of politics and hence as a species of metaphor that Jefferson could recognize.[30]

Rodgers's procedure with metaphor differs from Kolodny's. His orientation is towards politics and power, not literature and psychology. He searches the language for struggles, not motivations. And while, like Kolodny, his own public values are in the open, he does not arrive at the existentialist conclusion that Americans have a choice about their metaphors or keywords. Rather, his conclusion describes history as if it were a natural force, though one with a lesson:

> [E]very effort to alter the root metaphors of politics [has] inaugurated a furiously intense struggle over the control of words . . . But a public life without a strong deeply rooted repertoire of public words carries consequences. When the metaphors fail, legitimacy erodes.[31]

Where is Jefferson in this? Jefferson did not like struggle of any kind, and by metaphor he meant something much smaller and more mundane than Rodgers's keywords. But who in American history studied and employed political language to more effect? Who had a larger repertoire of public words? Who knew more than Jefferson how to control large metaphors in order to determine the character of public life? Jefferson would never have countenanced "land-as-woman" as a metaphor or have labeled "liberty" a metaphor. But he would have endorsed both Kolodny's freedom to choose the language of one's values and Rodgers's claim that language helps determine political legitimacy in the social order.

Both Kolodny and Rodgers are Jeffersonians in that they know the importance of rhetoric in public life. They also know how deeply Jefferson's rhetoric continues to affect Americans, especially through what they, though not Jefferson, consider metaphors. When an American says "liberty," what instantly comes to mind is Jefferson's "life, liberty, and the pursuit of happiness."

Recent evidence of the indissoluble tie between Jefferson and liberty appeared in *Thomas Jefferson: Genius of Liberty*, a book brought out by the Library of Congress in 2000. The Library of Congress is of course not able to turn a slaveholder into a genius of liberty, nor, notwithstanding some subtextual attempts, does the Library discover evidence that Jefferson was considered a genius of liberty in his own time. Yet Jefferson is a genius of

30. Rodgers, *Keywords* (1987), 15.
31. Ibid., 212, 224.

the *rhetoric* of liberty, and on this, almost in spite of itself, the book makes a valid and important point. If "liberty" is taken as a metaphor, and since metaphor is an element of rhetoric, then to say that Jefferson is a genius of the rhetoric of liberty is also to say that he is a genius of metaphor, or at least of one kind of large metaphor. And as this essay has demonstrated, Jefferson is also exceptionally talented, if he is not a genius, in his small metaphors. Thus through metaphor we may fairly take a new reckoning of the man.

The theory behind this reckoning has sound antecedents, going back to the classics. In the *Poetics,* Aristotle writes:

> It is a great thing to use properly each of the devices I have spoken of . . . but much the most important is the metaphor; this alone cannot be learned from others and its use is a sign of genius, for to use metaphors well is to see resemblance.[32]

In the *Essay Concerning Human Understanding* Locke writes that metaphor is about resemblance, though presumably because metaphor adds only to beauty and not to truth, he does not mention genius.[33] A few generations after Jefferson's time, William James seems to have drawn on both Aristotle and Locke with respect to resemblance, which he calls "association," and to have drawn on Aristotle with respect to genius, which he calls a capacity for association "to an extreme degree."[34] In the twentieth century, two American men of letters have extended the ideas of Aristotle, Locke, and James about the small metaphor (e.g., ship of state) so as to embrace the large metaphor (e.g., liberty) as well. Walker Percy explicitly interprets Aristotle on metaphor to embrace large metaphor, which he calls "prolonged analogy."[35] Robert Frost accomplishes the same end when he writes that poetry "begins in trivial metaphors, pretty metaphors, 'grace' metaphors, and goes on to the profoundest thinking that we have." Frost calls the profound thinking "beliefs," which, as he illustrates them, are belief-systems, one of which could be a belief system of liberty.[36] Using Frost's language to sum up these several thinkers, we may say that

---

32. *Poetics* 59a4; trans. Alfred Gudeman, in Gilbert, *Literary Criticism,* 103.

33. *Essay Concerning Human Understanding,* bk. II, ch.. xi, sec. 2; and bk. III, ch. x, sec. 34.

34. *Principles of Psychology,* ch. XXII ("Reasoning"), section on "Different Orders of Human Genius."

35. "Metaphor as Mistake" (1958), 81.

36. "Education by Poetry" (1930), 719, 726.

Jefferson's talent with resemblance through grace metaphors, together with his talent at carrying out a belief-system in liberty, substantiates the claim that at least part of his greatness lies in his mastery of metaphor. There is a final modern approach to thinking about metaphor through which Jefferson should be understood. It is an approach that takes small metaphor as its initial subject but makes something far grander out of it, something that is not metaphor at all, but philosophy. This is the approach of "metaphorology," a philosophy developed by Hans Blumenberg (1920-1996).

By metaphorology Blumenberg means the discovery of truth in the uncertainties of metaphor. In *Shipwreck with Spectator: Paradigm of a Metaphor for Existence* (1979), Blumenberg, rather amazingly for present purposes, develops his philosophy in an essay on the history of a particular nautical metaphor. The metaphor he chooses, "shipwreck with spectator," is rooted in classical antiquity, in Lucretius, and, as Blumenberg demonstrates, is interpreted throughout Western history by others, particularly Montaigne, Voltaire, Goethe, and Nietzsche. From this history Blumenberg creates a philosophy of existence.[37]

Blumenberg's philosophy could have been demonstrated through the study of other metaphors, but few could yield a paradigm for

37. Blumenberg wrote *Shipwreck with Spectator* in 1979. Steven Rendall's introduction to the English translation (1997) and an article by David Adams, "Metaphors for Mankind: The Development of Hans Blumenberg's Anthropological Metaphorology" (1991), are helpful in understanding where Blumenberg is situated in twentieth century philosophy. Blumenberg's original programmatic essay, "Paradigms for a Metaphorology" (1960; summarized in Shibles, *Metaphor,* 60) was later modified to hold that "metaphorics [is] merely a special case of nonconceptuality," where nonconceptuality is what we experience but cannot express except in non-literal ways; metaphor is but an example of these ways. See Blumenberg's essay, "Prospect for a Theory of Nonconceptuality," in *Shipwreck,* 81. David Adams presents Blumenberg as having chosen for his model the "philosophical anthropology" of Ernst Cassirer, with its "multitude of world-views and symbolic forms" (metaphor was Cassirer's leading symbolic form) over the metaphysics of Heidegger with its comprehension of existence through a single "absolute metaphor."

The nearest I have found to Blumenberg's approach to philosophy through nautical metaphor is W. H. Auden's *The Enchaféd Flood, Or the Romantic Iconography of the Sea* (1950). Auden's difficult book is wider (and more idiosyncratic) than its subtitle implies; it is also clearly the philosophy of a poet, not a historian.

existence as well as "shipwreck with spectator." Indeed, Blumenberg chose the metaphor precisely because of what it promises for philosophy as such. As explained by his translator, "spectator" in the essay's title embodies theory (the Greek word *theoria* derives from *theoros,* "spectator") and thus raises the question of what a theoretical perspective on the world entails.[38]

The exemplar passage from Lucretius comes at the opening of Book II of *De Rerum Natura:*

> When winds churn up a heavy storm at sea
> It is a pleasant thing to watch, from land,
> Another's mighty struggle with the waves:
> Not that delightful pleasure can be felt
> In someone's being buffeted, but that
> It is a pleasant thing to see that we
> Are being spared those troubles.

Blumenberg understands these lines to concern the spectator-philosopher's distance from, and relation to, human tribulation. But he interprets the passage not as about a relation between those who suffer and those who do not, but about

> the relationship between philosophers and reality; it has to do with the advantage gained through Epicurus's philosophy [in Lucretius], the possession of an inviolable, solid ground for one's view of the world.[39]

Blumenberg does not claim that those who use the shipwreck metaphor must be Lucretians in the rest of their philosophy, only that Lucretius points the way towards understanding what philosophy itself is. Jefferson, however, was a Lucretian in the substance of much of his philosophy, and since Blumenberg's interpretation of the original statement of the metaphor necessarily makes sense within Lucretian doctrine as a whole, it also makes sense for Jefferson. Jefferson's confidence in a "system of things in which we are placed," for instance, is contained within the "solid ground for one's view of the world" that Blumenberg finds in Lucretius.

There is more to a Blumenberg-Jefferson association than a connection to Lucretius. The two men are pluralist in their thought, drawing ideas from the widest learning available to them, and both men are

38. *Shipwreck with Spectator,* 2.
39. Ibid., 26.

concerned with the small metaphor, not the large. On the other hand, the two are starkly unalike in crucial ways. The modernist Blumenberg takes metaphor to reveal truth if not to constitute it, while the classicist Jefferson takes metaphor to adorn the truth as long as it does not obscure it. The scholar Blumenberg follows formulations of one nautical metaphor through history and makes an ontology of it. The writer Jefferson scatters his correspondence with his own formulations of several nautical metaphors (never including "shipwreck with spectator") for the purpose of utilitarian beauty.

These differences between the two thinkers may be seen in compressed form in Jefferson's library classification. That classification, which Jefferson developed from the three "faculties of the mind" proposed by Bacon, consists of Memory, Reason, and Imagination—history, philosophy, and fine arts (including literature). In this framework, Blumenberg's metaphors are data from Imagination (literature) organized according to Memory (history) for the purpose of Reason (philosophy). Jefferson, whose own metaphors are confined to Imagination, almost surely would have admired Blumenberg's expansive project.

* * * *

The initial justification for this essay was that Jefferson's nautical metaphors are so frequent and, within their range, so varied, as to deserve study. What have we learned at the end? Not surprisingly, the illumination of this small corner of Jefferson's life, no matter how brightly, has told little about many of the fields he roamed. Yet an examination of his nautical metaphors, along with examinations of his sources, his non-nautical metaphors, and the nautical metaphor and metaphor theory since his time, helps us understand a number of his views and often his mood on the many occasions he used the metaphors. With the theme of ship of state, those occasions were necessarily about public affairs. With the theme of voyage of life, the occasions were typically more private. Taken as a whole, the hundred nautical metaphors collected in Appendix I create an unusual lens on Jefferson's life and thought. Through it we have a new perspective on his rhetoric, one of his most recognized accomplishments in his own times and one of his most potent legacies to the future.

We have seen the source of Jefferson's understanding of metaphor in general and of the nautical metaphor in particular in his grounding in the classics. An examination of his metaphors has thereby enlarged an appreciation of the role of the classics in his life. We have also recognized the context for his using the nautical metaphor in the pervasive seafaring of his era, and in the assumption that most of his correspondents were familiar enough with the figure of speech to appreciate his talent with it. At the same time, we have found in his scientific outlook and his absorption of the lessons of Bacon and Locke a reason for his caution in using metaphor of any kind, limiting it with few exceptions to an ornamental role and keeping it away from argumentation.

Jefferson held his metaphors under tight rein as to both the occasions when he used them and the language that comprised them. In the range of nautical metaphors, from the unnoticeable and banal through the harmless and the worthy to the poetic and profound, Jefferson's belong almost entirely to the worthy. He is able to avoid writing metaphors that are overused, hackneyed, or cliché. He was a master of style in general because he was a master of style in the particular, and his nautical metaphors are a superlative example of the particular.

But metaphor lies not only in the biography of a man. Metaphor lies also in mankind. We have a distinctive and inherent capacity for comparison, with no provable beginning and no possible end. What we think about metaphor, and the kinds of metaphor we think up, naturally depend upon culture. We have found the Western tradition especially rich in the nautical metaphor. At the beginning this was presumably attributable to the metaphor's origin in the sea-based civilizations of Greece and Rome. These civilizations gave birth to a metaphor that Jefferson found in his education and that was also well suited to his own times. Since then, educational, geopolitical, and technological changes have diminished the effectiveness and reworked the use of the nautical metaphor. But these changes have not cut the metaphor off.

Indeed, the nautical metaphor cannot be cut off. It is too embedded in Western culture for that to happen. It may be too soon to know whether the end of the age of sail has affected its use, yet it is probable that ships are ships regardless how they are powered or how they look. And the sea is still the sea. Aside from the nautical metaphor's continuing in its traditional domains of literature and public rhetoric, it has been able to flow into some of the wide channels for modern metaphor, such as in the epistemology of Otto Neurath and the ontology of Hans Blumenberg. We must ask, too, whether anything could possibly replace some kind of "sea thinking." We live on land. To be on the water, especially on water beyond sight of land, is to transgress our natural boundaries. What stronger point of comparison to our condition exists than that of water? What more universally available perspective on our own circumstance? The nautical metaphor seems as innate to Jefferson as it is to mankind. To revise one of his ship-of-state figures, a nautical metaphor from him can show "by the beauty of [its] motion the skill of [its] builder."[40] Jefferson built his metaphors with skill, and the motion they supply to his writing is often beautiful. It is true that as a builder of nautical metaphors he was seldom searching for more than beauty or rhetorical effect. If he had understood metaphor differently, had his education been different, had he lived in different times, he might have achieved something else with nautical metaphors, such as more flexibility in his thinking or new truths in science, philosophy, or human understanding. His nautical metaphors are nevertheless evidence of the universal power of thinking at sea, even as his examples hold to a particular cultural tradition.

In his first inaugural address Jefferson spoke of "the vessel in which we are all embarked among the conflicting elements of a troubled world." A quarter century later he hoped future generations would enjoy "the Halcyon calms succeeding the storm which our Argosy has so stoutly weathered."[41] The American vessel still sails in a troubled world, and Halcyon calms seem beyond reach. But due in part to the vision and rhetoric of Jefferson, the ship of state endures.

40. TJ to John Dickinson, March 6, 1801.
41. TJ to John Adams, March 25, 1826.

APPENDIXES

THE APPENDIXES consist of (i) Jefferson's nautical metaphors, (ii) Jefferson's non-nautical metaphors, and (iii) nautical metaphors by other authors. Jefferson's metaphors are listed in chronological order. The nautical metaphors by other authors are divided into those written before and those written after Jefferson's death, and listed alphabetically by author. Brief annotations for many of the entries enable the metaphors to be self-interpreting at a basic level. The entries for metaphors mentioned in the text are followed by a page number in brackets, so that the appendixes also serve as an index to those metaphors.

The collection of Jefferson's nautical metaphors is incomplete, for two reasons. First, what counts as a nautical metaphor is to some degree necessarily subjective. Second, with few exceptions, the metaphors are derived from published sources, and a sizable portion of Jefferson's correspondence has not yet been published. The criteria for the selection of Jefferson's non-nautical metaphors are that they are striking or well-known or that they provide a good contrast with his nautical metaphors. In Appendix III, the first section gathers in one place the metaphors that Jefferson was either unquestionably familiar with or was likely to be familiar with; it therefore illustrates the metaphors that influenced his style. Conversely, several of the metaphors in Appendix III.B were presumably influenced by Jefferson—for instance the metaphors of his eulogists. Most of the metaphors in Appendix III.B, however, illustrate either different or more complex versions of the sorts of nautical metaphors that Jefferson himself used; or nautical metaphors employed for purposes quite different from his own—in particular for the purpose of argument rather than ornament.

Where possible, sources for Jefferson's metaphors, as well as for a number of the metaphors in Appendix III.A, are one of the following works. Priority is given to the Library of America edition of Jefferson's writings edited by Merrill Peterson because it is the most reliable, extensive, conveniently available, one-volume collection. (Its editorial procedures and sources are meticulously laid out in "Note on the Texts," 1532-48.) Other sources of Jefferson's writings, used in order of reliability, are Boyd, Ford, and Lipscomb-Bergh.

AJL   Lester J. Cappon, ed., *The Adams-Jefferson Letters: The Complete Correspondence between Thomas Jefferson and Abigail and John Adams.* 2 vols. Chapel Hill: Univ. of North Carolina Press, 1959.

B   Julian P. Boyd, et al., eds., *The Papers of Thomas Jefferson.* 28 vols. to date. Princeton: Princeton Univ. Press, 1950–.

F   Paul Leicester Ford, ed., *The Works of Thomas Jefferson.* Federal Edition. 12 vols. New York: G. P. Putnam's Sons, 1904-05. (This edition was also issued in a ten-volume format under *The Writings of Thomas Jefferson.* The indexes to the two sets lead to the identical material.)

LB   Andrew A. Lipscomb and Albert Ellery Bergh, eds., *The Writings of Thomas Jefferson.* Memorial Edition. 20 vols. Washington, D.C.: The Thomas Jefferson Memorial Association, 1903.

LoA   Merrill Peterson, ed., *Thomas Jefferson: Writings.* New York: Library of America, 1984.

LCB   Douglas L. Wilson, ed., *Jefferson's Literary Commonplace Book.* Princeton: Princeton Univ. Press, 1989.

APPENDIX I
Jefferson's Nautical Metaphors

Recipients or Occasions

John Adams, 1796, 1812, 1814,
1816, 1819, 1826
Samuel Adams, 1801
John Armstrong, 1809
James Breckinridge, 1821
John Breckinridge, 1800
Madame de Bréhan, 1787
Aaron Burr, 1797
Joseph C. Cabell, 1816
Arthur Campbell, 1797
Maria Cosway, 1786
County Lieutenants of Berkeley and
Frederick, 1781
John Dickinson, 1801
William Duane, 1810
Pierre Samuel Dupont de Nemours,
1809
Pierpont Edwards, 1801
John Wayles Eppes, 1813
Edward Everett, 1822
First Inaugural Address, 1801
Theodore Foster, 1801
Albert Gallatin, 1818
Elbridge Gerry, 1785, 1797, 1801
William Branch Giles, 1794
Claiborne W. Gooch, 1826
John Holmes, 1820
Francis Hopkinson, 1790
Richard M. Johnson, 1808
William Johnson, 1823
Walter Jones, 1810
Kentucky Resolutions, 1798
Samuel Kercheval, 1816
Lafayette, 1801, 1820
Richard Henry Lee, 1785
Nicholas Lewis, 1791

Edward Livingston, 1824
Robert R. Livingston, 1800
James Madison, 1794, 1795, 1796,
1797, 1797
James Maury, Jr., 1812
Philip Mazzei, 1796
John Melish, 1811
James Monroe, 1790, 1796, 1808,
1812, 1815, 1816, 1817, 1823, 1823
Nathaniel Niles, 1801
Mann Page, 1795
Thomas Paine, 1789
Charles Pinckney, 1809, 1820
Thomas Pinckney, 1797
Joseph Priestley, 1801
Thomas Mann Randolph, Jr., 1793
Thomas Ritchie, 1820
La Rochefoucauld, 1790
Richard Rush, 1820
Edward Rutledge, 1795, 1796
Correa de Serra, 1815
William Short, 1791, 1793
James Smith, 1822
Samuel H. Smith, 1823
Archibald Stuart, 1797
Eliza House Trist, 1783, 1785, 1786,
1814
St. George Tucker, 1793
Francis A. Van der Kemp, 1812
Jean Pierre Brissot de Warville, 1793
George Washington, 1792, 1792
James Wilkinson, 1811
Robert Wright, 1809
Charles Yancey, 1816
Isaac Zane, 1781

We are all embarked in one bottom, the Western end of which cannot swim while the Eastern sinks.

TJ to the County Lieutenants of Berkeley and Frederick, Feb. 16, 1781; B.IV.628. Jefferson, as governor of Virginia during the Revolution, seeks the military service of men in the state's western counties, reminding them that the entire state must be defended if the Revolution is to be successful.

His natural ill-temper was the tool worked with by another hand. He was like the minners which go in and out of the fundament of the whale. But the whale himself was discoverable enough by the turbulence of the water under which he moved.

TJ to Isaac Zane, Dec. 24, 1781; B.VI.143. The minnow is George Nicholas, who proposes an investigation of Jefferson as wartime governor. The whale is Patrick Henry.

I hope the day is near when Mr. Trist's return will make amends for the crosses and disappointments you complain of, and render the current of life as smooth and placid as you can wish.

TJ to Eliza House Trist, Dec. 11, 1783; B.VI.382.

They are throwing out another barrel for the political whales to play with. [34]

TJ to Richard Henry Lee, Feb. 7, 1785; B.VII.643. Jefferson writes from Paris about machinations in European politics. Literally, to throw a barrel or tub out to the whale referred to dumping harpoon line overboard that was stored in a tub, often a tub made of a barrel cut in half. A whale struck by a harpoon would then have enough free line so that its frantic dashing off across the water would not lead to harm to the whaleboat. I am indebted to John G. Arrison of the Penobscot Marine Museum for this information. To throw a barrel out to a whale was a common metaphor in Jefferson's time, often meaning to divert political opponents or to amuse political supporters while protecting the ship of state. For other examples see TJ to Albert Gallatin, Feb. 15, 1818, and TJ to Charles Pinckney, Sept. 30, 1820.

The arrêt [decree] on the West India commerce last winter raised a furious tempest against the minister. It has been with difficulty that he could keep the ground which that had gained. The storm is not yet over, but its force is so far spent that I think there is little danger of the merchants forcing him to retract. [34]

TJ to Elbridge Gerry, May 11, 1785; B.VIII.142-43.

Perhaps they [the French] may catch some moments of transport above the level of the ordinary tranquil joy we experience, but they are separated by long intervals during which all the passions are at sea without rudder or compass.

> *TJ to Eliza House Trist, Aug. 18, 1785; B.VIII.404.* Unlike Americans, who are moderate, the French cannot control their passions.

The art of life is the art of avoiding pain: and he is the best pilot who steers clearest of the rocks and shoals with which it is beset.

> *TJ to Maria Cosway, Oct. 12, 1786; LoA 872.* The Head is speaking to the Heart in Jefferson's "Dialogue Between My Head and My Heart."

Laid up in port, for life, as I thought myself at one time, I am thrown out to sea, and an unknown one to me. By so slender a thread do all our plans of life hang.

> *TJ to Eliza House Trist, Dec. 15, 1786; B.X.600.* Jefferson had hoped to leave public service after the Revolution and live permanently at Monticello. But the death of his wife in 1782 forced him to rearrange his life, and he became the American minister to France.

Heaven bless you, Madam, and guard you under all circumstances: give you smooth waters, gentle breezes, and clear skies, hushing all its elements into peace, and leading with its own hand the favored bark, till it shall have safely landed its precious charge on the shores of our new world.

> *TJ to Madame de Bréhan, Oct. 9, 1787; B.XII.222.* Writing from Paris, Jefferson sends an allegorical bon voyage to a woman who was accompanying her brother-in-law on a diplomatic mission to the United States.

I consider that [trial by jury] as the only anchor, ever yet imagined by man, by which a government can be held to the principles of its constitution. [33]

> *TJ to Thomas Paine, July 11, 1789; B.XV.269.*

They [Americans] think their own experience has so decidedly proved the necessity of two houses to prevent the tyranny of one, that they fear that this single error [of one house] will shipwreck your new constitution. [17, 33]

> *TJ to La Rochefoucauld, April 3, 1790; B.XVI.296.*

You will have heard of the vote of the representatives to remove to Baltimore. But it is doubted whether the Senate will concur. I am only a passenger in their voyages, and therefore meddle not. [41]

> *TJ to Francis Hopkinson, June 13, 1790; B.XVI.490.* The secretary of state reports on consideration by Congress of where to locate a temporary national capital.

After exhausting their arguments and patience on these subjects, they have for some time been resting on their oars, unable to get along as to these businesses, and indisposed to attend to any thing else till they are settled. [33]

> *TJ to James Monroe, June 20, 1790; B.XVI.536-37.* Congress has so far failed to act on the public debt and the location of the capital.

The prudence of the President is an anchor of safety to us. [18, 33]

> *TJ to Nicholas Lewis, Feb. 9, 1791; B.XIX.263.*

[The Arrêt du Conseil of December 1787] is in truth the sheet anchor of our connection with France, which will be much loosened when that is lost. [34]

> *TJ to William Short, March 15, 1791; B.XIX.571.* The decree granted the United States favorable terms of trade. A sheet anchor is used in emergencies; thus, a reliance in time of difficulty.

Your being at the helm will be more than an answer to every argument which can be used to alarm and lead the people in any quarter, into violence and secession. . . . I should repose among [my family, my farm, and my books], it is true, in far greater security, if I were to know that you remained at the watch. [33, 34]

> *TJ to George Washington, May 23, 1792; LoA 989, 990.* Jefferson fears disunion unless Washington is willing to continue in office for a second term, although he himself intends to retire from the cabinet.

I look to that period with the longing of a wave-worn mariner, who has at length the land in view, and shall count the days and hours which still lie between me and it. [10]

> *TJ to George Washington, Sept. 9, 1792; LoA 1000.* Anticipating retirement.

He [George Washington] added that he considered France as the sheet anchor of this country and its friendship as a first object. [34]
TJ to William Short, Jan. 3, 1793; LoA 1005. The secretary of state admonishes his friend, the American chargé in France, for public statements censuring the Jacobins. For "sheet anchor," see TJ to William Short, March 15, 1791.

This must depend in some degree on the will of those who troubled the waters before. When they suffer them to get calm, I will go into port.
TJ to Thomas Mann Randolph, Jr., Feb. 3, 1793; B.XXV.137. After publicly mentioning his wish to retire, Jefferson was attacked in the newspapers. He has decided to postpone retirement in order to avoid the imputation that he was driven from office.

We too have our aristocrats and monocrats, and as they float on the surface, they shew much, though they weigh little. [33]
TJ to Jean Pierre Brissot de Warville, May 8, 1793; B.XXV.679.

What an ocean is life! And how our barks get separated in beating through it! [4]
TJ to St. George Tucker, Sept. 10, 1793; B.XXVII.86. Jefferson looks forward to his retirement, now set for January 1794, and to seeing his old Virginia friend.

Hold on then like a good and faithful seaman till our brother-sailors can rouse from their intoxication and right the vessel. [5, 33]
TJ to William Branch Giles, Dec. 17, 1794; B.XXVIII.219. From retirement, Jefferson encourages Giles, a Congressman from Virginia.

However, the time is coming when we shall fetch up the leeway of our vessel. . . . Hold on then, my dear friend, that we may not shipwreck in the meanwhile. [17, 33]
TJ to James Madison, Dec. 28, 1794; LoA 1017. Madison should hold on in the House of Representatives until the Senate, too, becomes Republican. The context is Washington's condemnation, under the influence of Hamilton, of the "democratic societies"—organizations of Jeffersonian republicans.

[T]here is not another person in the U.S. who being placed at the helm of our affairs, my mind would be so completely at rest for the fortune of our political bark. [18, 34]

> *TJ to James Madison, April 17, 1795; LoA 1025.* Having retired from every office "without exception," Jefferson is unwilling to stand for president, but Madison would be excellent in the position.

Our part of the country is in considerable fermentation . . . . They say that while all hands were below deck mending sails, splicing ropes, and every one at his own business, and the captain in his cabin attending to his log book and chart, a rogue of a pilot has run them into an enemy's port. But metaphor apart, there is much dissatisfaction with Mr. Jay and his treaty. For my part, I consider myself but as a passenger, leaving the world, and its government to those who are likely to live longer in it. [35]

> *TJ to Mann Page, Aug. 30, 1795; LoA 1030.* The captain is George Washington. The pilot is John Jay, negotiator of an unpopular treaty with Great Britain.

But I am glad of the sentiment from you, my friend, because it gives a hope you will practice what you preach, and come forward in aid of the public vessel. [34]

> *TJ to Edward Rutledge, Nov. 30, 1795; B.XXVIII.542.* Jefferson declines Rutledge's urging to return to public service but hopes that Rutledge himself will consider holding office.

[Among many groups opposing republicanism] are all timid men who prefer the calm of despotism to the boisterous sea of liberty. [16]

> *TJ to Philip Mazzei, April 24, 1796; LoA 1037.* The first of several uses of "boisterous sea of liberty," this one appears in a letter castigating the Washington administration. Jefferson and many republicans were embarrassed when this letter became public a year later.

Republicanism must lie on its oars, resign the vessel to its pilot and themselves to the course he thinks best for them. [33]

> *TJ to James Monroe, June 12, 1796; F.VIII.244.* The pilot is still George Washington.

Let those come to the helm who think they can steer clear of the difficulties. [35]

> *TJ to James Madison, Dec. 17, 1796; F.VIII.255-56.* On foreign affairs in the coming Adams administration.

I have no ambition to govern men; no passion which would lead me to delight to ride in a storm. . . . The newspapers will permit me to plant my corn, peas, etc., in hills or drills as I please, . . . while our eastern friend will be struggling with the storm which is gathering over us; perhaps to be shipwrecked in it. This is certainly not a moment to covet the helm. . . . So far, I praise the wisdom which has descried and steered clear of a water-spout ahead.

> *TJ to Edward Rutledge, Dec. 27, 1796; F.VIII.257-58.* John Adams, the "eastern friend," has been elected president. Jefferson considers himself wise to have settled for the vice-presidency.

I leave to others the sublime delights of riding in the storm, better pleased with sound sleep and a warm berth below, with the society of neighbors, friends and fellow laborers of the earth, than of spies and sycophants.

> *TJ to John Adams, Dec. 28, 1796; LoA 1040.* Congratulating Adams on his election as president, Jefferson prefers Monticello, where he can remain most of the year even though he has become vice president. On Madison's advice, the letter, with its reference to spies, sycophants, and Hamilton as Adams's "arch-friend of New York," was never sent.

The only view on which I would have gone into it [the presidency] for awhile was to put our vessel on her republican tack before she should be thrown too much leeward of her true principles. [17]

> *TJ to James Madison, Jan. 1, 1797; LoA 1038.*

I have long thought . . . it was best for the republican interest to soothe him [George Washington] . . . in short to lie on their oars while he remains at the helm, and let the bark drift as his will and a superintending providence shall direct. [33]

> *TJ to Archibald Stuart, Jan. 4, 1797; F.VIII.266.* Washington has two months left in office.

I have been happy, however, in believing . . . that whatever follies we may be led into as to foreign nations, we shall never give up our Union, the last anchor of our hope, & that alone which is to prevent this heavenly country from becoming an arena of gladiators. [34]

> *TJ to Elbridge Gerry, May 13, 1797; LoA 1043-44.* Warning a moderate Federalist in Massachusetts that the "Hamiltons by whom [Adams] is surrounded" might plunge the United States into a European war on the side of England and divide the Union.

If those who are truly independent can so trim our vessel as to beat through the waves now agitating us, they will merit a glory the greater as it seems less possible. [16, 17. 34]

> *TJ to Thomas Pinckney, May 29, 1797; LoA 1045.* Encouraging a moderate Federalist on the need to keep peace with England.

During the present bankruptcy in England, [American] merchants seem disposed to lie on their oars. [35]

> *TJ to James Madison June 1, 1797 F.VIII.297.*

[W]e have been but a sturdy fish on the hook of a dexterous angler, who, letting us flounce till we have spent our force, brings us up at last. [35]

> *TJ to Aaron Burr, June 17, 1797; F.VIII.312.* The fish is republicanism. The angler is the pro-British party in Congress and in the executive.

They [the people] begin to see to what port their leaders were steering during their slumbers, and there is yet time to haul in, if we can avoid a war with France. [35]

> *TJ to Arthur Campbell, Sept. 1, 1797; F.VIII.337.* The port is British practices of government.

[Kentucky] doubts not [that resolutions passed by other states] will be so announced as to prove . . . that the rights and liberties of their co-States will be exposed to no dangers by remaining embarked on a common bottom with their own. [34]

> *TJ, Draft of the Kentucky Resolutions, October 1798; LoA 455.* A state can object to the Alien and Sedition Laws in a way that both protects its freedoms and shows its attachment to the Union. A "bottom" is a ship. The metaphor is an example of "we're all in the same boat."

Our vessel is moored at such a distance, that should theirs blow up, ours is still safe, if we will but think so.

> *TJ to John Breckinridge, Jan. 29, 1800; LoA 1075.* The United States is safe if France becomes embroiled in war.

Yet so long has the vessel run on this way and been trimmed to it, that to put her on her republican tack will require all the skill, the firmness and the zeal of her ablest and best friends. [16]

> *TJ to Robert R. Livingston, Dec. 14, 1800; F.IX.152.* Though under a republican constitution, the Federalists have administered the United States as if it were a monarchy.

To you, then, gentlemen, who are charged with the sovereign functions of legislation, and to those associated with you, I look with encouragement for that guidance and support which may enable us to steer with safety the vessel in which we are all embarked amidst the conflicting elements of a troubled world. [36]
> *TJ, First Inaugural Address, March 4, 1801; LoA 492.*

During the throes and convulsions of the ancient world . . . it was not wonderful that the agitation of the billows should reach even this distant and peaceful shore. [36]
> *Ibid., LoA 493.*

[Essential principles of American government include] the preservation of the general government in its whole constitutional vigor, as the sheet anchor of our peace at home and safety abroad. [36]
> *Ibid., LoA 494.*

The storm through which we have passed, has been tremendous indeed. The tough sides of our Argosie have been thoroughly tried. Her strength has stood the waves into which she was steered, with a view to sink her. We shall put her on her republican tack, & she will show by the beauty of her motion the skill of her builders. [38]
> *TJ to John Dickinson, March 6, 1801; LoA 1084.*

We have passed through an awful scene in this country. The convulsion of Europe shook even us to our centre. A few hardy spirits stood firm to their post, and the ship has breasted the storm. . . . I will only add that the storm we have passed through proves our vessel indestructible. [37]
> *TJ to Lafayette, March 13, 1801; The Letters of Lafayette and Jefferson, ed. Gilbert Chinard (Baltimore: Johns Hopkins Univ. Press), 1929, 212.*

As the storm is now subsiding, and the horizon becoming serene, it is pleasant to consider the phenomenon with attention. We can no longer say there is nothing new under the sun. For this whole chapter in the history of man is new. The great extent of our Republic is new. Its sparse habitation is new. The mighty wave of public opinion which has rolled over it is new. But the most pleasing novelty is, its so quickly subsiding over such an extent of surface to its true level again. [38-39]
> *TJ to Joseph Priestley, March 21, 1801; LoA 1086.*

It is pleasant for those who have just escaped threatened shipwreck, to hail one another when landed in unexpected safety. . . . I hope we shall now be permitted to steer her in her natural course, and to show by the smoothness of her motion the great skill with which she has been formed for it. [55]
TJ to Gen. James Warren; March 21, 1801; LB.X.231.

The times have been awful, but they have proved an useful truth, that the good citizen must never despair of the commonwealth. How many good men abandoned the deck, and gave up the vessel as lost.
TJ to Nathaniel Niles, March 22, 1801; F.IX.221.

However, the storm is over, and we are in port. The ship was not rigged for the service she was put on. We will show the smoothness of her motions on her republican tack.
TJ to Samuel Adams, March 29, 1801; F.IX.239-40.

The steady character of our countrymen is a rock to which we may safely moor.
TJ to Elbridge Gerry, March 29, 1801; LoA 1090. Republicans will not be led astray by the Federalist press.

They meant by crippling my rigging to leave me an unwielded hulk, at the mercy of the elements.
TJ to Theodore Foster, May 9, 1801; F.IX.252. The Federalists left Jefferson burdened with "midnight appointments" to the judiciary.

You will follow the bark of liberty only by the help of a tow-rope.
TJ to Pierpont Edwards, July 21, 1801; F.IX.279-80. Connecticut, which Jefferson found the most backward of states, is tied to the clergy and to the Federalists. Cf. TJ to Albert Gallatin, Feb. 15, 1818.

Let us not then, my dear friend, embark our happiness and our affections on the ocean of slander, of falsehood and of malice, on which our credulous friends are floating. . . . Having reached the harbor myself, I shall view with anxiety (but certainly not with a wish to be in their place) those who are still buffeting the storm, uncertain of their fate. Your voyage has so far been favorable. [39]
TJ to James Monroe, March 10, 1808; F.XI.14. Friendship between the two should not be disturbed by public criticism of Monroe's failed attempt to secure an acceptable treaty with England.

I hope . . . that my successor will enter on a calmer sea than I did. He will at least find the vessel of state in the hands of his friends, and not of his foes. [39]

> *TJ to Richard M. Johnson, March 10, 1808; LB.XII.10.* Madison succeeded Jefferson as president in March 1809; see also John Adams to Benjamin Rush, March 4, 1809.

Within a few days I retire to my family, my books and farms; and having gained the harbour myself, I shall look on my friends still buffeting the storm with anxiety indeed, but not with envy. . . . Nature intended me for the tranquil pursuits of science, by rendering them my supreme delight. But the enormities of the times in which I have lived, have forced me to take part in resisting them, and to commit myself on the boisterous ocean of political passions. [39]

> *TJ to Pierre Samuel Dupont de Nemours, March 2, 1809; LoA 1203.*

Safe in port myself, I shall look anxiously at my friends still buffeting the storm, and wish you all safe in port also. [39]

> *TJ to Gen. John Armstrong, March 5, 1809; LB.XII.262.*

The fog which arose in the east in the last moments of my service, will doubtless clear away and expose under a stronger light the rocks and shoals which have threatened us with danger.

> *TJ to Governor Robert Wright of Maryland, April 3, 1809; LB.XVI.361.* Two eastern states, Connecticut and Massachusetts, have defied Jefferson's embargo policy, but the policy will soon be seen as a wise one.

Satisfied as I am that the public vessel is in the hands of as able a pilot as could be found, I sleep soundly as a mere passenger without troubling myself with the courses pursued. [39]

> *TJ to Charles Pinckney, Aug. 29, 1809; Missouri Historical Society, from the Monticello Research Collection.* Madison is the pilot.

The system of government which shall keep us afloat amidst the wreck of the world will be immortalized in history.

> *TJ to Walter Jones, March 5, 1810; F.XI.139.*

Anxious, in my retirement, to enjoy undisturbed repose, my knowledge of my successor and late coadjutors, and my entire confidence in their wisdom and integrity, were assurances to me that I might sleep in security with such watchmen at the helm, and that whatever difficulties and dangers should assail our course, they would do what could be done to avoid or surmount them. [40]

TJ to William Duane, Aug. 12, 1810; LoA 1228.

Our ship is sound, the crew alert at their posts, and our ablest steersman at its helm. That she will make a safe port I have no doubt. [18, 40]

TJ to John Melish, March 10, 1811; LB.XIII.24.

I look back with commiseration on those still buffeting the storm, and sincerely wish your argosy may ride out, unhurt, that in which it is engaged.

TJ to James Wilkinson, March 10, 1811; LB.XIII.23-24. Jefferson never completely gave up on Wilkinson, an army officer with an unquenchable taste for intrigue.

[The world at large would have to weigh whether it was more probable that] I should descend to so unmeaning an act of treason, or that he [General Wilkinson], in the wreck now threatening him, should wildly lay hold of any plank.

TJ to James Monroe, Jan. 11, 1812; F.XI.217. Denying a rumor that he had known of Wilkinson's schemes when the general served as governor of Louisiana in 1806.

A letter from you . . . carries me back to the times when . . . we were fellow laborers in the same cause, struggling for what is most valuable to man, his right of self-government. Laboring always at the same oar, with some wave ever ahead threatening to overwhelm us and yet passing harmless under our bark, we knew not how, we rode through the storm with heart and hand, and made a happy port. [42]

TJ to John Adams, Jan. 21, 1812; LoA 1259. Jefferson's first letter after the long break with Adams.

I hope . . . that my fellow citizens, warned in it [Van der Kemp's book] of the rocks and shoals on which other political associations have been wrecked, will be able to direct theirs with a better knowledge of the dangers in its way.

TJ to Francis A. Van der Kemp, March 22, 1812; LB.XIII.136. Encouraging the completion of a work on world history.

Reviewing the course of a long and sufficiently successful life, I find in no portion of it happier moments than those were. I think the old hulk in which you are, is near her wreck, and that like a prudent rat, you should escape in time.

TJ to James Maury, Jr., April 25, 1812; F.XI.243-44. To a friend from childhood, recalling their youth. The "old hulk" is England, where Maury is living.

The swaggering on deck as a passenger is so much more pleasant than clambering the ropes as a seaman, and my confidence in the skill and activity of those employed to work the vessel is so entire that I notice nothing en passant but how smoothly she moves.

TJ to John Wayles Eppes, Sept. 11, 1813; F.XI.306. Expressing confidence in the Madison administration.

You might as well, with the sailors, whistle to the wind, as suggest precautions against having too much money. We must scud then before the gale, and try to hold fast, ourselves, by some plank of the wreck.

TJ to John Adams, Jan. 24, 1814; AJL.II.425. On futile proposals to avert a financial crisis in Virginia.

We are feeding horses with our wheat and looking at the taxes coming on us, as an approaching wave in a storm. Still I think we shall live as long, eat as much, and drink as much, as if the wave had already glided under our ship.

TJ to Eliza House Trist, Dec. 26, 1814; Missouri Historical Society, from the Monticello Research Collection. Optimism in the face of hardship during the war against England.

A truth now and then projecting into the ocean of newspaper lies, serves like head-lands to correct our course. [59]

TJ to James Monroe, Jan. 1, 1815; F.XI.442.

The right of nations to self-government being my polar star, my partialities are steered by it, without asking whether it is a Bonaparte or an Alexander towards whom the helm is directed.

TJ to Correa de Serra, June 28, 1815; LB.XIV.330. Napoleon, who has returned from Elba, will not deflect the course of the republican ship.

I am sure their intentions are faithful; and embarked in the same bottom, I am willing to swim or sink with my fellow citizens. If the latter is their choice, I will go down with them without a murmur. But my exhortation would rather be "not to give up the ship."

> *TJ to Charles Yancey, Jan. 6, 1816; F.X.4.* Urging a representative from Albemarle County in the Virginia House of Delegates not to abandon the effort to establish a state university.

The objects of the two institutions are fundamentally distinct. The one is science, the other mere charity. It would be gratuitously taking a boat in tow which may impede, but cannot aid the motion of the principal institution.

> *TJ to Joseph C. Cabell, Jan. 24, 1816; LB.XIV.414.* Urging his most important ally in Richmond in the founding of the University of Virginia to oppose the establishment of a school for the deaf and dumb in Charlottesville.

[Your letter] tells me where I am; and that to a mariner who has long been without sight of land or sun, is a rallying of reckoning which places him at ease.

> *TJ to James Monroe, Feb. 4, 1816; F.X.19.*

My temperament is sanguine. I steer my bark with Hope in the head, leaving Fear astern. [17]

> *TJ to John Adams, April 8, 1816; LoA 1382.* For Adams's reply, see John Adams to TJ, May 3, 1816.

But I am now retired; I resign myself, as a passenger, with confidence to those at present at the helm, and ask but for rest, peace, and good will. [41]

> *TJ to Samuel Kercheval, July 12, 1816; LoA 1395.* Declining to comment publicly on reforming the Virginia constitution.

I salute you with all my wishes for a prosperous and splendid voyage over the ocean on which you are embarked.

> *TJ to James Monroe, April 8, 1817; LB.XIX.24.* Congratulating Monroe on becoming president.

Federalism is substantially defunct. . . . The most signal triumph is in Connecticut where it was least and last expected. As some tub, however, must always be thrown out to the whale, and a religious one is fittest to recall the priesthood within their proper limits, the questions of

unity and trinity are now set afloat in the eastern states, and are occupying there all the vehemence of the genus *irritabile vatum*.
  TJ to Albert Gallatin, February 15, 1818; LB.XIX.259. The last phrase, which comes from Horace, may be translated "the touchy tribe of poets." On throwing a tub out to the whale, see TJ to Richard Henry Lee, Feb. 7, 1785.

These [political controversies] are occurrences which like waves in a storm will pass under the ship. But the Missouri question is a breaker on which we lose the Missouri country by revolt, and what more, God only knows. [41, 55]
  TJ to John Adams, Dec. 10 1819; F.XII.151.

I had for a long time ceased to read newspapers, or pay any attention to public affairs, confident they were in good hands, and content to be a passenger in our bark to the shore from which I am not distant. [14, 29, 41]
  TJ to John Holmes, April 22, 1820; LoA 1433-34. For the non-nautical metaphors that follow this nautical one, see Appendix II.

The Missouri question is a mere party trick. The leaders of federalism . . . have changed their tack, and thrown out another barrel to the whale. [41]
  TJ to Charles Pinckney, Sept. 30 1820; F.XII.165. Some New Englanders, finding they cannot succeed politically at monarchism, have taken up the cause of anti-slavery. On throwing a barrel to the whale, see TJ to Richard Henry Lee, Feb. 7, 1785.

The boisterous sea of liberty is never without a wave. [16, 41, 55]
  TJ to Richard Rush, Oct. 20, 1820; LB.XV.283. On the Missouri Compromise.

I hope our political bark will ride through all its dangers; but I can in future be but an inert passenger. [41]
  TJ to Thomas Ritchie, Dec. 25, 1820; LoA 1447. Declining to comment on a book about the judiciary.

The boisterous sea of liberty indeed is never without a wave, and that from Missouri is now rolling towards us, but we shall ride over it as we have over all others. [16, 41]
  TJ to Lafayette, Dec. 26, 1820; F.XII.191.

I learn, with deep affliction, that nothing is likely to be done for our University this year. So near as it is to the shore that one shove more would land it there, I had hoped that would be given.
  TJ to Gen. James Breckinridge, Feb. 15, 1821; LoA 1452.

Tossed at random by the newspapers on an ocean of uncertainties and falsehoods, it is joyful at times to catch the glimmering of a beacon which shows us truly where we are.
  TJ to Edward Everett, March 2, 1822; LB.XV.354-55. Acknowledging receipt of a publication on Europe written by Everett's brother.

He [Priestley] proves, also, that man, once surrendering his reason, has no remaining guard against absurdities the most monstrous, and like a ship without a rudder, is the sport of every wind. With such persons, gullibility which they call faith, takes the helm from the hand of reason, and the mind becomes a wreck. [13]
  TJ to James Smith, Dec. 8, 1822; LB.XV.409.

In these short interviews with you, I generally get my political compass rectified, learn from you whereabouts we are, and correct my course again.
  TJ to James Monroe, June 11, 1823; F.XII.191. On the benefits of speaking with his neighbor, the President.

[T]o preserve the republican form and principles of our constitution and cleave to the salutary distribution of powers which that has established . . . are the two sheet anchors of our Union. If driven from either, we shall be in danger of foundering.
  TJ to Justice William Johnson, June 12, 1823; LoA 1477. Encouraging his first appointee to the Supreme Court to hold up under the dominance of Chief Justice Marshall.

I ought not to quit the port in which I am moored to commit myself again to the stormy ocean of political party contest, to kindle new enmities, and lose old friends.
  TJ to Samuel H. Smith, Aug. 2, 1823; F.XII.301-02.

[The Monroe Doctrine] sets our compass and points the course which we are to steer through the ocean of time opening on us. And never could we embark on it under circumstances more auspicious.
  TJ to James Monroe, Oct. 24, 1823; LoA 1481.

I resign myself cheerfully to the managers of the ship, and the more contentedly, as I am near the end of my voyage. [42]
> *TJ to Edward Livingston, April 4, 1824; F.XII.348-49.*

Yet although I have little hope that the torrent of consolidation can be withstood, I should not be for giving up the ship without efforts to save her. She lived well through the first squall, and may weather the present one.
> *TJ to Claiborne W. Gooch, Jan. 9, 1826; LB.XVI.152.* A plea for state government authority against internal improvements financed by the national government.

Like other young people, he [Jefferson's grandson] wishes to be able, in the winter nights of old age, to recount to those around him what he has heard and learnt of the Heroic age preceding his birth, and which of the Argonauts particularly he was in time to have seen. . . . Theirs [the younger generation's] are the Halcyon calms succeeding the storm which our Argosy has so stoutly weathered. [42]
> *TJ to John Adams, March 25, 1826; AJL.II.614.* In this last letter to Adams, Jefferson asks his old friend to receive his grandson, Thomas Jefferson Randolph, who is visiting Boston.

APPENDIX II
Jefferson's Non-Nautical Metaphors

The lamp of war is kindled here, not to be extinguished but by torrents of blood. [45]
TJ to James Madison, Nov. 11, 1784; B.VII.506. Writing from Paris.

I did not receive the money till it was not worth oak leaves. [45]
TJ to Alexander McCaul, April 19, 1786; B.IX.389. On having been paid late for the sale of lands.

Error is the stuff of which the web of life is woven and he who lives longest and wisest is only able to weave out the more of it. [56]
TJ to Chastellux, Oct. 1786; LoA 593. In a cover note to "Thoughts on English Prosody," Jefferson's scholarly reconsideration of views he had expressed on the subject earlier. Julian Boyd presents evidence that Chastellux never saw the note or the essay. B.X.499n.

I hold it that a little rebellion now and then is a good thing, and as necessary in the political world as storms in the physical. [51]
TJ to James Madison, Jan. 30, 1787; LoA 882. On Shays' Rebellion.

I like a little rebellion now and then. It is like a storm in the atmosphere. [51]
TJ to Abigail Adams, Feb. 22, 1787; LoA 889-90. On Shays' Rebellion.

State a moral case to a ploughman & a professor. The former will decide it as well, & often better than the latter, because he has not been led astray by artificial rules. [28]
TJ to Peter Carr, Aug. 10, 1787; LoA 902.

The tree of liberty must be refreshed from time to time, with the blood of patriots and tyrants. It is its natural manure. [45]
TJ to William Stephens Smith, Nov. 13, 1787; LoA 911. On Shays' Rebellion.

I dare say that in time all these [the state governments] as well as their central government, like the planets revolving round their common sun, acting and acted upon according to their respective weights and distances, will produce that beautiful equilibrium on which our Constitution is founded, and which I believe it will exhibit to the world in a degree of perfection, unexampled but in the planetary system itself. [52, 55]
TJ to Peregrine Fitzhugh, Feb. 23, 1798; F.VIII.377.

To separate Congress now will be withdrawing the fire from under a boiling pot. [46]

> *TJ to James Madison, June 21, 1798; F.VIII.441.* To avoid worsening the Republican cause, the House of Representatives should be adjourned.

They [the Republican Congress] have lopped off a parasite limb, planted by their predecessors on their judiciary body for party purposes. . . . The people are nearly all united; their quondam leaders, infuriated with the sense of their impotence, will soon be seen or heard only in the newspapers, which serve as chimnies to carry off noxious vapors and smoke.

> *TJ to Gen. Thaddeus Kosciusko, April 2, 1802; LoA 1103.* Assuring a foreign hero of the Revolution that republican principles have returned to American politics. The parasite limb is the Judiciary Act of 1800.

Our seventeen States compose a great and growing nation. Their children are as the leaves of the trees, which the winds are spreading over the forest. [48]

> *TJ to the Brothers of the Choctaw Nation, Dec. 17, 1803; LoA 558.*

If plants have sensibility, as the analogy of their organization with ours seems to indicate, it cannot but be proudly sensible of her fostering attentions. [40]

> *TJ to Mrs. Samuel H. Smith, March 6, 1809; LoA 1204.* On leaving the White House, Jefferson has given a geranium to Mrs. Smith.

The flowers come forth like the belles of the day, have their short reign of beauty and splendor, and retire like them to the more interesting office of reproducing their like. [47]

> *TJ to Anne Randolph Bankhead, May 26, 1811; The Family Letters of Thomas Jefferson, ed. Edwin Morris Betts and James Adam Bear, Jr. (Columbia: Univ. of Missouri Press, 1966), 400.* To his granddaughter, who has just given birth to his first great-grandchild.

The weakness of our enemy will make our first errors innocent, and the seeds of genius which nature sows with even hand through every age and country, and which need only soil and season to germinate, will develop themselves among our military men.

> *TJ to Col. William Duane, Aug. 4, 1812; F.XI.264-65.* The American army will soon be the equal of the British.

I stand like a solitary tree in a field, its trunk indeed erect, but its limbs fallen off and its neighboring plants eradicated from around it.

> *TJ to Dr. Samuel Brown, April 28, 1814; quoted in University of Virginia Alumni News, Sept.-Oct. 1984, 23, from a letter in the University of Virginia library.*

The work itself [*Notes on the State of Virginia*] indeed is nothing more than the measure of a shadow, never stationary, but lengthening as the sun advances, and to be taken anew from hour to hour. It must remain, therefore, for some other hand to sketch its appearance at another epoch, to furnish another element for calculating the course and motion of this member of our federal system. For this, every day is adding new matter and strange matter. That of reducing, by impulse instead of attraction, a sister planet into its orbit, will be as new in our political as in the planetary system. The operation, however, will be painful rather than difficult. The sound part of our wandering star will probably, by its own internal energies, keep the unsound within its course. [53]

> *TJ to John Melish, December 10, 1814; LB.XIV.220-21.* Melish, a British geographer who had frequently visited America and interviewed Jefferson when he was President, presented Jefferson with his *Travels in the United States*. Thanking Melish for the work, Jefferson declines to prepare a new edition of *Notes on Virginia* and comments on the idea that New England might secede from the Union. The sister planet, and wandering star with sound and unsound parts, is Massachusetts. (This interpretation is made clear in TJ to John Melish, Jan. 13, 1813; LoA 1267; and TJ to William Short, Nov. 28, 1814; LoA 1358.) Jefferson correctly predicts the collapse, at the Hartford Convention, of the secessionist movement.

[L]aws and institutions must go hand in hand with the progress of the human mind. . . . We might as well require a man to wear still the coat which fitted him when a boy, as civilized society to remain ever under the regiment of their barbarous ancestors.

> *TJ to Samuel Kercheval, July 12, 1816; LoA 1401.* Justifying a revision of Virginia's constitution.

We should be far, too, from the discouraging persuasion that man is fixed, by the law of his nature, at a given point; that his improvement is a chimera, and the hope delusive of rendering ourselves wiser, happier or better than our forefathers were. As well might it be urged that the wild and uncultivated tree, hitherto yielding sour and bitter fruit only, can never be made to yield better; yet we know that the grafting art implants a new tree on the savage stock, producing what is most estimable both in kind and degree. Education, in like manner, engrafts a new man on the native stock, and improves what in his nature was vicious and perverse into qualities of virtue and social worth. And it cannot be but that each generation succeeding to the knowledge acquired by all those who preceded it, adding to it their own acquisitions and discoveries, and handing the mass down for successive and constant accumulation, must advance the knowledge and well-being of mankind, not *infinitely*, as some have said, but *indefinitely*, and to a term which no one can fix and foresee. [54, 56]

> *Rockfish Gap Report (Report of the Commissioners for the University of Virginia), Aug. 4, 1818; LoA 461.*

I had for a long time ceased to read newspapers, or pay any attention to public affairs, confident they were in good hands, and content to be a passenger in our bark to the shore from which I am not distant. But this momentous question, like a firebell in the night, awakened and filled me with terror. I considered it at once as the knell of the Union. It is hushed, indeed, for the moment. But this is a reprieve only, not a final sentence. . . . [A]s it is, we have the wolf by the ear, and we can neither hold him, nor safely let him go. Justice is in one scale, and self-preservation in the other. [41, 46]

> *TJ to John Holmes, April 22, 1820; LoA 1433-34.* On the "Missouri Question" of admitting slave and free states to the Union, and on the status of slavery in the territories. Note the quiet nautical metaphor that precedes the dramatic non-nautical ones. Until recently "wolf by the ear" was mistranscribed as "wolf by the ears."

Man, like the fruit he eats, has his period of ripeness. Like that, too, if he continues longer hanging to the stem, it is but an useless and unsightly appendage.

> *TJ to Gen. Henry Dearborn, August 17, 1821; F.XII.205.* On the old age of Jefferson and his correspondent.

To attain all this, however, rivers of blood must yet flow, and years of desolation pass over. Yet the object [representative government in Europe] is worth rivers of blood, and years of desolation, for what inheritance so valuable can man leave to his posterity? [45, 47]

> *TJ to John Adams, Sept. 4, 1823; LoA 1478.*

[W]hile writing to you . . . I forget for a while the hoary winter of age, when we can think of nothing but how to keep ourselves warm, and how to get rid of our heavy hours until the friendly hand of death shall rid us of all at once. . . . [A]ll men who have attended to the workings of the human mind, who have seen the false colours under which passion sometimes dresses the actions of others, have seen also those passions subsiding with time and reflection, dissipating, like mists before the rising sun, and restoring to us the sight of all things in their true shape and colours. It would be strange indeed if, at our years, we were to go an age back to hunt up imaginary, or forgotten facts, to disturb the repose of affections so sweetening to the evening of our lives. Be assured, my dear Sir, that I am incapable of receiving the slightest impression from the effort now made to plant thorns on the pillow of age, worth, and wisdom, and to sow tares between friends who have been such for nearly half a century. [47]

> *TJ to John Adams, Oct. 12, 1823; LoA 1479, 1481.* Explaining, and quelling, "malignant falsehoods" that portrayed Jefferson and Adams as enemies.

APPENDIX III
Nautical Metaphors by Other Authors

III.A *Before Jefferson's Death in 1826*

John Adams
Aeschylus
Fisher Ames
Aristotle
The Aurora
William Bartram
John Bondfield
William Cowper
The Echo
Euripides
Benjamin Franklin
Horatio Gates
Elbridge Gerry
Homer
Horace
James Jackson
Immanuel Kant
John Langhorne
Lucretius

William Maclay
Andrew Marvell
John Milton
Samuel Latham Mitchill
Isaac Newton
Ossian
John Page
Plato
Matthew Prior
William Shakespeare
William Shenstone
Margaret Bayard Smith
Sophocles
Joseph Story
James Thomson
George Villers
George Washington
Edward Young

III.B *Since Jefferson's Death* (begins p. 149)

Henry Adams
Spiro Agnew
Anonymous
Robert Bolt
William J. Brennan, Jr.
William Jennings Bryan
William Cullen Bryant
Pat Buchanan
J. H. Buckingham
Ralph Bunche
George Bush [about]
George W. Bush [about]
Jimmy Carter [about]
Civil Rights Movement
Bill Clinton [about]
James Fenimore Cooper
John Dewey
John F. Dillon
William O. Douglas
Frederick Douglass
Dwight D. Eisenhower
Ralph Waldo Emerson
George Engelmann
Edward Everett
John Kenneth Galbraith
Leonard Garment
Henry George
U. S. Grant [about]
Alexander M. Haig, Jr.
Learned Hand
Garrett Hardin
George F. Hoar
David Hollinger
Oliver Wendell Holmes, Sr.
Henrik Ibsen
William James
Philip C. Jessup
Lyndon B. Johnson
William Johnson
Ward Just
Wassily Leontief
Sinclair Lewis

Abraham Lincoln
Romulus Linney
Henry Wadsworth Longfellow
James Russell Lowell
Thomas Babington Macaulay
Dumas Malone
Mike Mansfield
Mao Zedong
John P. Marquand
Otto Neurath
Richard Nixon [about]
William D. Nordhaus
Michael Oakeshott
Charles Sanders Peirce
Merrill Peterson
Prairie as a Sea of Grass
Ronald Reagan
Conrad Richter
David Rockefeller
O. E. Rölvaag
Franklin D. Roosevelt [about]
William Safire
Paul Sifton
Spirituals
Peleg Sprague
James Stephen
Edward R. Stettinius, Jr.
Henry David Thoreau
Alexis de Tocqueville
Harry S. Truman
United States Supreme Court
John Updike
Gore Vidal
Lech Walesa
Booker T. Washington
Daniel Webster
Dixon Wecter
Walter White
Walt Whitman
Woodrow Wilson
William Wirt
William Butler Yeats

Appendix III
Nautical Metaphors by Other Authors

III.A *Before Jefferson's Death in 1826*

John Adams

But America is a great, unwieldy Body. Its Progress must be slow. It is like a large Fleet sailing under convoy. The fleetest Sailors must wait for the dullest and slowest. [33]

> *Adams to Abigail Adams, June 17, 1775; in The Book of Abigail and John: Selected Letters of the Adams Family, 1762-1784, ed. L. H. Butterfield, et al. (Cambridge: Harvard Univ. Press, 1975), 89.* Adams writes home from the Second Continental Congress in Philadelphia, where he and Jefferson first met.

My little bark has been overset in a squall of thunder and lightning and hail attended with a strong smell of sulphur.

> *Adams to Thomas Boylston Adams, Dec. 17, 1800; Adams Papers, Mass. Historical Society.* To his son after losing the election of 1800.

What course is it we steer? To what harbor are we bound?

> *Adams to Elbridge Gerry, Dec. 30, 1800; The Works of John Adams, ed. Charles Francis Adams (Boston, 1850-56), IX.578.* The "dexterous" Aaron Burr has humiliated American constitutional government by tying up the election of Jefferson in the House of Representatives.

Jefferson expired and Madison came to Life last night. . . . I pity poor Madison. He comes to the helm in such a storm as I have seen in the Gulf Stream, or rather such as I had to encounter in the Government in 1797. Mine was the worst however, because he has a great Majority of the officers and Men attached to him and I had all the officers and half the Crew always ready to throw me overboard. [40]

> *Adams to Benjamin Rush, March 4, 1809; in Alexander Biddle (comp.), Old Family Letters (Philadelphia, 1892), 219.* Comparing his and Madison's difficulties on establishing foreign policy at the start of their presidencies. Cf. TJ to Richard M. Johnson, March 10, 1808.

I admire your Navigation and should like to sail with you, either in your Bark or in my own, along side of yours; Hope with her gay

Ensigns displayed at the Prow; fear with her Hobgoblins behind the Stern.

> *Adams to Jefferson, May 3, 1816; AJL.II.471.* Replying to Jefferson of April 8, 1816; see Appendix I.

The Missouri question I hope will follow the other waves under the ship and do no harm.

> *Adams to Jefferson, Dec. 21, 1819; AJL.II.551.* Replying to Jefferson of Dec. 10, 1819; see Appendix I.

It was only, as if one had met a brother sailor, after twenty-five years' absence, and had accosted him, "How fare you Jack?"

> *From the journals of John Pierce, Jan. 10, 1823; quoted in Donald H. Stewart and George P. Clark, "Misanthrope or Humanitarian? John Adams in Retirement," New England Qtly., 28 (1955):232.* Pierce records a conversation with Adams, who treats rather nonchalantly the resumption of communication with Jefferson eleven years earlier. "Brother sailor" has a democratic ring, which is more in keeping with Jefferson's political outlook than Adams's; but in their style, it is Adams who could be the familiar democrat, while Jefferson was always the aristocrat. "Brother sailor" also suits a New Englander who was comfortable among seamen, not an inland Virginian who was uncomfortable at sea.

Aeschylus

To the great torrent of heroes
There is none worthily equal
Who resist, by defenses secured,
The unconquerable billows of ocean. [11]

> *The Persians, 87-90, trans. Seth G. Benardete; in The Complete Greek Tragedies, vol. 1, ed. David Grene and Richmond Lattimore (Chicago: Univ. of Chicago Press, 1992).* The chorus of Persian elders comments on the naval expedition that has left for Greece.

O cities of Asia, or Persian land,
And wealth's great anchorage!
How at a single stroke prosperity's
Corrupted, and the flower of Persia falls,
And is gone. [11]

> *Ibid., 248-52.* The herald brings the news of the defeat at Salamis.

Herald: First the floods of Persians held the line,
But when the narrows choked them, and rescue hopeless,

Smitten by prows, their bronze jaws gaping,
Shattered entire was our fleet of oars.
The Grecian warships, calculating, dashed
Round, and encircled us; the ships showed their belly:
No longer could we see the water, charged
With ships' wrecks and men's blood.
Corpses glutted beaches and the rocks.
Every warship urged its own anarchic
Route: and all who survived that expedition,
Like mackerel or some catch of fish,
Were stunned and slaughtered, boned with broken oars
And splintered wrecks: lamentations, cries
Possessed the open sea, until the black
Eye of evening, closing, hushed behind them. . . .
Queen: Alas! a sea of troubles breaks in waves
On the Persians and barbarian tribes. [12}
  Ibid., 412-34. Description of the defeat at Salamis, and response.

First was Medus leader of the host;
Next his son fulfilled the office well,
Whose reason was the helmsman to his spirit. [12]
  Ibid., 765-67. The ghost of Darius recounts the line of Persian kings.

Fisher Ames
A monarchy is a merchantman, which sails well, but will sometimes
strike on a rock and go to the bottom; whilst a republic is a raft, which
would never sink, but then your feet are always in water. [33]
  *Quoted by Ralph Waldo Emerson in "Politics"; in Essays and Journals,
  ed. Lewis Mumford (Garden City, N.Y.: Doubleday & Co., 1968), 346.* An
  example of a "proportional metaphor." Ames was a Massachusetts
  Federalist and implacable anti-Jeffersonian.

Aristotle
Like the sailor, the citizen is a member of a community. Now, sailors have
different functions, for one of them is a rower, another a pilot, and a third
a look-out man, a fourth is described by some similar term; and while the
precise definition of each individual's virtue applies exclusively to him,
there is, at the same time, a common definition applicable to them all. For
they have all of them a common object, which is safety in navigation.
Similarly, one citizen differs from another, but the salvation of the

community is the common business of them all. This community is the constitution; the virtue of the citizen must therefore be relative to the constitution of which he is a member. [19]

> *Politics, 1276b, trans. Benjamin Jowett.*

The Aurora

The fed'ral rats have left the ship,
And we in turn will take a trip.
  Thro' the rough 'tempestuous seas,'
  We'll safely guard our liberty:
  Stop the leaks, the rigging clear,
  And to a peaceful haven steer.

> *The Aurora, March 11, 1801; in Vera Brodsky Lawrence, Music for Patriots, Politicians, and Presidents (New York: Macmilllan, 1975), 170.* A Republican newspaper celebrates Jefferson's first inaugural.

William Bartram

I was now in a very elevated situation from whence I enjoyed a view inexpressively magnificent and comprehensive. The mountainous region through which I had lately traversed . . . appearing regularly undulated as the great ocean after a tempest; the undulations gradually depressing, yet perfectly regular, as the squamae of fish or imbrications of tile on a roof: the nearest ground to me of a perfect full green, next more glaucous, and lastly almost blue as the ether with which the most distant curve of the horizon seems to be blended.

> *The Travels of William Bartram, ed. Francis Harper (New Haven: Yale Univ. Press, 1958; orig. 1791), 212.* Bartram, a friend of Jefferson's, describes a scene in the Blue Ridge Mountains in the spring of 1775. The view is from a ridge in Oconee County, South Carolina, now called Station Mountain.

John Bondfield

I conducted the Bark in a Stormy Season and if I judge myself as I would judge others when at Anchor, would have been glad to have enjoy'd the fruits of my Labour.

> *Bondfield to TJ, Oct. 8, 1790; B.XVII.580.* A longtime U.S. agent in Bordeaux requests reimbursement for expenses from the Secretary of State.

William Cowper
No voice divine the storm allayed,
   No light propitious shone;
When, snatched from all effectual aid,
   We perished, each alone:
But I beneath a rougher sea,
And whelmed in deeper gulfs than he. [21n]

> *From "The Castaway" (1803).* Behind this poem, writes Jonathan Raban, lay a "lifetime of sea-reading and sea-metaphors" that Cowper, who never went to sea, "plundered . . . for metaphors for his own condition." *Passage to Juneau* (1999), 431, 430. Jefferson probably did not read the poem since he did not own any of Cowper's works and it was published, posthumously, long after he was spending much time with English literature. But he was familiar with the incident of the 1740s that inspired it, the drowning of a sailor washed overboard in a storm.

The Echo
Hereafter free from care
Our skiff shall glide,
Its compass folly, theory its guide,
Adown the stream of state.

> *The Echo, March 4, 1805; quoted in Linda Kerber, Federalists in Dissent: Imagery and Ideology in Jeffersonian America (Ithaca: Cornell Univ. Press, 1970), 133.* A Federalist newspaper parodies Jefferson at the time of his second inaugural.

Euripides
Great prosperity abideth not amongst mankind; but some power divine, shaking it to and fro like the sail of a swift galley, plunges it deep into the waves of grievous affliction, boisterous and deadly as the waves of the sea. [15]

> *Orestes, 340-44; LCB.68, trans. Edward P. Coleridge; in The Complete Greek Drama, vol. 2, ed. Whitney J. Oates and Eugene O'Neill, Jr. (New York: Random House, 1938).* Spoken by the chorus of the women of Argos.

A trusty comrade is a more cheering sight in trouble than a calm is to sailors. [15]

> *Ibid., 727-29; LCB.69, trans. Coleridge.*

> As with sailing,
> so with politics: make your cloth too taut,
> and your ship will dip and keel, but slacken off
> and trim your sails, and things head up again. [15]

> *Ibid., 707-10, trans. William Arrowsmith; in The Complete Greek Tragedies, vol. 4, ed. David Grene and Richmond Lattimore (Chicago: Univ. of Chicago Press, 1992).* Menelaus proposes to smooth matters over with Tyndareus, the father of Clytemnestra (and mother of Orestes), whom Orestes has murdered out of revenge.

Benjamin Franklin

Had Newton been Pilot but of a single common Ship, the finest of his Discoveries would scarce have excus'd or atton'd for his abandoning the Helm one Hour in the Time of Danger; how much less if she had carried the Fate of the Commonwealth. [34n]

> Franklin to Cadwallader Colden, Oct. 11, 1750; Papers of Benjamin Franklin, ed. Leonard W. Larabee (New Haven: Yale Univ. Press, 1961), 4:68.

Horatio Gates

The Hermit of Rose Hill sees it confirmed by Yesterdays post, that you have actually Resign'd your Office! . . . If the best Seamen abandon the Ship in a Storm, she must Founder; and if all Human means are neglected, Providence will not Care for the Vessel; She must Perish! [34n]

> *Gates to TJ, Jan. 5, 1794; B.XXVIII.6.* The former Revolutionary general on Jefferson's resigning as secretary of state.

Elbridge Gerry

But with the qualities which he [John Adams] possesses, like a ship ballasted with iron he may meet with repeated and violent tempests none of which will be able to upset him; should however the convulsion of the elements be too great for the best constructed barque, he may like the best of mariners be overwhelmed, and every good man will lament his fate.

> *Gerry to Abigail Adams, Jan. 7, 1797; Adams Papers, Mass. Historical Society.* On the election of Adams to the presidency. Cf. TJ to Elbridge Gerry, May 13, 1797.

Homer

As when a swell of sea on a sounding beach,
urged wave on wave as the West Wind moves it on,

lifts whitecaps first in the open sea, then later
breaks on land with a great crash round the headlands,
and curls in crests and spits the salt foam back,
so wave on wave the Danaans' ranks kept marching on to war. [9]

> *Iliad, IV.422-28, trans. Denison Bingham Hull; in Homer's Iliad (Scottsdale, Ariz., 1982).* Sea simile applied to the Greeks.

As when rivers in winter spate running down from the mountains
throw together at the meeting of streams the weight of their water
out of the great springs behind in the hollow stream-bed,
and far away in the mountains the shepherd hears the thunder;
such, from the coming together of men, was the shock and the shouting. [9]

> *Iliad, IV.452-56; LCB.142, trans. Jefferson.* Sea simile applied to Greeks and Trojans joining in battle. Jefferson, who finds these lines comparable to lines in Ossian (see below), omitted the two previous lines of Homer, *Iliad,* IV.450-51, although they are compatible with the passage from Ossian that he commonplaced: "Then screams and shouts of triumph rose together / from killers and from killed; the earth ran blood." Trans. Hull.

So the Trojans held their night watches. Meanwhile immortal
Panic, companion of cold Terror, gripped the Achaians
as all their best were stricken with grief that passes endurance.
As two winds rise to shake the sea where the fish swarm, Boreas
and Zephyros, north wind and west, that blow from Thraceward,
suddenly descending, and the darkened water is gathered
to crests, and far across the salt water scatters the seaweed;
so the heart in the breast of each Achaian was troubled. [90]

> *Iliad, IX.1-8, trans. Richmond Lattimore; in The Iliad of Homer (Chicago: Univ. of Chicago Press, 1951).* Hannah Arendt illustrates the origins of metaphor in Greek poetry with this passage. *The Life of the Mind; Vol. I: Thinking* (1977), 106.

As when a great wave joins a swollen river
at its mouth, and roars against its stream,
and spits salt water spume against the headlands,
so with a roar the Trojans came. [9]

> *Iliad, XVII.263-66, trans. Hull.* Sea simile applied to the Trojans.

He [Poseidon] spoke, and pulled the clouds together, in both
  hands gripping
the trident, and staggered the sea, and let loose all the storm-blasts
of all the winds together . . . .
East Wind and South Wind clashed together, and the bitter blown
  West Wind
and the North Wind born in the bright air rolled up a heavy sea. [60]
> *Odyssey V.291-96, trans. Richmond Lattimore; in The Odyssey of Homer
> (New York: Harper and Row, 1965).* Cf. Daniel Webster, March 7, 1850 in
> Appendix III.B.

And as when the land appears welcome to men who are swimming,
after Poseidon has smashed their strong-built ship on the open
water, pounding it with the weight of wind and the heavy
seas, and only a few escape the gray water landward
by swimming, with a thick scurf of salt coated upon them,
and gladly they set foot on the shore, escaping the evil;
so welcome was her husband to her as she looked upon him,
and she could not let him go from the embrace of her white arms. [10]
> *Odyssey, XXIII.233-40, trans. Lattimore.*

Horace

On such billows as these you will again be swept
Out to sea, O my ship! What are you doing! Make
  Utmost effort to reach port!
  On your one side your oars are lost;

See, your mast has been split under the Southwind's gusts,
Yard-arms groan with the strain, and, with its cable burst,
  Not for long will the keel stand
  This implacably hurtling sea's

Force. Your sails are in shreds, battered and broken off
Stand the after-deck gods heedless of cries for help.
  Pontic pine though you are, still,
  Famous daughter of forests green,

It will do you no good boasting your race and name;
Daunted sailors do not pluck up their courage from
  Painted prows. Have a care *your*
  Fate is not to be gale-winds' toy.

Once my anxious concern and my most heartsick care,
Now, the theme of my thoughts, O my beloved ship,
Shun the sea lanes where thick strewn
Lie the glittering Cyclades. [16-17]
*Odes 1.14, trans. Charles Passage; in The Complete Works of Horace
(New York: Frederick Ungar, 1983) 149-50.* The most widely cited ship-
of-state image from antiquity.

James Jackson

Our constitution, sir, is like a vessel just launched, and lying at the
wharf; she is untried, you can hardly discover any one of her properties.
It is not known how she will answer her helm, or lay her course;
whether she will bear with safety the precious freight to be deposited in
her hold. But, in this state, will the prudent merchant attempt
alterations? Will he employ workmen to take off the planking and tear
asunder the frame? He certainly will not. Let us, gentlemen, fit out our
vessel, set up our masts, and expand her sails, and be guided by the
experiment in her alterations. If she sails upon an uneven keel, let us
right her by adding weight where it is wanting . . . . In short, Mr.
Speaker, I am not for adding amendments at this time. [33n]
*Speech, House of Representatives, June 8, 1789; Annals of Congress, 1st
Cong., 1st Sess., 442.* Jackson, a fiery Congressman from Georgia,
ordinarily agreed with Jefferson, but here he argues against adding a bill
of rights to the new Constitution.

Immanuel Kant

This domain [of pure understanding] is an island, enclosed by nature
itself within unalterable limits. It is the land of truth—enchanting
name!—surrounded by a wide and stormy ocean, the native home of
illusion, where many a fog bank and many a swiftly melting iceberg
give the deceptive appearance of farther shores, deluding the
adventurous seafarer ever anew with empty hopes, and engaging him in
enterprises which he can never abandon and yet is unable to carry to
completion. [88]
*Critique of Pure Reason, trans. Norman Kemp Smith (New York:
Macmillan, 1933), 257. Orig. 1781; A.235-36.*

John Langhorne

Life's ocean slept—the liquid gale
Gently mov'd the waving sail.

Fallacious *Hope!* with flattering eye
You smiled to see the streamers fly.
The thunder bursts, the mad wind raves,
From slumber wake the 'frighted waves:
You saw me, fled me thus distrest,
And tore your anchor from my breast. [27n]
>   From *"Hymn to Hope;" LCB.147.* Jefferson entered into his commonplace
>   book these lines by a contemporary English poet.

Lucretius

When winds churn up a heavy storm at sea
It is a pleasant thing to watch, from land,
Another's mighty struggle with the waves:
Not that delightful pleasure can be felt
In someone's being buffeted, but that
It is a pleasant thing to see that we
Are being spared those troubles. [99-100]
>   *De Rerum Natura, II.1-6, trans. Palmer Bovie; in Lucretius: On the
>   Nature of Things (New York: New American Library, 1974).* No classical
>   philosopher was more influential on Jefferson's thinking than Lucretius,
>   the poet-interpreter of Epicurus to the Roman world. The passage above is the
>   primary metaphor in Hans Blumenberg's essay in philosophy and cultural his-
>   tory, *Shipwreck with Spectator: Paradigm of a Metaphor of Existence* (1979).

William Maclay

This is the important week, and perhaps the important day, when the
question will be put on the assumption of the State debts. I suspect this
from the rendezvousing of the crew of the Hamilton galley. It seems all
hands are piped to quarters.
>   *The Journal of William Maclay, United States Senator from Pennsylvania,
>   1789-1791 (New York: Frederick Ungar, 1965; repr.), 202-03; entry of
>   March 8, 1790.*

Andrew Marvell

The mind, that Ocean where each kind
Does straight its own resemblance find;
Yet it creates, transcending these,
Far other worlds, and other seas. [21n, 58]
>   *From "The Garden" (1650-1652).*

John Milton
What Pilot so expert but needs must wreck,
Imbark'd with such a Steermate at the Helm? [29]
> *Samson Agonistes, 1044-45; LCB.126.* Samson is the Pilot, Dalila the
> Steermate. The lines are spoken by the Chorus.

Samuel Latham Mitchill
The modern Argonautic expedition, whereby our Jason has enriched his
country with the invaluable treasure of the golden fleece.
> *Toast at a sheepshearing at Clermont, New York, the estate of Robert*
> *Livingston, 1810; quoted in The Papers of James Madison, Presidential*
> *Series, ed. Robert A. Rutland, et al. (Charlottesville: Univ. Press of Virginia,*
> *1984-), 3:47 n.1.* Honoring Livingston's role in importing Merino sheep
> from Spain during America's "Merino mania." Several of the sheep ended
> up at Monticello.

Isaac Newton
I do not know what I may appear to the world, but to myself I seem to
have been only a boy playing on the seashore, and diverting myself in
now and then finding a smoother pebble or a prettier shell than ordinary,
whilst the great ocean of truth lay all undiscovered before me. [88n]
> *In Robert K. Merton, On the Shoulders of Giants (San Diego: Harcourt,*
> *Brace, Jovanovich, 1985 ed.), 205-06; quoting from a biography of*
> *Newton by David Brewster, 1855.* In an Afterword, Denis Donoghue
> brings Newton's metaphor into the twentieth century with lines from W.
> B. Yeats, "At Algeciras—A Meditation upon Death" (1933): "Often at
> evening when a boy / Would I carry to a friend—Hoping more substantial
> joy / Did an older mind commend— / Not such as are in Newton's
> metaphor, / But actual shells of Rosses' lovely shore."

Ossian
The chief like a whale of ocean, whom all his billows follow, poured
valor forth as a stream, rolling his might along the shore. [10]
> *Fingal, An Ancient Epic Poem, LCB.141.*

As two dark streams from high rocks meet, and mix and roar on the
plain; loud, rough, and dark in battle meet Lochlin and Innis-fail: chief
mixed his strokes with chief, and man with man; steel clanging sounded
on steel, helmets are cleft on high. [10]
> *Ibid., LCB.142.*

As roll a thousand waves to the rocks, so Swaran's host came on: as meets rock a thousand waves, so Innis-fail met Swaran. [10]

> *Ibid., LCB.143.* In the 1760s a Scottish scholar, James McPherson, announced that he had discovered and translated the poetry of Ossian, an ancient Celtic bard. Jefferson was among many enthusiasts who accepted McPherson's claims as genuine, entering passages from Ossian into his commonplace book along with similar lines from Homer (see above). He was not much concerned by the discrediting of McPherson shortly after the poetry appeared, and in old age still found it "equal to the best morsels of antiquity." TJ to Lafayette, Nov. 4, 1823; F.XII.324.

John Page

Consider how inconsistently we shall act, if you should leave the Helm when it requires such Vigilance, Activity, Spirit and Dextrous Skill to steer us through the Storm, and if [he] who had quitted the Ship confessedly because worn down with Fatigue and unable to hand a rope or keep the Deck, even in a Calm, should presume to take your Helm out of your Hands. It will never do indeed. [33]

> *Page to TJ, Oct. 20, 1780; B.IV.53.* Page, having recently resigned as lieutenant governor, rejects the idea that he should now succeed Jefferson as governor of Virginia.

Plato

It is our duty to do one of two things: either to ascertain the facts . . . or, if this is impossible, to select the best and most dependable theory which human intelligence can supply, and embark on it, like a mariner going to sea on a raft, and sail through the voyage of life—unless we can proceed on some firmer vessel, such as a divine revelation.

> *Phaedo, 85d, trans. Hugh Tredennick; in The Last Days of Socrates (Harmondsworth, England: Penguin Books, 1954).* Simmias is speaking to Socrates.

Imagine this state of affairs on board a ship or a number of ships. The master is bigger and burlier than any of the crew, but a little deaf and short-sighted and no less deficient in seamanship. The sailors are quarrelling over the control of the helm; each thinks he ought to be steering the vessel, though he has never learnt navigation and cannot point to any teacher under whom he has served his apprenticeship; what is more, they assert that navigation is a thing that cannot be taught at all, and are ready to tear in pieces anyone who says it can. Meanwhile they besiege the master himself, begging him urgently to trust them with the helm; and sometimes, when others have been more successful in gaining his ear, they kill them or throw them overboard, and, after somehow stupefying the worthy master with strong drink or an opiate, take control of the ship, make free with its stores, and turn the voyage, as might be expected of such a crew, into a drunken carousal. Besides all this, they cry up as a skilled navigator and master of seamanship anyone clever enough to lend a hand in persuading or forcing the master to set them in command. Every other kind of man they condemn as useless. They do not understand that the genuine navigator can only make himself fit to command a ship by studying the seasons of the year, sky, stars, and winds, and all that belongs to his craft; and they have no idea that, along with the science of navigation, it is possible for him to gain, by instruction or practice, the skill to keep control of the helm whether some of them like it or not. If a ship were managed in that way, would not those on board be likely to call the expert in navigation a mere star-gazer? [17-18]

> *Republic VI.488, trans. Francis MacDonald Cornford; The Republic of Plato (London: Oxford Univ. Press, 1941).* Socrates is speaking.

We see many instances of cities going down like sinking ships to their destruction. There have been such wrecks in the past and there surely will be others in the future, caused by the worthlessness of captains and crews alike. For these are guilty of supreme ignorance of what matters most. They are men who know little or nothing of real political truth. [17n]

> *Statesman 302a, trans. J. B. Skemp; Plato's Statesman (New York: Liberal Arts Press, 1957).* The speaker is the Eleatic Stranger, the principal figure in the dialogue.

Matthew Prior

Did I but purpose to embark with thee
On the smooth surface of a summer's sea,
While gentle zephyrs play with prosperous gales,
And future's favor fills the swelling sails;
But would forsake the ship, and make the shore,
When the winds whistle, and the tempests roar? [26]

> *Henry and Emma (1709); quoted in Hugh Blair Lectures on Rhetoric, 167.* Blair cites this allegorical passage from Prior, 1664-1721, as an example of a "continued metaphor." Jefferson considered Blair's *Lectures* the finest contemporary treatise on rhetoric.

William Shakespeare

[W]hen the Sea was calm, all Boats alike,
Shew'd Mastership in floating. [21]
> *Coriolanus, IV.i.6-7; LCB.108.* Spoken by Coriolanus.

To take arms against a sea of troubles. [27]
> *Hamlet, III.i.59; quoted in Kames, Elements of Criticism, 289, and Blair,*
> *Lectures on Rhetoric, 164.* Kames considered the line a mixed metaphor;
> Blair found it "a most unnatural medley [that] confounds the imagination
> entirely." Jefferson, though he admired both critics, was probably un-
> moved by the criticism.

There is a tide in the affairs of men,
Which, taken at the flood, leads on to fortune;
Omitted, all the voyage of their life
Is bound in shallows and in miseries.
On such a full sea are we now afloat;
And we must take the current while it serves,
Or lose our ventures. [27]
> *Julius Caesar, IV.iii.217; quoted in Kames, Elements of Criticism, 276.*
> Kames cites Brutus' lines to illustrate the metaphor of "human life [as] a
> voyage at sea."

In struggling with Misfortunes
Lies the true Proof of Virtue. On smooth Seas
How many Bawble Boats dare set their Sails,
And make an equal Way with firmer Vessels:
But let the Tempest once enrage the Sea,
And then behold the strong ribb'd Argosie
Bounding between the Ocean & the Air,
Like Perseus mounted on his Pegasus;
Then where are those weak Rivals of the Main?
Or to avoid the Tempest, fled to port,
Or made a Prey to Neptune. Even thus
Do empty Shew & true-priz'd Worth divide
In Storms of fortune. [21]
> *Troilus & Cressida (Dryden adaptation), I.i.13-25 (Shakespeare, I.iii.33-*
> *47); LCB.109-10.* Spoken by Nestor.

O, how I faint when I of you do write,
Knowing a better spirit doth use your name,

And in the praise thereof spends all his might,
To make me tongue-tied, speaking of your fame!
But since your worth, — wide as the ocean is, —
The humble as the proudest sail doth bear,
My saucy bark, inferior far to his,
On your broad main doth wilfully appear.
Your shallowest help will hold me up afloat,
Whilst he upon your soundless deep doth ride;
Or, being wrack'd I am a worthless boat,
He of tall building and of goodly pride:
Then if he thrive and I be cast away,
The worst was this; — my love was my decay. [21n]

> *Sonnet 80.* A modern critic finds the ocean metaphor "almost to have wandered in from a different poem." Helen Vendler, *The Art of Shakespeare's Sonnets* (Cambridge: The Belknap Press of Harvard Univ. Press, 1997), 358.

William Shenstone

Shores there are, bless'd shores for us remain,
And favor'd isles with golden fruitage crown'd
Where tufted flow'rets paint the verdant plain,
Where ev'ry breeze shall med'cine every wound.

There the stern tyrant that embitters life,
Shall vainly suppliant, spread his asking hand;
There shall we view the billow's raging strife,
Aid the kind breast, and waft his boat to land. [29]

> *From Elegy XX; Jefferson's Memorandum Books, ed James Bear and Lucia Stanton (Princeton: Princeton Univ. Press, 1997), I:246; the full poem may be found in Shenstone, Works (1791 ed.), 82.* Jefferson copied these verses out in 1771 for an intended but never implemented "Inscription for an African Slave" at a burial site at Monticello. Jefferson appreciated Shenstone (1714-1763) as much for his landscape gardening as his verse; he visited Shenstone's estate on his tour of English gardens in 1786. The attribution of the verses to Shenstone is a recent one. The normally reliable Paul Leicester Ford, in his 1890s edition of Jefferson's writings, concluded that the inscription was Jefferson's own composition, because it was in Jefferson's hand on a blank page at the end of his copy of the Virginia Almanack for 1771, and Ford had not been able to find it in print. F.II.8. In the 1940s, two scholars, relying on Ford, continued to hold the lines were Jefferson's own, while a third silently deleted them

when otherwise quoting the memorandum by Jefferson in which they appeared. Saul K. Padover. *The Complete Jefferson* (New York Duell, Sloan & Pearce, 1943), 822; Eleanor Davis Berman. *Thomas Jefferson among the Arts* (New York: Philosophical Library, 1947), 243; Edwin Betts, *Thomas Jefferson's Garden Book, 1766-1824, With relevant extracts from his other writings* (Philadelphia: American Philosophical Society, 1944), 26. Neither the Lipscomb and Bergh nor the Boyd editions of Jefferson's writings includes the verses, presumably because they do not touch Jefferson's memorandum books, which, for the Boyd edition, were set aside for separate editing. It was that editing, in 1997, that settled the question of authorship.

Margaret Bayard (Mrs. Samuel Harrison) Smith

He [Jefferson] has passed through the tempestuous sea of political life, has been enveloped in clouds of calumny, the storms of faction . . . and often threatened with a wreck, of happiness and fame. But these things are now all passed away, and like the mountain on which he stands, fogs and mists and storms gather and rage below, while he enjoys unclouded sunshine. . . . The morning after my arrival . . . the space between Monticello and the Allegany . . . was covered with a thick fog, which had the appearance of the ocean and was unbroken except when wood covered hills rose above the plain and looked like islands. . . . [Mr. Jefferson] had now reached the haven of domestic life. Here while the storm roared at a distance, he could hear its roaring and be at peace. . . . As a ship long tossed by the storms of the ocean casts anchor and lies at rest in a peaceful harbour, he is retired from an active and restless scene to this tranquil spot. [40]

> *From Mrs. Smith's notebook, Aug. 1, 1809; in Smith, The First Forty Years of Washington Society (1906), ed. Gaillard Hunt, 65, 69 75, 79-80.*
> Margaret Bayard Smith, whose husband was the founding editor of the Republican-oriented *National Intelligencer,* was in at the beginning of Washington society. At Jefferson's invitation the couple visited Monticello shortly after he retired from the presidency.

Sophocles

Gentlemen: as for our city's fortune,
the gods have shaken her, when the great waves broke;
but they have brought her through again to safety. [14]

> *Antigone, 179-81. These and the following passages are adapted from translations by David Grene and Robert F. Goheen.* Creon is speaking.

A man with the task of guiding [steering] a whole city,
if he does not reach for the best counsel for her,
I judge the worst of any.   [14]
   Ibid., 198-201.

It is the city which gives us our security. While she sails
steady under us, friends will be ours for the making.   [14]
   Ibid., 207-09.

O harbor of Death, hard to cleanse. Why? Why do you destroy me?   [14]
   Ibid., 1361-63.

Joseph Story
When I examine a question, I go from headland to headland, from case
to case. Marshall has a compass, puts out to sea, and goes directly to his
result.   [58-59]
   Quoted from an 1867 essay on John Marshall in Fred R. Shapiro, Oxford
   Dictionary of American Legal Quotations (1933), 307.

James Thomson
[In a dream, a crazed lover] wades
The turbid stream below, and strives to reach
The farther shore; where succorless, and sad,
Wild as a Bacchanal she spreads her arms,
But strives in vain, born by th'outrageous flood
To distance down, he rides the ridgy wave,
Or whelm'd beneath the boiling eddy sinks.   [27n]
   From "Spring," The Seasons; LCB.112.

George Villers
Physician: Sir, to conclude, the place you fill has more than amply
exacted the talents of a wary pilot; and all these threatening storms,
which like impregnate clouds, hover o'er our heads, will, when they
once are grasp'd but by the eye of reason, melt into fruitful showers of
blessings on the people.
Bayes: Pray mark that allegory. Is not that good?
Johnson: Yes, that grasping of a storm with the eye is admirable.   [27n]
   The Rehearsal (1672), quoted in Kames, Elements of Criticism, 287. An
   example, according to Kames, of a "faulty metaphor . . . pleasantly
   ridiculed." *The Rehearsal,* a parody of contemporary drama attributed to a
   member of the nobility, was performed throughout the eighteenth century.

George Washington
I am embarked on a wide ocean, boundless in its prospect, and from whence, perhaps, no safe harbor is to be found. [33]

> *Washington to John Augustine Washington, June 20, 1775; in Ralph K. Andrist, ed. George Washington: A Biography in His Own Words (New York: Newsweek/Harper & Row, 1972), 104.* Appointed commander in chief of the Continental Army a few days earlier, Washington writes to his brother.

Edward Young
Walk thoughtful on the silent, solemn shore
Of that vast ocean, it must sail so soon;
And put good works on board; and wait the wind
That shortly blows us into worlds unknown. [27]

> *From Night Thoughts (1742-45); quoted in Blair, Lectures on Rhetoric, 167.* Criticizing this passage on old age by one of Jefferson's favorite authors, Blair writes: "The first two lines are uncommonly beautiful; . . . but when he continues, the metaphor . . . plainly becomes strained and sinks in dignity."

Appendix III
Nautical Metaphors by Other Authors

III.B *Since Jefferson's Death*

Henry Adams

The President may indeed in one respect resemble the commander of an army in peace, but in another and more essential sense he resembles the commander of a ship at sea. He must have a helm to grasp, a course to steer, a port to seek; he must sooner or later be convinced that a perpetual calm is as little to his purpose as a perpetual hurricane, and that without headway the ship can arrive nowhere. President Grant assumed at the outset that it was not his duty to steer, that his were only duties of discipline.

> *"The Session, 1869-1870," in The Great Winter of 1860-61 and Other Essays, ed. George Hochfield (New York: Sagamore Press, 1958), 197.*

Of all the travels made by man since the voyages of Dante, this new exploration along the shores of Multiplicity and Complexity promised to be the longest, though as yet it had barely touched two familiar regions—race and sex. Even within these narrow seas the navigator [Adams] lost his bearings and followed the winds as they blew. [92]

> *The Education of Henry Adams (Boston: Houghton Mifflin, 1918), 449.*

At last [the universe of the uniformitarians of one's youth] had been wrecked by rays [the x-rays of Roentgen], and Karl Pearson [in *The Grammar of Science,* 1892] undertook to cut the wreck loose with an axe, leaving science adrift on a sensual raft in the midst of a supersensual chaos. The confusion seemed, to a mere passenger, worse than that of 1600 when the astronomers upset the world; . . . he knew that his opinion was worthless; only, in this case, he found himself on the raft, personally and economically concerned in its drift. [92]

> *Ibid., 452-53.*

Spiro Agnew

When the winds and tides were favorable, the military outlook promising, the American ship of state sailed on with the enthusiastic backing of Senator Fulbright and his contented crew. But when the seas became choppy, one could soon glance down from the bridge and see

Senator Fulbright on deck demanding that the ship be abandoned and staking out a claim to the nearest life boat. [76]

> *In James Calhoun, The Real Spiro Agnew: Commonsense Quotations of a Household Word (Gretna, La.: Pelican, 1970), 57; no original source provided.*

Anonymous

An American Democrat orator once declaimed, "We will burn our ships, and with every sail unfurled steer boldly out into the ocean of freedom."

> *Quoted in W. B. Stanford, Greek Metaphor, 32.*

Robert Bolt

What Englishman can behold without Awe
The Canvas and the Rigging of the Law!
Forbidden here the galley-master's whip—
Hearts of Oak, in the Law's Great Ship! . . .

So now we'll apply the good, plain sailor's art,
And fix these quicksands on the Law's plain chart! [78]

> *A Man for All Seasons (New York: Vintage Books, 1960), 85-86.*

William J. Brennan, Jr.

[T]he Court now needlessly departs from its generous tradition and improvidently sets sail on a journey whose landing point is uncertain. [76]

> *In re MacDonald, 489 U.S. 180, at 188 (1989), dissenting opinion.*

William Jennings Bryan

The ship of state may be intrusted to pilots during fair weather; but, in hours of storm, the people turn to the Sage of Monticello, the greatest of the world's constructive statesmen. [74-75]

> *"Jeffersonian Principles," North American Review, 168 (June 1899):672.*

William Cullen Bryant

       Lo! they stretch,
In airy undulations, far away,
As if the ocean, in his gentlest swell,
Stood still, with all his rounded billows fixed,
And motionless forever. [73]

> *From "The Prairies" (1834). Based on a trip to Illinois from New York in the spring of 1831.*

Pat Buchanan, see Richard Nixon

J. H. Buckingham
For miles we saw nothing but a vast prairie of what can compare to nothing else but the ocean itself. The tall grass, interspersed occasionally with fields of corn, looked like the deep sea; it seemed as if we were out of sight of land, for no house, no barn, no tree was visible, and the horizon presented the rolling of waves in the afar-off distance. There were all sorts of flowers—as if the sun were shining upon the gay and dancing waters. [73]
> *Quoted in The American Land (Washington: Smithsonian Exposition Books, 1979), 113.* A Boston journalist traveling with Congressman Abraham Lincoln in Illinois in the 1840s.

Ralph Bunche
The good ship "Humanity" often lists badly from an over ballast of cold intellectuality. [76]
> *"The Fourth Dimension of Personality" (UCLA Commencement Address), June 1967; in Ralph Bunche: The Man and His Times, ed. Benjamin Rivlin (New York: Holmes and Meier, 1990), 221.*

George Bush [about]
The ship of state's course may not be precisely plotted, and its fuel reserves may be somewhat depleted; but the machinery is well-oiled, the crew is superbly trained, and the seas are calm. No crisis seems likely to be serious enough to interrupt the voyage. [76]
> *Terry L. Deibel, "Bush's Foreign Policy: Mastery and Inaction," Foreign Policy, No. 84 (fall 1991):22.*

George W. Bush [about]
Let's not make waves, so we don't cause a train wreck. [76]
> *Mark Sanford, New York Times, Sept. 12, 2000, A16.* Sanford, a Republican Congressman from South Carolina, explains why, during the presidential campaign, he and other conservatives were not speaking about the political values they hoped would be served by electing Mr. Bush. Bush was the more likely to be elected, according to Sanford, if voters did not know what supporters like himself actually stood for.

Moderates say the lesson in this [the defection of Senator Jeffords of Vermont from the Republican Party] is that George Bush and the

Congressional leadership ought to let them steer the ship. But they are, after all, the tail and not the dog. [76]

> *David Keene, chairman of the American Conservative Union; New York Times, May 31, 2001, A24.*

Jimmy Carter [about]

A Politician Without Metaphor is a Ship Without Sails [76]

> *Henry Fairley, "A Sense of Metaphor," New Republic, March 3, 1979, 10-13.* A critique of Carter's rhetorical style.

Civil Rights, see Dwight Eisenhower, Richard Nixon, Paul Sifton, and Walter White

Civil Rights Movement [variously attributed]

We may have come on different ships, but we are in the same boat now. [77]

> An unusual metaphor because both elements are nautical and the first could be just as figurative as the second. The metaphor has become a popular saying, almost a proverb, variously attributed to Jesse Jackson, Barbara Jordan, John Lewis, Whitney Young and, most commonly, Martin Luther King, Jr. I have been unable to discover a reliable original source.

Bill Clinton [about], see also Leonard Garment

Five months into the Clinton Administration its pattern of governing is now starting to emerge.

The best way to capture it is to compare this Administration to the previous one. The Bush Administration on domestic affairs was like a boat that was perfectly trimmed, fore and aft, with the captain dressed to the nines. But it never left the dock. The Clinton Administration, it is now becoming clear, is like a boat headed out to sea, dragging its anchor, with half the passengers seasick and several of the crew having fallen overboard. There's constant trouble in the mate's mess, and the captain is navigating by the stars, having long ago lost his charts.

But, by gosh, it is forging along.

Hang on to your deck chairs, folks. This is the Clinton Administration. Its seamanship may leave something to be desired, but you may just get where you are going, and if you like the unexpected, you may even enjoy it. [76]

> *Thomas L. Friedman, "Clinton's Sailing Isn't Smooth, But It's Sailing," New York Times, June 20, 1993, sec. 4, p. 1.*

The majority leader, Senator Trent Lott, emphasized throughout the day that the [impeachment] proceeding was now firmly positioned for no more surprises and a finish by Friday of next week, as planned.

Or maybe even a day sooner, the Senate leader suddenly began suggesting, sounding like a sea captain holding out the promise of an extra grog ration to a crew grown weary of the bounding main of impeachment. [76]

Francis X. Clines, New York Times, Feb. 5, 1999, A16.

James Fenimore Cooper

From the summits on the swells [of the trans-Mississippi prairie], the eye became fatigued with the sameness and chilling dreariness of the landscape. The earth was not unlike the ocean, when its restless waters are heaving heavily, after the agitation and fury of the tempest have begun to lessen. There was the same waving and regular surface, the same absence of foreign objects, and the same boundless extent to the view. Indeed so very striking was the resemblance between the water and the land, that, however much the geologist might sneer at so simple a theory, it would have been difficult for a poet not to have felt that the formation of the one had been produced by the subsiding dominion of the other. Here and there a tall tree rose out of the bottoms, stretching its naked branches abroad, like some solitary vessel; and, to strengthen the delusion, far in the distance appeared two or three rounded thickets, looming in the misty horizon like islands resting on the waters. It is unnecessary to warn the practised reader, that the sameness of the surface, and the low stands of the spectators, exaggerated the distances; but, as swell appeared after swell, and island succeeded island, there was a disheartening assurance that long and seemingly interminable tracts of territory must be passed, before the wishes of the humblest agriculturist could be realized. [73]

The Prairie (New York: Dodd, Mead & Co., 1954), 6-7; orig. 1827. One of the subtitles of *The Prairie* is "The Skimmer of the Seas." Another of Cooper's Leather-Stocking Tales is *The Pathfinder, or, The Inland Sea* (1840).

John Dewey

Whether or no we are, save in some metaphorical sense, all brothers, we are at least all in the same boat traversing the same turbulent ocean.

A Common Faith (New Haven: Yale Univ. Press, 1934), 84. A philosopher may notice one metaphor without noticing others.

John F. Dillon

[Courts are the] only breakwater against the haste and the passions of the people—the tumultuous ocean of democracy. [74]

> *Presidential address to the American Bar Association, 1892; quoted in Arnold Paul, Conservative Crisis and the Rule of Law: Attitudes of Bar and Bench, 1887-1895 (Ithaca: Cornell Univ. Press, 1960), 81.*

William O. Douglas

Your message, written on my retirement from the Court, filled my heart with overflowing emotion.

You were kind and generous and made every hour, including the last one on our arduous journey, happy and relaxed.

I am reminded of many canoe trips I have taken in my lifetime. Those who start down a water course may be strangers at the beginning but almost invariably are close friends at the end. There were strong headwinds to overcome and there were rainy as well as sun drenched days to travel. The portages were long and many and some were very strenuous. But there were always a pleasant camp in a stand of white bark birch and water concerts held at night to the music of the loons; and inevitably there came the last camp fire, the last breakfast cooked over last night's fire, and the parting was always sad.

And yet, in fact, there was no parting because each happy memory of the choice parts of the journey—and of the whole journey—was of a harmonious united effort filled with fulfilling and beautiful hours as well as dull and dreary ones. The greatest such journey I've made has been with you, my Brethren, who were strangers at the start but warm and fast friends at the end.

The value of our achievements will be for others to appraise. Other like journeys will be made by those who follow us, and we trust that they will leave those wilderness water courses as pure and unpolluted as we left those which we traversed. [76]

> *423 U.S. ix-x (1975).* Justice Douglas's farewell to the Supreme Court.

Frederick Douglass

I have often, in the deep stillness of a summer's Sabbath, stood all alone upon the lofty banks of that noble bay, and traced . . . the countless number of sails moving off to the mighty ocean. . . . I would pour out my soul's complaint, in my rude way, with an apostrophe to the moving multitude of ships: —

"You are loosened from your moorings, and are free; I am fast in my chains, and am a slave! You move merrily before the gentle gale, and I sadly before the bloody whip! You are freedom's swift-winged angels, that fly around the world; I am confined in bands of iron! O that I were free!" [62]

Narrative of the Life of Frederick Douglass, An American Slave (1845; repr. Garden City, N.Y.: Doubleday, 1963), 66-67. Douglass's soliloquy sets the scene for his plan to escape into freedom. William Lloyd Garrison, in his preface to the Narrative, considered these lines "the most thrilling" in the book and rephrased them: "receding vessels as they flew with their white wings . . . animated by the living spirit of freedom." xv.

As the sheet anchor takes a firmer hold, when the ship is tossed by the storm, so did the cause of your fathers grow stronger as it breasted the chilling blasts of kingly displeasure . . . . [But now,] from the round top of your ship of state, dark and threatening clouds may be seen. Heavy billows, like mountains in the distance, disclose to the leeward huge forms of flinty rocks! That blot drawn, that chain broken, and all is lost. Cling to this day—cling to it, and to its principles, with the grasp of a storm-tossed mariner to a spar at midnight. [62-63]

"The Meaning of July Fourth for the Negro," speech at Rochester, N.Y. July 5, 1852; in The Life and Writings of Frederick Douglass, ed. Philip Foner (New York: International Publishers, 1950), 2:184-85. Douglass asks his white audience to cling to Jeffersonian principles. On sheet anchor, see TJ to William Short, March 15, 1791.

Dwight D. Eisenhower

Possibly I am something like a ship which, buffeted and pounded by wind and wave, is still afloat and manages in spite of frequent tacks and turnings to stay generally along its plotted course and continue to make some, even if slow and painful, headway. [76]

To Everett Hazlett, July 22, 1957; in Stephen E. Ambrose, Eisenhower, Vol. 2, The President (New York: Simon & Schuster, 1984), 410. On the school desegregation crisis in Little Rock. The biographer continues: "But to many observers, it appeared that the ship of state was in fact caught in a storm without a rudder, without power, without a captain; that it was, if the truth be told, drifting aimlessly in unknown and uncharted waters."

Ralph Waldo Emerson
They [the ancients] preferred the noble vessel too late for the tide, contending with winds and waves, dismantled and unrigged, to her companion borne into harbor with colors flying and guns firing.

> From "Conduct of Life" (1860); in Essays and Journals, ed. Lewis Mumford (Garden City, N.Y.: Doubleday, 1968), 438. Unconcerned about the history of firearms, the philosopher nods.

George Engelmann
Many a young life is battered and forever crippled in the breakers of puberty; if it crosses these unharmed and is not dashed to pieces on the rock of childbirth, it may still ground on the ever-recurring shallows of menstruation, and lastly, upon the final bar of the menopause ere protection is found in the unruffled waters of the harbor beyond the reach of sexual storms. [75n]

> The American Girl of Today: Modern Education and Functional Health (1900), 9-10; quoted in Roger B. Stein, "Realism and Beyond," in Springer (ed.), America and the Sea (1995), 207. Engelmann was president of the American Gynecological Society.

Edward Everett
The men, who, when the wisest and most sagacious were needed to steer the newly launched vessel through the broken waves of the unknown sea, sat calm and unshaken at the helm. [58]

> "Address, Delivered at Charleston [Mass.], August 1, 1826, in Commemoration of John Adams and Thomas Jefferson"; in Orations and Speeches on Various Occasions (Boston: 1836; repr. 1972), 124.

John Kenneth Galbraith
It is a far, far better thing to have a firm anchor in nonsense than to put out on the troubled seas of thought. [76]

> The Affluent Society (Boston: Houghton Mifflin, 1958), 154. A barb directed at his opponents and their conventional economic reasoning.

Leonard Garment
As late as November 1972, less than two years before Watergate forced his resignation, Nixon's enterprise seemed as unsinkable as the Titanic. It had state-of-the-art, watertight political construction, an experienced captain and crew, and a course well marked by historical example. Then came that oblique, sideways swipe from an iceberg, causing a breach below the water line.

The breach was invisible; but, while first-class passengers partied on, Nixon's underlying structural defense failed. Blunder followed blunder, flooding proceeded, and the vessel sank—with the loss of many reputations and calamitous consequences for American politics. . . .

Thus the sideways "bump" from the iceberg was just the proximate cause of Nixon's demise. The fundamental reasons lay deeper.

In the current intense scrutiny of the Clinton White House, the wounds that are apparent so far have mostly to do with campaign money. Though deeply embarrassing, or wrong, such disclosures are unlikely to sink the Administration.

[While at a news conference Mr. Clinton appeared as Mr. Cheerful] on a comparable occasion, Nixon looked like Mr. Gloom, sweaty and defensive ("I am not a crook"). So President Clinton sails on majestically.

Of course, it is possible that Mr. Clinton may sink in some other manner. His Administration, while not weakened by a personally scarred President, may have some equally fundamental, as-yet-unseen fault. [76]

> *"Scandals Past and Present," New York Times, March 13, 1997, A16.*

Henry George
Let us not think that after the stormy seas and head gales of all the ages, *our* ship has at last struck the trade winds of time. [74]

> *Quoted in Edward J. Rose, Henry George (New York: Twayne Publishers, 1968), 34.*

U. S. Grant, see Henry Adams

Alexander M. Haig, Jr.
In those early days . . . the [foreign policy] course of the nation was set for the voyage through the Reagan years. But to me, the White House was as mysterious as a ghost ship; you heard the creak of the rigging and the groan of the timbers and sometimes even glimpsed the crew on deck. But which of the crew had the helm? . . . It was impossible to know for sure. [76]

> *Caveat: Realism, Reagan, and Foreign Policy (New York: Macmillan, 1984), 85.* The bafflement of Ronald Reagan's first secretary of state.

Learned Hand
[There is] no point in nailing your colors to the mast in a cyclone. [76]

> *Hand to Felix Frankfurter, Dec. 3, 1919; in Gerald Gunther, Learned Hand, The Man and the Judge (New York: Knopf, 1994), 359.* Urging his friend to restrain himself at the time of Red-baiting.

Perhaps if we cannot build breakwaters, we may be able to deepen the bottom. [76]

> *"Sources of Tolerance" (1930); in The Spirit of Liberty: Papers and Addresses of Learned Hand, ed. Irving Dilliard (New York: Knopf, 1952),* 78. In the protection of liberty, the study of literature and history is a needed supplement to building institutions of government.

The American people is getting used to the idea that when the wind blows, the Captain is the boss, and that what he says goes. . . . If you once get used to browbeating the whole crew and the passenger list whenever the wind rises to a half-gale, your Beaufort scale will be half-gale whenever you don't have your way. [76]

> *Hand to Felix Frankfurter, July 23, 1933; in Gunther, Learned Hand, 440-41.* A reaction to President Roosevelt. Sir Francis Beaufort, a British admiral, developed a scale in the early nineteenth century to estimate the effects of the wind based on observations of the sea.

Garrett Hardin [paraphrased]

[His metaphor] conceives each nation as a lifeboat with limited carrying capacity, cast on turbulent seas, and surrounded by a diverse array of other lifeboats. About one-third of the world's population lives on relatively spacious, well-stocked lifeboats. The other two-thirds live on poor and more crowded lifeboats, and some have been spilling excess people overboard for some time. The U.S. lifeboat is among the well-to-do . . . . We must recognize that the irresponsible population growth of two-thirds of the world is depleting the ecological structure to the point where every life saved today in a floundering lifeboat diminishes the quality of life for all subsequent generations. . . . [They] must learn to fend for themselves or perish in the sea. [76]

> *John G. Thompson and James E. Trinnaman, "The Spaceship and the Lifeboat: Metaphors for the 1990's" (Carlisle Barracks, Pa.: Army War College Strategic Studies Institute, 1975), 3; citing Garrett Hardin, "Living on a Lifeboat" (1974).* The ideas of an environmental pessimist.

George F. Hoar

I ask you to keep in the old channels, and to keep off the old rocks laid down in the old charts, and to follow the old sailing orders that all the old captains of other days have obeyed, to take your bearings, as of old . . . and not from this meteoric light of empire. [74]

> *On the floor of the U. S. Senate, late 1890s; quoted in Peterson, The Image of Jefferson in the American Mind (1960), 267-68.* Hoar, a senator

from Massachusetts, relies on Jefferson in arguing against American imperialism.

David Hollinger
It is not enough to see [William] James as a "trimmer," trying to restore balance by getting any lop-sided ship of thought to throw overboard ideas he did not like, or to at least move them across the deck where their weight would function differently in the maintenance of the craft. James was concerned with the seaworthiness of certain fleets: Those sailing for the most cosmopolitan ports in the West, laden with cargoes of traditions he regarded as the most promising resources for the further exploration and enrichment of the world. The mariners he most wanted to encourage were those with at least some appreciation of those traditions, but he found many of them slouching in their cabins, taking their destiny for granted. The mariners, on the other hand, of whom James was most suspicious were those so infatuated with the newly designed vessels of science that they were willing to sail without the ballast that sustained even science itself. The proper manning and equipping of these fleets was the chief business of James's career. [79]

> *In the American Province; Studies in the History and Historiography of Ideas (Bloomington: Univ. of Indiana Press, 1985), 22.* The concluding paragraph of "William James and the Culture of Inquiry"; orig. 1981.

Oliver Wendell Holmes, Sr., see also William James
I find the great thing in this world is not so much where we stand, as in what direction we are moving. To reach the port of heaven, we must sail sometimes with the wind and sometimes against it, —but we must sail, and not drift, nor lie at anchor. [79-80]

> *The Autocrat of the Breakfast Table (1858), chap. 4; quoted by Samuel Eliot Morison as an epigram to his Oxford History of the American People (New York: Oxford Univ. Press, 1965), omitting "to reach the port of heaven."*

Henrik Ibsen
Billing: Society is like a ship: every man must put his hand to the helm.
Horster: That may be all right on shore; but at sea it wouldn't do at all. [78]

> *An Enemy of the People (1882), Act I, trans. William Archer.*

William James, see also David Hollinger
Sir James Stephen compares our belief in the uniformity of nature, the congruity of the future with the past, to a man rowing one way and

looking another, and steering his boat by keeping her stern in line with an object behind him. In Dr. Holmes's phrase, stories in passing from mouth to mouth make a great deal of lee-way in proportion to their headway. In Mr. Lowell's description of German sentences, they have a way of yawing and going stern-foremost and not minding the helm for several minutes after it has been put down. [83]

> *Principles of Psychology (1890), chap. xiv.* James illustrates "association by similarity" with a string of nautical metaphors. See also David Hollinger.

Philip C. Jessup
It is the part of statesmanship to steer a steady course between the Scylla of impatience and the Charybidis of inflexibility. It is the part of the United Nations not to try to blast out the rocks on either side of the channel, but like some deus ex machina to disperse the storm clouds and provide favoring winds. [76]

> *Address to Ottawa Women's Canadian Club, Sept. 25, 1952; Dept. of State Bulletin, Oct. 13, 1952, 572.*

Lyndon B. Johnson
When a ship cuts through the sea, the waters are always stirred and troubled. And our ship is moving—and it's moving through troubled and new waters, and it's moving toward new and better shores. [76]

> *State of the Union Message, Jan. 17, 1968; New York Times, Jan. 18, 1968, 16.* Commenting on American "restlessness," i.e., urban rioting.

William Johnson
Are the value, the protection, the political bearings of the Fisheries to be reported on? The sage of Monticello descends from the mountain to the ocean; he grasps the line and the oar; every sea is ransacked; every market explored; the ocean to be cultivated; a rich harvest to be gathered from its barren waves; and the hardy son of the trident to be fostered, that he may bear our enterprise and our thunder to wherever the ocean flows.

> *"Eulogy to Jefferson, Charleston, S.C, Aug. 3, 1826," in A Selection of Eulogies Pronounced in the Several States, in Honor of John Adams and Thomas Jefferson (1826), 308.* Johnson, 1771-1834, was Jefferson's first appointee to the Supreme Court, serving for thirty years.

Ward Just
A publisher has the responsibility of a skipper on the bridge of a vessel, mindful always of the rigging, the weather, the course, the morale below

decks and, not least, the safe delivery of the cargo, the news, good and bad. The news business has its own amendment of the Constitution of the United States, which gives the cargo a special value and the skipper a special duty.

> *"The Reign of a Great Publisher;" New York Times, July 19, 2001, A25.* Tribute to Katherine Graham of the *Washington Post.*

Wassily Leontief

The captain is dismissing a large part of his crew and has ordered the sails set so that the canvas would catch the full force of the wind, that is, for the pursuit of the highest possible profits. He has also directed the helmsman to take his hand off the tiller so that, unimpeded by an attempt to steer it, the ship could sail in the direction in which the wind happens to propel it. Most passengers seem to be enjoying the cruise except, of course, the poor, the old, and the sick who are being lowered in leaky dinghies overboard. This, the captain explains, has to be done to lighten the load.

But the mood will change, and I think quite soon when everyone hears and feels the rocks scraping the bottom of the vessel. Emergency measures will certainly be taken, but after having been pulled out into deeper water, should we resume experimentation with the same kind of policies based on the same kind of theories that permitted the American economy to reach the stage in which it finds itself today? Let's hope not. The waters that we are about to enter are much more treacherous than those we were navigating up until now. [76]

> *Testimony before the Joint Economic Committee of Congress, 1982, in James Galbraith, "Wassily Leontief: An Appreciation," Challenge, 41 (May/June, 1999):103.* A Nobel laureate on the economic policies of the Reagan administration.

Sinclair Lewis

Miss Sherwin's trying to repair the holes in this barnacle-covered ship of a town by keeping busy bailing out the water. And Pollock tries to repair it by reading poetry to the crew! Me, I want to yank it up on the ways, and fire the poor bum of a shoe-maker that built it so it sails crooked, and have it rebuilt right, from the keel up. [75]

> *Main Street (1920), chap. 10.* Miles Bjornstam to Carol Kennikott.

Abraham Lincoln

The very figure-head of the ship of state. [63]

> *Speech at Peoria, Oct. 16, 1854; Collected Works of Abraham Lincoln, ed. Roy P. Basler (New Brunswick: Rutgers Univ. Press, 1953), II:275.* Referring

to slavery, which through the Kansas-Nebraska Act had replaced freedom as the symbol of the United States. "Figure-head" did not at the time have its modern meaning of "in name only," but referred exclusively to a statue carved on the prow of a ship. Thus Lincoln's phrase ingeniously combines a literal nautical symbol with a political-nautical metaphor.

Mr. Lincoln shook hands with him [a man who had voted for Stephen A. Douglas] and said if he and the other friends of Mr. Douglas would assist in keeping the ship of state afloat, that perhaps Mr. Douglas might be selected to pilot it sometime in the future. [63-64]

> *Remarks at Wellsville, Ohio, Feb. 14, 1861; ibid., IV:208.* The first of three nautical metaphors on the way from Illinois to Washington for his inauguration.

If all do not join now to save the good old ship of the Union this voyage, nobody will have a chance to pilot her on another voyage. [64]

> *Speech at Cleveland, Feb. 15, 1861; ibid., IV:216.*

I understand a ship to be made for the carrying and preservation of the cargo, and so long as the ship can be saved with the cargo, it should never be abandoned. This Union should likewise never be abandoned unless it fails and the possibility of its preservation shall cease to exist without throwing the passengers and cargo overboard. So long, then, as it is possible that the prosperity and the liberties of the people can be preserved in the Union, it shall be my purpose at all times to preserve it. [64]

> *"Reply to Mayor Fernando Wood at New York City," Feb. 20, 1861; ibid., IV:233.*

As I am not much impressed with the belief that the present Constitution can be improved, I make no recommendations of amendments. I am, rather, for the old ship, and the chart of the old pilots. If, however, the people desire a new, or an altered vessel . . . I shall place no obstacle in the way of what may appear to be their wishes. [64]

> *First Inaugural Address, March 4, 1861; ibid., IV:260.*

[T]his class of men will do nothing for the government, nothing for themselves, except demanding that the government shall not strike its open enemies, lest they be struck by accident! . . . They are to touch neither a sail nor a pump, but to be merely passengers—deadheads at that—to be carried snug and dry, throughout the storm, and safely landed right side up. Nay, more; even a mutineer is to go untouched lest these sacred passengers receive an accidental wound. [64]

> *Lincoln to Cuthbert Bullitt, July 28, 1862; ibid., V:345.* Replying to a group of professed Union loyalists in Louisiana who complain that the presence of the Union army in the state interferes with their rights as slaveholders.

I shall do my utmost that whoever is to hold the helm for the next voyage, shall start with the best possible chance to save the ship. [64]

> *Response to a Group of Loyal Citizens of Maryland, resident in Washington, D.C., Oct. 19, 1864; ibid., VIII:52.* The presidential election is to be held in three weeks; the next voyage begins on inauguration day in March 1865.

Romulus Linney

There, at the end of the third month, three elderly ladies of the church, trim frigates in full sail under breezes of joy and innocence, moored themselves around Starns and attempted his conversion.

"Mister Starns," said one, a stately vessel in harbor water, "it is but a step into the arms of the Lord." . . .

"I scrub floors here. That's all. You old bitches can go to hell."

And he threw a duster at them.

Instantly the ladies reversed their tackle. Foregoing the breezes of innocence and joy, they set sail toward the Reverend of the church under black winds of indignation. Sales was overwhelmed [and] cast Starns from the Temple and hired another janitor. . . .

[Later] launched against their will by an adamant Bishop, the three frigates, sails drooping, glided silently to the church. At anchor, the offending Christians apologized. [75]

> *Heathen Valley (New York: Atheneum, 1962), 31, 32, 50.* In this novel set in the Appalachians in the 1840s, Reverend Sales [sails] dismisses and is later forced by his bishop to rehire Starns [stern], the heathen caretaker of a fallen church.

Henry Wadsworth Longfellow

Cedar of Maine and Georgia pine
Here together shall combine.
A goodly frame, and a goodly fame,
And the UNION be her name. . .
Thou, too, sail on, O Ship of State!

Sail on, O UNION, strong and great!
Humanity with all its fears,
With all the hopes of future years
Is hanging breathless on thy fate!
We know what Master laid thy keel,
What Workmen wrought thy ribs of steel,
Who made each mast and sail, and rope,
What anvils rang, what hammers beat,
In what a forge and what a heat
Were shaped the anchors of thy hope!
Fear not each sudden sound and shock,
'T is of the wave and not the rock;
'T is but the flapping of the sail
And not a rent made by the gale!
In spite of rock and tempest's roar,
In spite of false lights on the shore,
Sail on, nor fear to breast the sea!
Our hearts, our hopes, are all with thee,
Our hearts, our hopes, our prayers, our tears,
Our faith triumphant o'er our fears,
Are all with thee, —are all with thee! [60-61]

> *"The Building of the Ship," 1849; The Poetical Works of Longfellow (Boston: Houghton Mifflin, 1975; orig. 1893), 100, 103.*

James Russell Lowell, see William James

Thomas Babington Macaulay
Your constitution is all sail and no anchor. [65-66, 75n]

> *Macaulay to Henry S. Randall, May 23, 1857; The Letters of Thomas Babington Macaulay ed. Thomas Pinney (Cambridge: Cambridge Univ. Press, 1981), 6:96; from recipient's copy, New York Public Library.* The mistranscription of Macaulay's phrase to "Your Constitution . . . " began a few years after his letter was written and has continued to the present. See *Southern Literary Messenger,* xxx (March 1860):227; New York Times, March 24, 1860, p. 3, col. 5; *Harper's New Monthly Magazine,* LIV (Feb. 1877):461 (claiming that "all [Macaulay's] letters are here given as they were written"); Merrill Peterson, *The Image of Jefferson in the American Mind* (1960), 160; *American Heritage,* Feb. 1974, 104; Michael Kammen, *A Machine That Would Go of Itself: The Constitution in American Culture* (1986), 17; *Time,* July 6, 1987, 27; *Bartlett's Familiar Quotations* (16th

ed., 1992), 426. The only source I have discovered with the correct orthography is *Oxford Dictionary of American Legal Quotations* (1993), citing the Pinney edition of Macaulay's letters. Merrill Peterson, despite reprinting the faulty transcription, correctly explicates Macaulay's ideas on the American "constitution."

Dumas Malone
[At the end of his second administration Jefferson] talked plaintively of having gained the harbor, sounding as though he wished he had never set sail. At that time, acutely conscious of the discomforts and perils of the voyage he had made, he was in no position to realize that it was to prove one of the most memorable in the annals of his country. We shall not attempt to assess it here, but we may ask what sort of captain he essayed to be, and what sort of men he had with him as mates. [78]
   Jefferson the President, First Term, 1801-1805 (Boston: Little, Brown, 1970), 50.

Mike Mansfield
It is as though we were passing through a stretch of stormy seas in a ship which is obviously powerful and luxurious, but a ship, nevertheless, frozen in a dangerous course and with a hull in pressing need of repair. [76]
   Speech in the U.S. Senate, April 14, 1960; Congressional Record, 106:8053. On a "deepening disquiet" in America.

Mao Zedong [attributed]
The people are like water and the army is like fish. [77]

John P. Marquand
Thomas Apley, like every other New England industrialist, was piloting his craft through difficult financial waters, where politics not infrequently were lashed to banking. [75n]
   The Late George Apley (Boston: Little Brown, 1937), 42. Said of George Apley's father at the time of financial scandals during the Grant administration.

Otto Neurath
We are like sailors who must reconstruct their ship on the open sea but are never able to start afresh from the bottom. Where a beam is taken away a new one must at once be put there, and for this the rest of the ship is used

as support. In this way, by using old beams and driftwood, the ship can be shaped entirely anew, but only by gradual reconstruction. [94-95]

> *Quoted in Nancy Cartwright, et al., Otto Neurath: Philosophy Between Science and Politics (Cambridge: Cambridge Univ. Press, 1996; orig. 1921), 139.*

Richard Nixon [about], see also Leonard Garment

The second era of Re-Construction is over; the ship of integration is going down; it is not our ship . . . and we cannot salvage it; and we should not be aboard. [76, 77]

> *Pat Buchanan, memo to President Nixon, spring 1970; quoted in Tom Wicker, One of Us: Richard Nixon and the American Dream (New York: Random House, 1991), 502.* A speech-writer for the president argues against the administration's support of racial integration.

William D. Nordhaus

Just a year ago, most economists fretted that the American economy was headed for shipwreck on the reefs of budgetary and external deficits. Yet today, thanks to favorable trade winds, skies look brighter as the economy gathers steam for a sustained powerful boom. Four factors have turned the economic tide . . . .

Everyone agrees we must trim our fiscal sails . . . . [But] what lies downwind from these four converging zephyrs? I believe the American economy will soon weigh anchor on a record-breaking economic expansion. . . .

Of course, no one can guarantee a safe voyage, for in economic affairs shifting winds can throw even the sturdiest economy off course. It is a safe bet that at some point over the next year, the Federal Reserve will divine inflationary squalls ahead and lean against the prevailing winds.

But for now we can postpone such gloomy thoughts and bask in Prosperity's smile. After a decade of turbulent economic weather we can thank our stars that fickle Fortune sometimes brings in boats that have no helmsman. [76]

> *"On the Eve of a Historic Economic Boom," New York Times, April 6, 1986, sec. 3, p. 5.*

Michael Oakeshott

In political activity, then, men sail a boundless and bottomless sea; there is neither harbor for shelter nor floor for anchorage, neither starting-place nor appointed destination. The enterprise is to keep afloat on an

even keel; the sea is both friend and enemy; and the seamanship consists in using the resources of a traditional manner of behavior in order to make a friend of every hostile occasion. [87]
   "Political Education," in Rationalism and Other Essays (New York: Basic Books, 1962), 127.

Charles Sanders Peirce
The problems which present themselves to such a mind [directed wholly to practical subjects] are matters of routine which he has learned once for all to handle in learning his business. But let a man venture into an unfamiliar field, or where his results are not continually checked by experience, and . . . he is like a ship on the open sea, with no one on board who understands the rules of navigation. [88]
   "The Fixation of Belief," 1877; in Selected Writings, ed. Philip P. Wiener (New York: Dover Publications, 1966), 97.

If we desire to rescue the good ship Philosophy for the service of Science from the hands of lawless rovers of the sea of literature, we shall do well to keep [the terms] prescind, preciss, precission, and precissive [apart from] precide, precise, precision, and precisive. [88]
   "Issues of Pragmaticism," 1905; ibid., 212.

Merrill Peterson
Jefferson, for all the freight of idealism, had always steered a close-reefed political craft. The voyage of the embargo was under full sail, and the helmsman's single-minded commitment to the principle, with the rational hope it embodied, obscured his view of the navigational hazards. . . . The result was drift. [78-79]
   Thomas Jefferson and the New Nation: A Biography (New York: Oxford Univ. Press, 1970), 918. Summarizing the embargo of 1807, which failed to bring England to terms and at the same time virtually destroyed American commerce.

Prairie as a Sea of Grass, see William Cullen Bryant, J. H. Buckingham, James Fenimore Cooper, Conrad Richter, and O. E. Rölvaag

Ronald Reagan, see also Alexander M. Haig, Jr., Wassily Leontief, and William Safire
We and our trading partners are in the same boat. If one partner shoots a hole in the bottom of the boat, does it make sense for the other partner to shoot another hole in the boat? . . . We must plug the holes in the boat

of open markets and free trade and set sail again in the direction of prosperity. No one should mistake our determination to use our full power to prevent anyone from destroying the boat and sinking us all. [76]

> *To the Annual Joint Meeting of the Board of Governors of the World Bank and the International Monetary Fund, Sept. 27, 1983; New York Times, Sept. 28, 1983, D27.*

Born in the safe harbor of freedom, economic growth gathered force and rolled out in a rising tide that has reached distant shores. [76]

> *To the Annual Joint Meeting of the Board of Governors of the World Bank and the International Monetary Fund, Sept. 25, 1984; New York Times, Sept. 26, 1984, D5.*

Conrad Richter
I saw a wave of antelope flowing inquisitively toward the buggy far ahead, a wave rusty as with kelp, rising and falling over the grassy swells and eventually turning in alarm, so that a thousand white rumps, whirled suddenly into view, were the breaking of that wide prairie wave on some unseen reef of this tossing upland sea. [74n]

> *The Sea of Grass (New York: Alfred A. Knopf, 1936), 48.*

David Rockefeller
[Certain factors and actions] enabled most LDCs [Less-Developed Countries] to weather these earlier rough waters fairly handily.

For the ships of most less-developed states, the 1974-75 period was one of rising economic seas and gusting financial winds; for good seafarers in the international economic seas, there was challenge—but no threat.

The seascape facing these same nations in the days ahead, however, is markedly different—and rather more threatening. What we see ahead are treacherous economic seas and gale-force financial winds, strong enough to capsize even large and well-manned ships—unless sails are reefed early, and all hands are ready at their stations when the gale hits. [76]

> *"Rough Seas Ahead: The LDCs and the Credit Squeeze," address to the Chase Econometrics Luncheon, New York City, Jan. 10, 1980, 6.*

O. E. Rölvaag
It was late afternoon. A small caravan was pushing its way through the tall grass. The track that it left behind was like the wake of a boat—except that instead of widening out astern it closed in again. [73]

> *Giants in the Earth (New York: Harper & Brothers, 1927), 3.* Norwegian immigrants to the Great Plains hold on to their seafaring past.

The boat that he steered [a wagon pulled by oxen] was behaving very badly; it wouldn't answer to the helm; it didn't ride the swell like a sea-worthy craft; it had no speed or power to lift itself over the rough waves. . . . Per Hansa felt as if he were sliding down one huge wave after another; the boat was scudding now with terrific speed! [73]
> *Ibid., 269-70.*

Franklin D. Roosevelt [about]

He was captain of the ship of state, but many hands reached for the tiller, and a rebellious crew manned the sails. It was only natural that this vessel should move ahead by hugging the shore, threading its way past shoal and reef, putting into harbor when the storm roared. [76]
> *James MacGregor Burns, Roosevelt: The Lion and the Fox (New York: Harcourt, Brace, & World, 1956), 401.* For an opposite view of FDR, see Learned Hand to Felix Frankfurtrer, July 23, 1933.

William Safire

In our last gloom-and-doom installment, Captain Reagan was at the bridge, smiling amiably into the fog, as the ship of state headed straight for the iceberg of a second-term, trillion-dollar deficit. [76]
> *"The Iceberg Cometh," New York Times, Aug. 11, 1985, E25.*

Paul Sifton

[In civil rights] neither the Congress nor the executive branch has taken the lead or even acted to implement the pioneering work of the courts, usually looked upon as the keel, rudder, and sea anchor of our system of government. Lacking sail or propeller, the courts, though unaided by the other two branches of Government, have managed to hold a steady forward course in the great currents of change that sweep the world. [77]
> *Hearings before Subcommittee No. 5, Committee on the Judiciary, House of Representatives, March 12, 1959, 86th Cong., 1st Sess., 392.* Testifying for the United Auto Workers on behalf of civil rights legislation.

Spirituals [representative lines]

Deep river, my home is over Jordan.

I wanter go to heav'n when I die, to hear ol' Jordan roll.

O, de river of Jordan is so wide. One more river to cross.

Hallelujah, Lord! I been down into the sea.

De ol' ark she reel, de ol' ark she rock, d'ol' ark she landed on the mountain top. O, de ol' ark's a-moverin, an' I'm goin' home.

My ship is on de ocean, Po' sinner, fare you well. [62n]
> *James Weldon Johnson and J. Rosamond Johnson, The Books of American Negro Spirituals (New York: Da Capo, 1969; orig. 1925, 1926), I:100, I:104, I:152, I:172, II:25, II:150.*

Peleg Sprague

But when the storm rages, and all feel that they are embarked together upon the waves—then, when the timid quail, and the feeble tremble, and the short-sighted are confounded—none but the strong hand, and the firm heart, and the unblenched eye, can hold the helm and direct the course. [57-58]
> *"Eulogy to Thomas Jefferson and John Adams at Hallowell, Maine, July 1826," in A Selection of Eulogies, 147. Sprague was a Congressman from Maine.*

James Stephen, see William James

Edward R. Stettinius, Jr.

The ship whose keel was laid at Dumbarton Oaks and launched at San Francisco has put to sea—fully equipped and manned. [76]
> *Communication to President Truman, May 31, 1946; Dept. of State Bulletin, June 9, 1946, 989.* The U.S. representative to the United Nations on the recently established international organization.

Henry David Thoreau

In the midst of this chopping sea of civilized life, such are the clouds and storms and quicksands and thousand-and-one items to be allowed for, that a man has to live, if he would not founder and go to the bottom and not make his port at all, by dead reckoning, and he must be a great calculator indeed who succeeds.
> *Walden, ed. J. Lyndon Shanley (Princeton: Princeton Univ. Press, 1971), 91 ("Where I Lived and What I Lived For").*

I had withdrawn so far within the great ocean of solitude, into which the rivers of society empty, that for the most part, so far as my needs were concerned, only the finest sediment was deposited around me. Beside, there were wafted to me evidences of unexplored and uncultivated continents on the other side. [68]
> *Ibid., 144 ("Visitors").*

It was very pleasant, when I staid late in town, to launch myself into the night, especially if it was dark and tempestuous, and set sail from some bright village parlor or lecture room, with a bag of rye or Indian meal upon my shoulder, for my snug harbor in the woods, having made all tight without and withdrawn under hatches with a merry crew of thoughts, leaving only my outer man at the helm when it was plain sailing. I had many a genial thought by the cabin fire "as I sailed." I was never cast away nor distressed in any weather, though I encountered some severe storms. [68]

    Ibid., 169 ("The Village").

What I have observed of the pond is no less true in ethics. It is the law of average. . . . [D]raw lines through the length and breadth of the aggregate of a man's particular daily behaviors and waves of life into his coves and inlets, and where they intersect will be the height or depth of his character. Perhaps we need only to know how his shores trend and his adjacent country or circumstances, to infer his depth and concealed bottom. If he is surrounded by mountainous circumstances, an Achillean shore, whose peaks overshadow and are reflected in his bosom, they suggest a corresponding depth in him. But a low and smooth shore proves him shallow on that side. In our bodies, a bold projecting brow falls off to and indicates a corresponding depth of thought. Also there is a bar across the entrance of our every cove, or particular inclination; each is our harbor for a season, in which we are detained and partially land-locked. These inclinations are not whimsical usually, but their form, size, and direction are determined by promontories of the shore, and ancient axes of elevation. When this bar is gradually increased by storms, tides, or currents, or there is a subsidence of the waters, so that it reaches to the surface, that which was at first but an inclination in the shore in which a thought was harbored becomes an individual lake, cut off from the ocean, wherein the thought secures its own conditions, changes, perhaps, from salt to fresh, becomes a sweet sea, dead sea, or a marsh. At the advent of each individual into this life, may we not suppose that such a bar has risen to the surface somewhere? It is true, we are such navigators that our thoughts, for the most part, stand off and on upon a harborless coast, are conversant only with the bights of the bays of poesy, or steer for the public ports of entry, and go into the dry docks of science, where they merely refit for this world, and no natural currents concur to individualize them. [68]

    Ibid., 291-92 ("The Pond in Winter").

Yet we should oftener look over the tafferel of our craft, like curious passengers, and not make the voyage like stupid sailors picking oakum. The other side of the globe is but the home of our correspondent. Our voyaging is only great-circle sailing, and the doctors prescribe for diseases of the skin merely. . . . What was the meaning of that South-Sea Exploring Expedition, with all its parade and expense, but an indirect recognition of the fact, that there are continents and seas in the moral world, to which every man is an isthmus or an inlet, yet unexplored by him, but that it is easier to sail many thousand miles through cold and storm and cannibals, in a government ship, with five hundred men and boys to assist one, than it is to explore the private sea, the Atlantic and Pacific Ocean of one's being alone. . . . England and France, Spain and Portugal, Gold Coast and Slave Coast, all front on this private sea; but no bark from them has ventured out of sight of land, though it is without doubt the direct way to India.

Ibid., 320-22 ("Conclusion").

Alexis de Tocqueville
The federal judges . . . must know how to understand the spirit of the age, to confront those obstacles that can be overcome, and to steer out of the current when the tide threatens to carry them away. [66]

Democracy in America (1835), vol. I, pt. I, chap. 8, "The Federal Constitution," trans. George Lawrence (New York: Harper & Row, 1966), 150-51.

A lawgiver is like a man steering his route over the sea. He, too, can control the ship that bears him, but he cannot change its structure, create winds, or prevent the ocean stirring beneath him. [66]

Ibid., 163.

Harry S. Truman
You will remember that Saint Paul, the Apostle of the Gentiles, and his companions, suffering shipwreck, "cast four anchors out of the stern and wished for the day." Happily for us, whenever the American Ship of State has been storm-tossed we have always had an anchor to the windward.

We are met on the South Lawn of the White House. The setting is a reminder of Saint Paul's four anchors. To one side is the . . . Washington Monument—fit symbol of our first anchor. On the opposite end of Potomac Park is the memorial to another of the anchors which we see when we look astern of the Ship of State—Abraham Lincoln. . . . Between them is the memorial to Thomas Jefferson, the anchor of democracy. On the other side of the White House, in bronze, rides Andrew Jackson—the fourth of our anchors. [76]

Address at the Lighting of the National Community Christmas Tree, Dec. 24, 1945; Public Papers of the Presidents of the United States: Harry S. Truman

(Washington, D.C.: Government Printing Office, 1961), 1:584-85. In a lay sermon not long after the end of World War II, President Truman vivifies a phrase from Acts 27:29.

United States Supreme Court, see also William J. Brennan, Jr., and William O. Douglas

Miranda's opponents . . . should have expected heavy waters but can be excused for not having anticipated the shoals on which the statute foundered and ultimately sunk.
Linda Greenhouse, New York Times, June 27, 2000, A20. The Supreme Court holds unconstitutional a section of a 1968 law that sought to overturn Miranda v. Arizona (1964).

Safe Harbor.
A quasi-technical term prominent in judicial proceedings surrounding the November 2000 presidential vote in Florida. It refers to a provision in federal law that protects states—providing them a "safe harbor"—against challenges in Congress to presidential electors chosen according to state rules that are in place before election day. See "Legal fog around safe harbor," *New York Times*, Dec. 12, 2000, A23.

John Updike
Writing criticism is to writing fiction and poetry as hugging the shore is to sailing in the open sea. At sea, we have that beautiful blankness all around, a cold bright wind, and the occasional thrill of a gleaming dolphin-back or the synchronized leap of silverfish; hugging the shore, one can always come about and draw even closer to land with another nine-point quotation. [76]
Hugging the Shore: Essays and Criticism (New York: Alfred A. Knopf), 1983, xv.

Gore Vidal
"The ship of state is in the open sea at last," said Hay. "Ship is the right image," said Lodge, somewhat grimly. "And I've just spent a month in the engine room."
Hay completed the nautical image. "Let's hope the barometer's not falling, now that we're on the high seas."
"So I'll keep killing Capitoline geese until I find one whose liver predicts good sailing weather."
"Let us say the ships are afloat, and the legions are fighting on the Asian marches."

"Ave Caesar!" Lodge laughed.

"Hail McKinley." Hay smiled in the icy darkness. "Pacific lord of the Pacific Ocean." [75n]

  Empire (New York: Random House, 1987), 115-16 (ellipses omitted).

Lech Walesa

Can you fully democratically steer a ship through a stormy sea? [77]

  Quoted by Timothy Garten Ash in " 'Refolution' in Hungary and Poland," New York Review, Aug. 17, 1989, 10.

Booker T. Washington

A ship lost at sea for many days suddenly sighted a friendly vessel. From the mast of the unfortunate vessel was seen a signal, "Water, water; we die of thirst!" The answer from the friendly vessel at once came back, "Cast down your bucket where you are." A second time the signal, "Water, water; send us water!" ran up from the distressed vessel, and was answered, "Cast down your bucket where you are." The captain of the distressed vessel, at last heeding the injunction, cast down his bucket, and it came up full of fresh, sparkling water from the mouth of the Amazon River. To those of my race who depend on bettering their condition in a foreign land or who underestimate the importance of cultivating friendly relations with the Southern white man, who is their next-door neighbour, I would say: "Cast down your bucket where you are"—cast it down in making friends in every manly way of the people of all races by whom we are surrounded. [75n]

  Atlanta Exposition Address, Sept. 18, 1895; in Leslie H. Fishel, Jr. and Benjamin Quarles, The Negro American: A Documentary History (Glenview, Ill.: Scott, Foresman, 1967), 342-43. Washington holds out prosperity for Negroes who labor in southern fields and factories and cause no trouble.

Daniel Webster

Like the mariner, whom the currents of the ocean and the winds carry along till he sees the stars which have directed his course and lighted his pathless way descended, one by one, beneath the rising horizon, we should have felt that the stream of time had borne us onward till another great luminary, whose light had cheered us and whose guidance we had followed, had sunk away from our sight. [58]

  "A Discourse in Commemoration of the Lives and Services of John Adams and Thomas Jefferson, Delivered in Faneuil Hall, Boston, on the 2nd of

August, 1826," in The Bunker Hill Monument; Adams and Jefferson. Two
Orations (Houghton Mifflin: Riverside Literature Series, 1893), 40.

When the mariner has been tossed for many days in thick weather, and
on an unknown sea, he naturally avails himself of the first pause in the
storm, the earliest glance of the sun, to take his latitude, and ascertain
how far the elements have driven him off his true course.

From "Second Reply to Hayne," Jan. 26-27, 1830; in Paul D. Erickson,
The Poetry of Events: Daniel Webster's Rhetoric of the Constitution and
Union (New York: New York Univ. Press, 1986), 98.

We may be tossed upon an ocean where we can see no land—nor,
perhaps, the sun or stars. But there is a chart, and a compass for us to
study, to consult, and to obey. That chart is the Constitution.

"The Mexican War," speech at Springfield, Mass.; Sept. 29, 1847; The
Writings and Speeches of Daniel Webster Hitherto Uncollected (Boston:
Little, Brown, 1903), 1:365.

The imprisoned winds are let loose. The East, the North, and the stormy
South combine to throw the whole sea into commotion, to toss its billows to
the skies, and disclose its profoundest depths. I do not affect to regard
myself, Mr. President, as holding, or as fit to hold, the helm in this combat
with the political elements; but I have a duty to perform, and I mean to
perform it with fidelity. . . . I have a part to act, not for my own security or
safety, for I am looking out for no fragment upon which to float away from
the wreck, if wreck there must be, but for the good of the whole and the
preservation of all; and there is that which will keep me to my duty during
this struggle, whether the sun and stars shall appear, or shall not appear for
many days. I speak today for the preservation of the Union. [59-60]

"The Constitution and Union" ("Seventh of March" speech), to the U.S.
Senate, March 7, 1850; in Erickson, 120. Cf. Homer, Odyssey, V.291-96.

New England is a ship, staunch, strong, well built, and particularly well
manned. She may be occasionally thrown into the trough of the sea by
the violence of winds and waves, and may wallow there for a time; but,
depend on it, she will right herself. She will ere long come round to the
wind, and obey her helm.

At the Pilgrim Festival, New York, Dec. 22, 1850; in The Writings and
Speeches of Daniel Webster: Speeches on Various Occasions (Boston:
Little, Brown, 1903), 4:223.

Dixon Wecter

Jefferson the man was easy to know, but impossible to know well. Many called him "a trimmer." Sometimes it appeared that he steered a circuitous course, catching the prevailing winds as he went along, to reach in the end a wholly honorable port. [79n]

> *The Hero in America: A Chronicle of Hero-Worship (New York: Charles Scribner's Sons, 1941), 170.*

Walter White

All the peoples of the world are in the same boat now. Today that vessel is unseaworthy because we have not yet mastered the science of living together. Through a major leak caused by color prejudice the waters of hate are rushing in. Our survival may depend on how swiftly and expertly that leak is caulked. [76]

> *How Far the Promised Land? (New York: Viking, 1955), 28. White was executive director of the NAACP.*

Walt Whitman

O Captain! my Captain! our fearful trip is done,
The ship has weather'd every rack, the prize we sought is won,
The port is near, the bells I hear, the people all exulting,
While follow eyes the steady keel, the vessel grim and daring;
But O heart! heart! heart!
O the bleeding drops of red,
Where on the deck my Captain lies,
Fallen cold and dead.

O Captain! my Captain! rise up and hear the bells;
Rise up—for you the flag is flung—for you the bugle trills,
For you bouquets and ribbon'd wreaths—for you the shores a-crowding,
For you they call, the swaying mass, their eager faces turning;
Here Captain! dear father!
This arm beneath your head!
It is some dream that on the deck,
You've fallen cold and dead.

My Captain does not answer, his lips are pale and still,
My father does not feel my arm, he has no pulse nor will,

The ship is anchor'd safe and sound, its voyage closed and done,
From fearful trip the victor ship comes in with object won;
  Exult O shores, and ring O bells!
   But I with mournful tread,
    Walk the deck my Captain lies,
     Fallen cold and dead. [65]
    "O Captain! My Captain!" in Leaves of Grass: The Collected Writings of
    Walt Whitman, ed. Harold W. Blodgett and Sculley Bradley (New York:
    New York Univ. Press, 1965), 337-38.

Woodrow Wilson

Political liberty consists in the best practicable adjustment between the power of the government and the privilege of the individual; and the freedom to alter the adjustment is as important as the adjustment itself for the ease and progress of affairs and the contentment of the citizen.

There are many analogies by which it is possible to illustrate the idea, if it needs illustration. We say of a boat skimming the water with light foot, "How free she runs," when we mean, how perfectly she is adjusted to the force of the wind, how perfectly she obeys the great breath out of the heavens that fills her sails. Throw her head up into the wind and see how she will halt and stagger, how every sheet will shiver and her whole frame be shaken, how instantly she is "in irons," in the expressive phrase of the sea. She is free only when you have let her fall off again and get once more her nice adjustment to the forces she must obey and cannot defy. [75]
    Constitutional Government in the United States (New York: Columbia
    Univ. Press, 1908), 5. "Being in irons" is the embarrassing situation of a
    boat that begins to move backwards because the steersman has been
    unable successfully to tack (move upwind in the desired direction by
    steering first to the right and then to the left, etc.). "We say of a boat
    skimming the water with light foot" may be Wilson's creation, perhaps
    drawn from ballroom dancing. It does not appear to derive from the
    language of sailing. I am indebted to Roger J. Faber for this information
    and conjecture.

William Wirt

They felt that they were Apostles of human liberty [and] rested not until they had . . . given such an impulse to the great ocean of mind, that they saw the waves rolling on the farthest shore, before they were called to their reward. [58]

> *"Eulogy on Thomas Jefferson and John Adams," Washington, D.C., Oct. 19, 1826, in the chamber of the House of Representatives; in A Selection of Eulogies Pronounced in the Several States, in Honor of Those Illustrious Patriots and Statesmen, John Adams and Thomas Jefferson (Hartford, 1826), 382; an incomplete but more accessible printing is LB.XIII.ix-lvii.* Wirt (1772-1834) was a close friend of Jefferson's and an acquaintance of Adams. He was also a novelist, a biographer of Patrick Henry, a renowned orator, a constitutional lawyer, and the longest-serving attorney general in American history, 1817-1829.

[During the seventeenth century] Massachusetts had been buffeting with the storm. Virginia, resting on a halcyon sea, had been cultivating the graces of science and literature. [57]

> *Ibid., 394; also LB.XIII.x.*

Together, and stroke for stroke, [the two states] breasted the angry surge [against Independence], and threw it aside . . . until they reached that shore from which we now look back with so much pride and triumph. [57]

> *Ibid., 399.*

The objections of [Adams's] adversaries were seen no longer but in a state of wreck; floating, in broken fragments, on the billows of the storm; and over rocks, over breakers, and amid ingulfing whirlpools, that everywhere surrounded him, he brought the gallant ship of the nation safe into port.

> *Ibid., 405; also LB.XIII.xxv.*

[On assuming the presidency, Jefferson] had the good fortune to find, or to make a smoother sea. The violence of the party storm gradually abated, and he was soon able to pursue his peaceful course without any material interruption. . . . Mr. Jefferson continued at the helm for eight years. [57]

> *Ibid., 414, 415; also LB.XIII.xxxviii, xxxix.*

William Butler Yeats, see Isaac Newton, Appendix III.A.

ACKNOWLEDGMENTS

MY DEEPEST ACKNOWLEDGEMENT for this study is to the Swarthmore College honors program of the 1950s. It was in that program, with its unmatched freedom to learn, that I was inspired by Felix Frankfurter's definition of research: "the systematic indulgence of one's curiosity." Applied to my curiosity about Jefferson's nautical metaphors, that indulgence has been enabled by editors and scholars, philosophers and poets—the systematizers whose names appear throughout the book.

A fellowship at the International Center for Jefferson Studies at Monticello allowed convenient access to the University of Virginia libraries. Through its generous interlibrary loan policy, Eastern Mennonite University added access to another dozen libraries. David E. Graybill provided skillful editing and indispensable technical aid. Friends and relatives supported the project along the way: Lucia Stanton, senior research historian at Monticello; Michael A. Miller and Arthur Zilversmit, critical readers of the manuscript; David H. Porter, my model humanist for more than forty years; and Barbara P. Brennan, who supports so many things in my life.

SELECT BIBLIOGRAPHY

Abrams, M. H. *The Mirror and the Lamp: Romantic Theory and the Critical Tradition.* New York: Oxford Univ. Press, 1953.

Adams, David. "Metaphors for Mankind: The Development of Hans Blumenberg's Anthropological Metamorphology." *Jnl. of the History of Ideas* 52 (Jan. 1991):152-66.

Adams, Henry. *The Education of Henry Adams.* Boston: Houghton Mifflin, 1918.

Adams, John Quincy. *Lectures on Rhetoric and Oratory.* 1810. Repr. New York: Russell & Russell, 1962.

Adams, Richard P. "Emerson and the Organic Metaphor." In *Interpretations of American Literature*, ed. Charles Feidelson, Jr. and Paul Brodtkorb, Jr. New York: Oxford Univ. Press, 1959, 137-52.

Addison, Joseph. *The Spectator,* No. 595, Sept. 17, 1714. In *The Spectator*, ed. Gregory Smith. London, 1907, 4:361-62.

Arendt, Hannah. *The Life of the Mind; Vol. I: Thinking.* New York: Harcourt Brace Jovanovich, 1978, pp. 98-125.

Arthos, John. "Figures of Speech." In *Princeton Encyclopedia of Poetry and Poetics.* Princeton: Princeton Univ. Press, 1965.

Auden, W. H. *The Enchafèd Flood, Or the Romantic Iconography of the Sea.* New York: Random House, 1950.

Baym, Nina. "From Metaphysics to Metaphor: The Image of Water in Emerson and Thoreau." *Studies in Romanticism* 5 (1966): 231-43.

Beardsley, Monroe C. "Metaphor." *Encyclopedia of Philosophy.* New York: Macmillan, 1967. 5:284-89.

Beller, Manfred. "Staatschiff und Schiff des Lebens als Gleichnisse der barocken Geschichtsdichtung." *Arcadia* 15 (1980): 1-13.

Bender, Bert. *Sea-Brothers: The Tradition of American Sea Fiction from Moby-Dick to the Present.* Philadelphia: Univ. of Pennsylvania Press, 1988.

Berman, Eleanor Davidson. *Thomas Jefferson among the Arts: An Essay in Early American Esthetics.* New York: Philosophical Library, 1947.

Berman, Eleanor Davidson, and E. C. McClintock, Jr. "Thomas Jefferson and Rhetoric." *Qtly. Jnl. of Speech* 33 (Feb. 1947):1-8.

Berry, Christopher J. "Eighteenth-Century Approaches to the Origin of Metaphor." *Neuphilologische Mitteilungen* 74 (1973):690-713.

Black, Max. "More About Metaphor." In *Metaphor and Thought,* ed. Andrew Ortony. Cambridge: Cambridge Univ. Press, 1979, 19-43.

Blair, Hugh. *Lectures on Rhetoric and Belles Lettres.* New York, 1833.

Blumenberg, Hans. *Shipwreck with Spectator: Paradigm of a Metaphor for Existence.* 1979. Trans. Steven Rendall. Cambridge, Mass.: MIT Press, 1997.

Bokenkamp, Stephen R. "Chinese Metaphor Again: Reading—and Understanding—Imagery in the Chinese Poetic Tradition." *Jnl. of the American Oriental Society* 109 (1989):211-21.

Bonner, Willard C. *Harp on the Shore: Thoreau and the Sea.* Albany: SUNY Press, 1985.

Boyd, Julian P., et al., eds. *The Papers of Thomas Jefferson.* 28 vols. to date. Princeton: Princeton Univ. Press, 1950- .

Brooks, Cleanth, and Robert Penn Warren. *Fundamentals of Good Writing* ("Metaphor," 361-89). New York: Harcourt Brace, 1950.

Brown, Stephen J. *The World of Imagery: Metaphor and Kindred Imagery.* 1927. Repr. New York: Russell and Russell, 1966.

Bullitt, John, and W. Jackson Bate. "The Distinctions between Fancy and Imagination in Eighteenth-Century English Criticism." *Modern Language Notes* 60 (1945): 8-15.

Burke, Edmund. *A Philosophical Enquiry into the Origin of our Ideas of the Sublime and Beautiful.* 1756. Ed. J. T. Boulton. London: Routledge and Kegan Paul, 1958.

Burstein, Andrew. *The Inner Jefferson: Portrait of a Grieving Optimist.* Charlottesville: Univ. Press of Virginia, 1995.

Campanile, Enrico. "Indo-European Metaphors and Non-Indo-European Metaphors." *Jnl. of Indo-European Studies* 2 (Fall 1974):247-58.

Cantor, Paul. "Friedrich Nietzsche: The Use and Abuse of Metaphor." In David Miall, ed., *Metaphor: Problems and Perspectives.* Brighton: Harvester Press, 1982, 71-88.

Cartwright, Nancy, et al. *Otto Neurath: Philosophy Between Science and Politics.* Cambridge: Cambridge Univ. Press, 1996.

Chilton, Paul. *Security Metaphors: Cold War Discourse from Containment to Common House.* New York: Peter Lang, 1996.

Clark, S. H. " 'The Whole Internal World his Own': Locke and Metaphor Reconsidered." *Jnl. of the History of Ideas,* 59 (April 1998):241-65.

Coetzee, J. M. "Newton and the Ideal of a Transparent Scientific Language." *Jnl. of Literary Semantics* 11 (1982):3-13.

Cohen, Felix S., "Transcendental Nonsense and the Functional Approach," in Lucy Kramer Cohen, ed., *The Legal Conscience: Selected Papers of Felix S. Cohen* (New Haven: Yale Univ. Press, 1960), 33-76 (orig. 1935).

Conkin, Paul K. "The Religious Pilgrimage of Thomas Jefferson." In *Jeffersonian Legacies,* ed. Peter S. Onuf. Charlottesville: Univ. Press of Virginia, 1993, pp. 19-49.

Dallmayr, Fred R. *Language and Politics—Why Does Language Matter to Political Philosophy?* Notre Dame: Univ. of Notre Dame Press, 1983.

Davis, David Brion, and Steven Mintz, eds. *The Boisterous Sea of Liberty: A Documentary History of America from Discovery Through the Civil War.* New York: Oxford Univ. Press, 1998.

Dawidoff, Robert. "Man of Letters." In *Thomas Jefferson: A Reference Biography,* ed. Merrill Peterson. New York: Scribner, 1986, 181-98.

de Baecque, Antoine. *The Body Politic: Corporeal Metaphor in Revolutionary France, 1770-1800.* Trans. Charlotte Mandell. Palo Alto: Stanford Univ. Press, 1997.

de Grazia, Emilio. "The Great Plain: Rölvaag's New World Sea." In *Literature and Love of the Sea,* ed. Patricia Carlson. Amsterdam: Rodopi, 1986, 244-55.

Dreistadt, Roy. "An Analysis of the Use of Analogies and Metaphors in Science." *Jnl. of Psychology* 68 (Jan. 1968):97-116.

Drucker, H. M. "Just Analogies?: The Place of Analogies in Political Thinking." *Political Studies* 18 (1970):448-60.

Eco, Umberto. "The Scandal of Metaphor. Metaphorology and Semiotics." *Poetics Today* (Tel Aviv) 4 (1984):217-57.

Edwards, Philip. *Sea-Mark: The Metaphorical Voyage, Spenser to Milton.* Liverpool: Liverpool Univ. Press, 1997.

_____. *The Story of the Voyage: Sea Narratives in Eighteenth-Century English Literature.* Cambridge: Cambridge Univ. Press, 1994.

Erickson, Paul D. *The Poetry of Events: Daniel Webster's Rhetoric of the Constitution and Union.* New York: Columbia Univ. Press, 1987.

Eubanks, Philip. *A War of Words in the Discourse of Trade: The Rhetorical Constitution of Metaphor.* Carbondale: Southern Illinois Univ. Press, 2000.

Fenollosa, Ernest. "The Chinese Written Character as a Medium for Poetry." In Ezra Pound, *The Instigations of Ezra Pound, Together with an Essay on the Chinese Written Character.* New York: Boni & Liveright, 1920, 357-88.

Ferguson, Robert A. " 'With What Majesty Do We There Ride above the Storms!' Jefferson at Monticello." *Virginia Qtly. Rev.* 74 (Autumn 1998):581-96.

Fernandez, James W., ed. *Beyond Metaphor: The Theory of Tropes in Anthropology.* Palo Alto: Stanford Univ. Press, 1991.

Fitzosborne, Sir Thomas [pseud. William Melmoth]. *Letters on Several Subjects,* Letter LI. London, 1749. Repr. New York: Garland Publishing, 1971.

Foley, John P., ed. *The Jefferson Cyclopedia: A Comprehensive Collection of the Views of Thomas Jefferson, Classified and Arranged in Alphabetical Order under Nine Thousand Titles.* New York: Funk and Wagnalls, 1900.

Follett, Wilson. *Modern American Usage: A Guide.* New York: Hill and Wang, 1966 ("Metaphor," 226-30).

Ford, Paul Leicester, ed. *The Works of Thomas Jefferson* (Federal Edition). 12 vols. New York: G. P. Putnam's Sons, 1904-05.

Fowler, H. W. *A Dictionary of Modern English Usage.* Oxford: Oxford Univ. Press, 1926 ("Metaphor," 348-52).

Frost, Robert. "Education by Poetry: A Meditative Monologue." 1930. In *Collected Poems, Prose, and Plays.* New York: Library of America, 1995, 717-28.

Frye, Northrop. *Anatomy of Criticism: Four Essays.* Princeton: Princeton Univ. Press, 1957.

Fussell, Paul. *The Rhetorical World of Augustan Humanism: Ethics and Imagery from Swift to Burke.* Oxford: Oxford Univ. Press, 1965.

Gerschenkron, Alexander. "Figures of Speech in Social Sciences." *Proceedings of the American Philosophical Society* 118 (1974):431-48.

Gibbs, Raymond W., Jr. *The Poetics of Mind: Figurative Thought, Language, and Understanding.* New York: Cambridge Univ. Press, 1994.

Gilbert, Allan H. *Literary Criticism: Plato to Dryden.* New York: American Book Company, 1940.

Gill, Jerry H. *Wittgenstein and Metaphor* (new and rev. ed.). Atlantic Highlands, N.J.: Humanities Press, 1996.

Goatly, Andrew. *The Language of Metaphors*. London: Routledge, 1997.

Goheen, Robert F. *The Imagery of Sophocles' "Antigone": A Study of Poetic Language and Structure*. Princeton: Princeton Univ. Press, 1951.

Gould, Stephen Jay. *Time's Arrow, Time's Cycle: Myth and Metaphor in the Discovery of Geological Time*. Cambridge: Harvard Univ. Press, 1987.

Gozzi, Raymond, Jr. "Metaphor by the Seashore." *Etc.: A Review of General Semantics* 54 (Fall 1997):348-52.

Hawkes, Terence. *Metaphor*. London: Methuen, 1972.

Hoenigswald, Henry M., and Linda F. Wiener, eds. *Biological Metaphor and Cladistic Classification: An Interdisciplinary Perspective*. Philadelphia: Univ. of Pennsylvania Press, 1987.

Hollinger, David A. "T. S. Kuhn's Theory of Science and Its Implications for History." 1973. In *In The American Province: Studies in the History and Historiography of Ideas*. Bloomington: Indiana Univ. Press, 1985, 105-29.

Home, Henry (Lord Kames). *Elements of Criticism*. 2 vols. 1785 ed. Repr. New York: Garland Publishing, 1972.

Howell, Samuel. *Logic and Rhetoric in England, 1500-1700*. Princeton: Princeton Univ. Press, 1956.

Hume, David. "Of the Standard of Taste." 1742. In *Essays: Moral, Political and Literary,* ed. Eugene F. Miller. Indianapolis: Liberty Classics, 1985, pp. 226-49.

James, William. *Principles of Psychology.* 1890. In *Great Books of the Western World*, ed. Mortimer J. Adler. Chicago: Encyclopedia Britannica, 1952.

Jefferson, Thomas. *Notes on the State of Virginia,* ed. William Peden. Chapel Hill: Univ. of North Carolina Press, 1954.

Jenks, Edward. *The Ship of State: The Essentials of Political Science*. London: Duckworth, 1949.

Johnson, Nan. *Nineteenth-Century Rhetoric in North America*. Carbondale: Southern Illinois Univ. Press, 1991.

Jones, Roger S. *Physics as Metaphor*. Minneapolis: Univ. of Minnesota Press, 1982.

Kammen, Michael. *A Machine that Would Go of Itself: The Constitution in American Culture*. New York: Knopf, 1986.

Kofman, Sarah. *Nietzsche and Metaphor*. 2nd ed., 1983. Trans. Duncan Large. Palo Alto: Stanford Univ. Press, 1993.

Kolodny, Annette. *The Lay of the Land: Metaphor as Experience and History in American Life and Letters*. Chapel Hill: Univ. of North Carolina Press, 1975.

Krahé, Peter. " 'Sir Christopher Wren Had Made Everything Shipshape': Schiffsmetaphorik und historische Bezüge in MacNeices 'Homage to Wren.' " *Sprachkunst: Beiträge zur Literaturwissenschaft* 16 (1985): 66-73.

Kuhn, Thomas S. *The Structure of Scientific Revolutions*. Chicago: Univ. of Chicago Press, 1962.

Lai, Whalen. "Ch'an Metaphors: Waves, Water, Mirror, Lamp." *Philosophy East and West* 29 (July 1979):243-53.

Lakoff, George, and Mark Johnson. *Metaphors We Live By*. Chicago: Univ. of Chicago Press, 1980.

Leary, David E. "Psyche's Muse: The Role of Metaphor in the History of Psychology." In Leary, ed., *Metaphors in the History of Psychology*. Cambridge: Cambridge Univ. Press, 1990, 1-78.

Leatherdale, W. H. *The Role of Analogy, Model and Metaphor in Science*. Amsterdam: North Holland Publishing, 1974.

Leetz, Kenneth L. "Abraham Lincoln, Psychotherapist to the Nation: The Use of Metaphors." *American Jnl. of Psychotherapy* 51 (Winter 1997):45-53.

Lehmann, Karl. *Thomas Jefferson: American Humanist*. New York: Macmillan, 1947.

Lewis, Jan. " 'The Blessings of Domestic Society': Thomas Jefferson's Family and the Transformation of American Politics." In *Jeffersonian Legacies*, ed. Peter S. Onuf. Charlottesville: Univ. Press of Virginia, 1993, 109-46.

Lewis, Jan, and Peter S. Onuf. "American Synecdoche: Thomas Jefferson as Image, Icon, Character, and Self." *American Historical Rev.* 103 (Feb. 1998):125-36.

[Library of Congress]. *Thomas Jefferson: Genius of Liberty*. Washington: Library of Congress, 2000.

Lipscomb, Andrew A., and Albert Ellery Bergh, eds. *The Writings of Thomas Jefferson, Memorial Edition*. 20 vols. Washington, 1904.

Love, Walter D. "Edmund Burke's Idea of the Body Corporate: A Study in Imagery." *Rev. of Politics* 27 (April 1965):184-97.

McPherson, James M. "How Lincoln Won the War with Metaphors." In

Abraham Lincoln and the Second American Revolution. New York: Oxford Univ. Press, 1990, 93-112.

Malone, Dumas. *Jefferson and His Time.* 6 vols. Boston: Little, Brown, 1948-1981.

Martin, Wallace. "Metaphor." In *The New Princeton Encyclopedia of Poetry and Poetics.* Princeton: Princeton Univ. Press, 1993.

Mazzeo, Joseph Anthony. "Notes on John Donne's Alchemical Imagery." *Isis* 48 (June 1957):103-23.

Miller, Charles A. *Jefferson and Nature: An Interpretation.* Baltimore: Johns Hopkins Univ. Press, 1988.

Miller, Eugene F. "Metaphor and Political Knowledge." *American Political Science Rev.* 73 (March 1979):155-70.

Mindel, Joseph. "Uses of Metaphor: Henry Adams and the Symbols of Science." *Jnl. of the History of Ideas* 26 (Jan.1965):89-102.

Mio, Jeffrey Scott, and Albert N. Katz, eds. *Metaphor: Implications and Applications.* Mahwah, N.J.: Erlbaum, 1996.

Moran, Michael G., ed. *Eighteenth-Century British and American Rhetorics and Rhetoricians: Critical Studies and Sources.* Westport, Conn.: Greenwood Press, 1994.

Murry, John Middleton. "Metaphor" (1927). In *John Clare and Other Studies.* New York: Peter Nevill, 1950, pp. 85-97.

Nicolson, Marjorie Hope. *The Breaking of the Circle: Studies in the Effect of the 'New Science' upon 17th Century Poetry.* Rev. ed. New York: Columbia Univ. Press, 1960.

Nietzsche, Friedrich. "On Truth and Lies in a Nonmoral Sense." In Daniel Breazeale, ed. and trans. *Philosophy and Truth: Selections from Nietzsche's Notebooks of the Early 1870's.* Atlantic Highlands, N.J.: Humanities Press, 1979, 79-97.

Noonan, John T., Jr. *Persons and Masks of the Law: Cardozo, Holmes, Jefferson and Wythe as Makers of the Masks.* New York: Farrar, Straus and Giroux, 1976.

Nuyen, A. T. "The Kantian Theory of Metaphor," *Philosophy and Rhetoric* 22(2) (1989):95-109.

Ozick, Cynthia. "The Moral Necessity of Metaphor: Rooting History in a Figure of Speech." *Harper's,* May 1986, 62-68.

Passage, Charles E. *The Complete Works of Horace.* New York: Frederick Ungar, 1983.

Peil, Detmar. " 'Im selben Boot': Variationen über ein metaphorisches Argument." *Archiv für Kulturgeschichte* (Köln) 68 (1986):269-93.

Pepper, Stephen C. *World Hypotheses, a Study in Evidence.* Berkeley: Univ. of California Press, 1948.

Percy, Walker. "Metaphor as Mistake." *Sewanee Rev.* 66 (Winter 1958):79-99.

Peterson, Merrill D. *The Jefferson Image in the American Mind.* New York: Oxford Univ. Press, 1960.

_____. *Thomas Jefferson and the New Nation: A Biography.* New York: Oxford Univ. Press, 1970.

_____. "Thomas Jefferson and the Enlightenment: Reflections on Literary Influence." *Lex et Scientia* 11 (1975):89-127.

Porter, David H. *Horace's Poetic Journey: A Reading of Odes 1-3.* Princeton: Princeton Univ. Press, 1987.

_____. "The Imagery of Greek Tragedy: Three Characteristics," *Symbolae Osloenses* 61 (1986):19-42.

_____. "Violent Juxtaposition in the Similes of the *Iliad.*" *Classical Jnl.* 68 (1972-73):11-21.

Raban, Jonathan, ed. *The Oxford Book of the Sea.* New York: Oxford Univ. Press, 1992.

_____. *Passage to Juneau: A Sea and Its Meanings.* New York: Pantheon, 1999.

Rabassa, Gregory. "No Two Snowflakes Are Alike: Translation as Metaphor." In *The Craft of Translation,* ed. John Bignuenot and Ranier Schulte. Chicago: Univ. of Chicago Press, 1989, 1-12.

Richard, Carl J. *The Classics and the Founders.* Cambridge: Harvard Univ. Press, 1994.

Ricoeur, Paul. *The Rule of Metaphor: Multi-disciplinary Studies of the Creation of Meaning in Language.* Trans. Robert Czerny. Toronto: Univ. of Toronto Press, 1977.

Rodgers, Daniel T. *Contested Truths: Keywords in American Politics Since Independence.* New York: Basic Books, 1987.

Rölvaag, O. E. *Giants in the Earth.* New York: Harper & Brothers, 1927.

Rorty, Richard. "Philosophy as Science, as Metaphor, and as Politics." In *Essays on Heidegger and Others: Philosophical Papers,* 2:9-26. Cambridge: Cambridge Univ. Press, 1991.

Schäfer, Eckart. "Das Staatsschiff: Zur Präzision eines Topos." In *Toposforschung; eine Dokumentation,* ed. Peter Jehn. Frankfurt: Athenäum, 1972, 259-92.

Searle, John R. *Expression and Meaning: Studies in the Theory of Speech*

Acts. Cambridge: Cambridge Univ. Press, 1979 ("Metaphor," 76-116).

Shibles, Warren A. *Metaphor: An Annotated Bibliography and History*. Whitewater, Wis.: The Language Press, 1971.

Sontag, Susan. *AIDS and Its Metaphors*. New York: Farrar, Straus and Giroux, 1989.

_____. *Illness as Metaphor*. New York: Farrar, Straus and Giroux, 1977.

Sowerby, E. Millicent, comp. *Catalogue of the Library of Thomas Jefferson*. 5 vols. Washington: Government Printing Office, 1952-59.

Springer, Haskell S. "The Nautical *Walden*." *New England Qtly* 57 (March 1984): 84-97.

_____, ed. *America and the Sea: A Literary History*. Athens: Univ. of Georgia Press, 1995.

Spurgeon, Caroline F. E. *Shakespeare's Imagery and What It Tells Us*. Cambridge: Cambridge Univ. Press, 1935.

Stambovsky, Phillip. *The Depictive Image: Metaphor and Literary Experience*. Amherst: Univ. of Massachusetts Press, 1988.

Stanford, William Bedell. *Greek Metaphor: Studies in Theory and Practice*. Oxford: Blackwell, 1936.

Stanton, Lucia. "'Those Who Labor for My Happiness': Thomas Jefferson and His Slaves." In *Jeffersonian Legacies*, ed. Peter S. Onuf. Charlottesville: Univ. Press of Virginia, 1993, 147-80.

Stewart, Keith. "Samuel Johnson and the Ocean of Life: Variations on a Commonplace." *Papers on Language and Literature* 23 (Summer 1987):305-17.

Taub, Sarah F. *Language from the Body: Iconicity and Metaphor in American Sign Language*. New York: Cambridge Univ. Press, 2001.

Thomas, Francis-Noël, and Mark Turner. *Clear and Simple as the Truth: Writing Classic Prose*. Princeton: Princeton Univ. Press, 1994.

Tocqueville, Alexis de. *Democracy in America*, trans. George Lawrence, ed. J. P. Mayer. New York: Harper & Row, 1966.

Turner, Terence. "'We are Parrots,' 'Twins are Birds': Play of Tropes as Operational Structure." In *Beyond Metaphor: The Theory of Tropes in Anthropology*, ed. James W. Fernandez. Palo Alto: Stanford Univ. Press, 1991, 121-58.

Tymieniecka, Anna-Teresa, ed. *Poetics of the Elements in the Human Condition: The Sea: From Elemental Stirrings to Symbolic Inspiration,*

Language, and Life-Significance in Literary Interpretation and Theory. Dordrecht, Holland: D. Reidel: Analecta Husserliana, 1985.

Vaihinger, Hans, *The Philosophy of 'As If': A System of the Theoretical, Practical and Religious Fictions of Mankind,* trans. C. K. Ogden (New York, 1924).

van Noppen, Jean-Pierre, et al., comps. *Metaphor: A Bibliography of Post-1970 Publications.* Amsterdam: John Benjamins, 1985.

van Noppen, Jean-Pierre, and Edith Hols, comps. *Metaphor II: A Classified Bibliography of Publications, 1985 to 1990.* Amsterdam: John Benjamins, 1990.

Vitzthum, Richard C. *Land and Sea: The Lyric Poetry of Philip Freneau.* Minneapolis: Univ. of Minnesota Press, 1978.

Vogt, Philip. "Seascape with Fog: Metaphor in Locke's *Essay.*" *Jnl. of the History of Ideas* 54 (Jan. 1993):1-18.

Watson, George. "Hobbes and the Metaphysical Conceit," *Jnl. of the History of Ideas,* 16 (Oct. 1955): 558-62.

Weinberg, Florence M. *The Cave: The Evolution of a Metaphoric Field from Homer to Ariosto.* New York: Peter Lang, 1986.

Wellek, René, and Austin Warren. *Theory of Literature.* 3rd ed. New York: Harcourt, Brace and World, 1956.

Whalley, George. "Metaphor." In *Princeton Encyclopedia of Poetry and Poetics.* Princeton: Princeton Univ. Press, 1965.

Williams, C. A. S. *A Manual of Chinese Metaphor, Being a Selection of Typical Chinese Metaphors, with Explanatory Notes and Indices.* 1920. Repr. New York: AMS Press, 1974.

Wilson, Douglas L. "Jefferson's Library." In *Thomas Jefferson: A Reference Biography,* ed. Merrill Peterson. New York: Scribner, 1986, 157-79.

_____, ed. *Jefferson's Literary Commonplace Book.* Princeton: Princeton Univ. Press, 1989.

Wolf, Gunther. "Ueber die Geschichte der Staatsschiffmetaphor," *Geschichte in Wissenschaft u. Unterricht,* 10 (Nov. 1959):696-98.

Wong, Samuel G. "Some Baconian Metaphors and the Problems of Pure Prose." *Texas Studies in Literature and Language* 36 (Fall 1994):233-58.

Wright, Louis B. "Thomas Jefferson and the Classics." *Proceedings of the American Philosophical Society* 87 (July 1943):222-33.

Yasuda, Kenneth. *The Japanese Haiku.* Rutland, Vt.: Charles Tuttle, 1957.

Yeh, Michelle. "Metaphor and *bi:* Western and Chinese Poetics." *Comparative Literature* 39 (Summer 1987):237-54.

Young, Robert M. "Darwin's Metaphor: Does Nature Select?" *Monist* 55 (July 1971):442-503.

Yu, Pauline. "Metaphor and Chinese Poetry." *Chinese Literature* (Madison, Wis.) 3 (1981): 205-24.

Zacharias, Greg W. "The Marine Metaphor, Henry James, and the Moral Center of *The Awkward Age*." *Philological Qtly.* 69 (Winter 1990):91-105.

INDEX

Metaphors discussed in the text are indexed in the appendixes.

ABOUT THE AUTHOR

CHARLES A. MILLER, professor emeritus of politics and American studies at Lake Forest College in Illinois, is the author of *The Supreme Court and the Uses of History, A Catawba Assembly, Isn't That Lewis Carroll?* and *Jefferson and Nature: An Interpretation.* He lives in the Shenandoah Valley of Virginia.